# PHILOSOPHICAL PERSPECTIVES ON MODERN QUR'ĀNIC EXEGESIS

## Themes in Qur'ānic Studies

*Series Editors*

Mustafa Shah, School of Oriental and African Studies, University of London, and Abdul Hakim al-Matroudi, School of Oriental and African Studies, University of London

This series aims to introduce critical issues in the academic study of The Qur'ān and offers a variety of topics essential to providing an historical overview of The Qur'ān and the interrelated traditional teachings and beliefs which issue from it.

### Forthcoming

*Contemporary Qur'ānic Exegesis in Historical Perspective*
Johanna Pink

*Prophets and Prophecy in the Qur'ān*
*Narratives of Divine Intervention in the Story of Humankind*
Anthony H. Johns

*The Qur'ān and Kerygma*
*Christian Readings and Literary Renditions*
*from Late Antiquity to Postmodernity*
Jeffrey Einboden

*The Qur'ān and its Concepts*
*Disciplinary Perspectives*
Ulrika Mårtensson

# PHILOSOPHICAL PERSPECTIVES ON MODERN QUR'ĀNIC EXEGESIS

## KEY PARADIGMS AND CONCEPTS

*Massimo Campanini*

SHEFFIELD UK    BRISTOL CT

Published by Equinox Publishing Ltd.

UK: Office 415, The Workstation, 15 Paternoster Row, Sheffield, South Yorkshire, S1 2BX
USA: ISD, 70 Enterprise Drive, Bristol, CT 06010

www.equinoxpub.com

First published 2016

**British Library Cataloguing-in-Publication Data**
A catalogue record for this book is available from the British Library.

**Library of Congress Cataloging-in-Publication Data**
Names: Campanini, Massimo, 1954- author.
Title: Philosophical perspectives on modern Qur'åanic exegesis : key
  paradigms and concepts / Massimo Campanini.
Description: Bristol, CT : Equinox Pub. Ltd., 2016. | Includes
  bibliographical references and index.
Identifiers: LCCN 2016007866 (print) | LCCN 2016008645 (ebook) | ISBN
  9781781792308 (hb) | ISBN 9781781792315 (pb) | ISBN 9781781794609 (e-PDF)
  | ISBN 9781781794616 (e-epub)
Subjects: LCSH: Qur®an--Hermeneutics.
Classification: LCC BP130.2 .C36 2016 (print) | LCC BP130.2 (ebook) | DDC
  297.1/22601--dc23
LC record available at http://lccn.loc.gov/2016007866


ISBN:  978 1 781792 30 8  (hardback)
       978 1 781792 31 5  (paperback)

Typeset by CA Typesetting Ltd, www.publisherservices.co.uk
Printed and bound in the UK by Lightning Source UK Ltd., Milton Keynes and
Lightning Source Inc., La Vergne, TN

# CONTENTS

## Part I
## THE PROBLEMS OF MODERN
## HERMENEUTICS OF THE QUR'ĀN

# OBJECTIVES

This book ties together the results of many years of research and thinking. The thesis and arguments of some previous documents are reconsidered in the text.[1] The book seeks to elaborate the prolegomena of a future 'philosophical Qur'anology'. In (Western) Christian thought, a 'philosophical Christology' developed long ago (Sabetta 2015) aiming to stress not only the presence of Christ in the philosophers' reflection but also how Christ has been the inspirational principle of a significant part of Western philosophy (Tilliette 1993). As the role of Christ is played in Islam by the Qur'ān, it is not absurd to seek a 'philosophical Qur'anology' as it were – laying the foundations of a 'new' science.

This book's object is then the Qur'ān as the inspirational principle of philosophy, not only of Islamic philosophy. Philosophy is a method. The Qur'ān is a goal. No one who has studied Islam with a minimum of empathy can do without the Qur'ān. Writing on the Qur'ān and about the Qur'ān is an unavoidable duty for anyone wishing to understand Islam. Many hermeneutical paths have been gone through in order to fathom and disclose the secrets of a Scripture so multi-layered and complex. Here I propose a philosophical path.

This book is divided into two parts. The first is the *pars destruens*. It examines a number of hermeneutical problems from the point of view of content, history, methodology and implications, showing their values and advantages and disadvantages and the need to go further. I will discuss themes such as the relation between subjectivity and objectivity, language and Being, *tafsīr* and *ta'wīl* in the larger framework of the history of the contemporary hermeneutics of the Qur'ān. As Francis Bacon would have put it, the *pars destruens* will help the reader to remove as far as possible prejudices and errors paving the way to the second part, that is the *pars construens*. Part two explains the 'conditions of possibility' of a philosophical – and more specifically phenomenological – hermeneutics of the Qur'ān. 'Conditions of possibility' means that hermeneutics is always a work in progress. It is challenging and difficult for us to gain '*truth*' through philosophy: philosophy is an open space of research and questioning and would be self-contradictory if it would claim to have achieved '*The Truth*' with both capital letters. But we can try to gain more knowledge; and phenom-

---

1.   The book extends and develops an article which is to be published in the *Oxford Handbook of Qur'ānic Studies* (forthcoming), hopefully deepening its perspectives.

enology will be chosen as a useful key to open the door of the secrets of Being. Being in Islam is God and God discloses Himself in the Qur'ān. Thus, phenomenology is a key to probing the Qur'ān. Ontology is a focus of phenomenological inquiry. God as Being is the supreme reality. Thus, phenomenology offers a direct route to an investigation of the ontological reality of God.

In Part I, I will follow a precise plan: after stating what hermeneutics is and why, hermeneutically, the Qur'ān is an 'event' (in Heidegger's terms), I will peruse various hermeneutical approaches to the text with their applications. Decoding symbols (Islam is a symbolic culture and the Qur'ān is replete with symbols) is of course a highly hermeneutical activity. The Ka'ba is a symbol of the believer's orientation towards his/her God. Prophet Muhammad's very life is a living interpretation/hermeneutics of the Holy Book. The so-called 'scientific exegesis' (*tafsīr 'ilmī*) represents a symbolic hermeneutics passing widely over the literality of the text. Last but not least, a Qur'ānic translation is a highly hermeneutical work. A final paragraph will sum up these apparently disconnected investigations paving the way to the arguments that follow. The same discussion of modern literary hermeneutics is functional to underline the possibility to transcend philosophically the simply literary character of the text.

In Part II, I propose a theoretical path within the Qur'ān, searching to demonstrate that God's transcendence (*tanzīh*) can be read in phenomenological terms. Classic and contemporary authors, like al-Ghazālī and Hasan Hanafī, will be of help along this walk.

# ACKNOWLEDGEMENTS

Over the years, many people have helped me to mature and develop my thoughts. I cannot name all of them here and I apologize for this. However, among those I must acknowledge are: Hasan Hanafī and Nasr Hāmid Abū Zayd who have honoured me with their friendship and taught me so much about Islam. I thank the many friends and associates from the universities of Milan, Naples l'Orientale and Trent who have given me their time to discuss so many philosophical and theological topics. All have contributed to my thoughts and so to the writing and completion of this book. Caroline Higgitt, Livia Revelli and Norma Beavers contributed their linguistic expertise. It goes without saying that any mistakes are my own responsibility.

Last but not least, my grateful thanks go to Mustafa Shah, of the London School of Oriental and African Studies, whose proposition it was that I publish this book in the series that he is editing with Professor Abdul Hakim al-Matroudi. My thanks also to my publisher Equinox Publishing.

I could not have completed this work without the love and support of my wife, Donatella, and my son Emanuele to whom this work is dedicated.

**Wa Bi'llah faqat al-tawfīq**

NB: I have adopted a very simplified transliteration of Arab words and names, marking only the *'ayn* (') and the *hamza* (') when they appear within a word, and the macrons ā, ī, and ū. No diacritical signs are reported. When not explicitly indicated, all the Qur'ānic renderings are mine.

# PART I

# THE PROBLEMS OF MODERN
# HERMENEUTICS OF THE QUR'ĀN

# INTRODUCTION

Hermeneutics is a pivotal science in the understanding of religions and their holy texts. Bibliographies on hermeneutics or on hermeneutical applications to the holy texts continue to flourish. This book is a contribution to the exploration of the conditions of possibility of a *philosophical* hermeneutics of the Qur'ān – a subject rarely explored in literature. Philosophy has been widely used to interpret the Qur'ān, but here, paraphrasing Ayman El-Desouky 'What is of immediate concern to us here is the postulate of a modern literary approach to the Qur'ān as literature' (El-Desouky 2014), in a similar fashion I intend to consider that: 'what is of immediate concern to us here is the postulate of a modern philosophical approach to the Qur'ān as *philosophy*'. Thus, it is equally important to outline the 'conditions of possibility' of that enterprise. 'Conditions of possibility' means that hermeneutics is always a work in progress, the attained results are always open to revision and what seems today an end can tomorrow become a starting point. Thus, any stop needs reconsideration and new conditions of possibility can be realized. In order to promote a renewal and a fresh revision of hermeneutics of the Qur'ān, a thorough reflection on the theoretical and methodological aspects of hermeneutics is required.

In the last century, Muslim hermeneutics of the Qur'ān has witnessed a rejuvenation, both with traditional and innovative authors (Taji-Farouki 2004, 2015; Campanini 2011). From the so-called Salafī commentary of the *Manār* by Muhammad 'Abduh (1849–1905) and Rashīd Ridà (1865–1935) until the methodologically 'revolutionary' exegesis of Muhammad Arkoun (1928–2010) and Nasr Abū Zayd (1943–2010) (pathmarks on the road of Islamic modernity I will quote many times in the following pages), through to the more traditional but equally important *tafāsīr* of, to give just a few examples, the Shiite 'Allāma Sayyid Muhammad Husayn Tabātabā'ī (1903–1981) (the *Tafsīr al-mīzān* [*The Balance*]), and the Sunni Tunisian Muhammad Tāhir Ibn 'Ashūr (1879–1973) (*Tahrīr al-ma'nà al-sadīd wa tanwīr al-'aql al-jadīd fī'l-kitāb al-majīd* [*Explanation of the correct meaning and the illumination of the new intellect in the Glorious Book*]), contemporary Muslim hermeneutics looks like a hermeneutics of praxis. This means that Qur'ānic exegesis is not merely a philological or a theological enterprise, but an effort to change the present (political too) situation. As Hasan Hanafī explains (a *topos* I have quoted elsewhere): 'Returning to the Qur'an, source of all religious thought, both theological and otherwise, God does not present Himself on a theoretical level but on a practical level. God is not Logos, but Praxis. God is not rational object, concept, category or idea, but behaviour or conduct' (Hanafi 1972: 241). The Qur'ān thus provides the basis for reversal of religious epistemology where there is, at the centre of the experience of the sacred, a *teleological, phenomenological* God, a God who is the end of human actions.

# 1

## WHAT IS HERMENEUTICS?

We are surrounded by things (*res*), they are absolutely real and objective, but we communicate – and act accordingly – through signs (*signa*) that are only reproductions of those things. Even if I am not wearing my glasses at this moment, I can nevertheless speak of them with a friend using a *signum*, the word 'glasses'. This sign replaces perfectly the real object and I don't need any previous objective reality to acquire or keep knowledge, because, even if the glasses were to cease existing tomorrow, I am able to keep the knowledge of them in my mind and communicate it. The *signum* is not *flatus vocis*, it is the substantial representation of the *res*. Unavoidably, the signs 'interpret' the things insofar as they abstract them and can do without their objective reality. Thus, it is important to analyse the relationship between the things and the interpretative signs that abstract them from their objective reality.

This book sets off from Friedrich Nietzsche's radical assumption that there are no facts but only interpretations:

> Against positivism, which halts at phenomena – "there are only facts" – I would say: No, facts is precisely what there is not, only interpretations. We cannot establish any fact "in itself": perhaps it is folly to want to do such a thing.
> "Everything is subjective", you say; but even this is *interpretation*. The "subject" is not something given, it is something added and invented and projected behind what there is. – Finally, is it necessary to posit an interpreter behind the interpretation? Even this is invention, hypothesis.
> In so far as the word "knowledge" has any meaning, the world is knowable; but it is *interpretable* otherwise, it has no meaning behind it, but countless meanings. – "Perspectivism" (Nietzsche 1999, §481).[1]

---

1.  This passage is so important in my perspective that I am including the German text here: 'Gegen den Positivismus, welcherbei den Phänomenenstehnbleibt "esgiebtnur *Thatsachen*", würdeichsagen: nein, gerade Thatsachengiebtes nicht, nur *Interpretationen*. Wirkönnenkein Faktum "an sich" feststellen: vielleichtistesein Unsinn, so etwaszuwollen. "Esistalles *subjektiv*" sagtihr: aberschon Das ist-*Auslegung*. Das "Subjekt" istnichts Gegebenes, sondernetwas Hinzu-Erdichtetes, Dahinter-Gestecktes – Isteszuletztnöthig, den Interpretennoch hinter die Interpretation zusetzen? Schon das ist Dichtung, Hypothese. Soweitüberhaupt das Wort "Erkentniß" Sinn hat, ist die Welt erkennbar: abersieistanders *deutbar*, sie

*Prima facie*, this assertion is squarely nihilistic: the objective reality of things is denied in favour of a linguistic elusiveness. Furthermore, if Nietzsche is right, the (real/objective) world becomes a mere (subjective) production of the self/mind; moreover, the ontological nihilism leads to an ethical and axiological nihilism. If 'nothing is', 'nothing has a value' (see Ferraris 2014: 53).[2] Nietzsche would say: *transvaluation of all values*. Others would say: dangerous relativism. Nietzsche's assertion implies a deeper and more substantial outcome, however. Perspectivism recognizes that reality is multifarious and that, also when we believe we are grasping the substance of things, this certainty can be called into question by other discoveries. This is particularly important in natural sciences, but even for ideologies, global *Weltanschauungen*: to believe that an ideology is mono-directional implies the impossibility of contesting it, struggling against it, or achieving liberation through other ideologies. Johann Fichte would say that realism is 'dogmatic' insofar as it allows the permanence of a gap between the things and their representations, between reality and mind.

Perspectivism is the view that there are many possible conceptual schemes, but it does not mean relativism, rather pluralism. If there is a positive ontological ground for reality – and there is as I argued in the previous example of the glasses – we can speak of reality in different ways (as we will see with Ibn Rushd/Averroes below). This differentiation pluralizes both our interpretations of reality, our speaking of reality and our capacity to carry on praxis on the basis of such comprehension. The debate, or better the contrast, between the searching of a 'truth' based upon an objective, verifiable and formalizable criterion along with logical, mathematical and linguistic patterns (the analytical method), on the one hand, and the historicization and humanization of knowledge so that it does not exist in fact but only in interpretations (the 'continental' way), on the other hand, finds a common ground of interaction in language: we can understand man and world only analysing language and other means of communication and expression (see Eco and Fedriga 2015: 292–93).

However, even if 'truth' seems elusive of our grasp; even if nihilism were the only implication of Nietzsche's perspectivism, we would be fortunate: we have the Qur'ān. This is a solid certainty, irrespective of whether the Qur'ān was composed just after the Prophet's death, or in 'Abd al-Malik's

hat keinen Sinn hinter sich, sondernunzählige Sinne – "Perspektivismus" (*Der Wille zur Macht*, 481). See the English translation by Kaufmann (1968).
2.   Ferraris argues that from Descartes to Nietzsche going through Kant and Hegel modern philosophy is a negative philosophy: certainty must be sought in what we know and think, not in what (objectively) exists. He undervalues the importance of signs for communication and action far beyond the self (*ego*) and the subject, however. So, in my view, his critique misses the point here.

time or later. Although we circulate and meditate essentially interpretations of the Qur'ān, the Qur'ān is a fact like the world, existing before interpretation. We have the *mushaf* in our hands, it is there and produces its effects,[3] it is *le fait coranique* as Muhammad Arkoun (1928–2010) would put it.[4] The opening words of the Qur'ān after the *Fātiha* are clear: '*This is* the Book, no doubt in this, a guide for the pious' (*dhalika al-kitāb lā rayb fihi hudā li'l-muttaqīn*) (Q. 2:2). '*This Qur'ān* (*hadhā al-Qur'ān*', emphasizing the presence and concreteness of the Book), is a relatively common expression in the Qur'ān (for example Q. 6:19; 10:37, etc.). The Book is a firm reality just as God is a firm reality, the revealer of the Book: 'God: there is no God but Him'[5] (*Allāh lā ilāh illā huwa*) (Q. 2:255); 'He is God, there is no other god than Him' (*Huwa Allāh, alladhī lā ilāh illā huwa*)[6] (Q. 59:63). The Qur'ānic God is eminently self-conscious, affirming his absolute reality: 'I

3.  See Eco (1986: 509): 'Il testo è lì e produce i propri effetti... L'autore dovrebbe morire dopo aver scritto. Per non disturbare il cammino del testo' ('The author would have to die after writing in order to not disturb the journey of the text').

4.  It is not always clear what *le fait coranique* really is, at least to my mind. Arkoun distinguished between the Qur'ānic 'fact' and the Islamic 'fact'. Both are historical, but the 'Islamic fact' is, so to speak, a betrayal of the 'Qur'ānic fact'. Arkoun acquired great fame, maybe a bit beyond his actual exegetic merits, on the grounds of an innovative method. He was among the first to stress the importance of the historicization of the Holy Book. In Islamic thought, a great part of 'unthought-of' has remained, meaning that Islamic thought has not been able to face the great problems of history, democracy, secularism, human rights and so on, because the tradition enclosed all that is 'thinkable'. And even further: the unthought-of has become 'unthinkable' and modernity and knowledge's conquests are ghettoized in the limbo of impossibility (Arkoun 2002). These assumptions are applied by Arkoun to the Qur'ān, whose interpretation needs to be based on three pillars: linguistics and semiotics; social criticism and historical psychology. Arkoun's analysis of the Qur'an has been justly criticized by Farid Esack who notes: 'When one pursues "independent knowledge" with "exact methods" and ignores the meaning of the text [the Qur'an] for the contemporary situation and for people of faith, then one effectively places oneself and a small group of other "objective" intellectuals outside and above the vast majority of believers for whom the text is a living document' (Esack 2002: 73). The same critique, in substance, has been put forward by Muhammad Talbī when he complains that, in his writings, Arkoun has never openly claimed to be a Muslim. The scientific use of scientific categories of study and interpretation does not detract from the fact that the eye of the believing beholder is different from the pure orientalist beholder.

5.  I decided to use 'He', 'Him' and so on in relation to God although I am perfectly convinced that 'It' or other neutral expressions would have been more appropriate. God is not a 'male', a 'father', but transcends every gender attribute. 'He' and 'Him' are commonly used, however.

6.  The metaphysical importance of the term *huwa* will be duly emphasized in Part II of this book.

am God, there is no god but Me' (*anā allāhu lā ilāh illā anā*) (Q. 20:14). The existence of the Book is a proof of the existence of its Author, given that rational proofs of the existence of God can be questioned and voided from many points of view.[7] Obviously, using David Hume's paradigm, we can put forward a comparison: according to Hume, we cannot infer from the existence of a house (i.e. the universe) that its architect (i.e. God) is eternal, omnipotent, omniscient and so on. *Mutatis verbis*, we cannot infer from the existence of the Qur'ān that its author is God (and not Muhammad, for example). Nevertheless, the very fact that we possess a Book, whose existence is absolutely objective and whose very content testifies that the reality of the Book depends on the reality of its author, demonstrates that the two realities confirm one another.

That said, however, the weakening of metaphysical objectivity is a path that leads towards a whole world of chances and potentialities. If we objectivize reality up to a high degree, no room is left for creation and alternation. Although this is not the place to examine this assertion in depth, it follows that it is hermeneutics, then, which builds up the sense of the world in every thinking being, and particularly philosophical hermeneutics as will be argued here.

Although an excess of realism is equally dangerous, the danger of idealism is unavoidable. Thus, it is necessary to operate precautionary corrections and distinctions. In this framework, the problem of the use of contemporary hermeneutics in the analysis and commentary of the Qur'ān stands out as a complex and multifaceted issue. It actually implies the answer to a number of questions.

First of all, which hermeneutics are we speaking of? Generally, we can say that hermeneutics is: to 'express' (utter or describe); to 'explain' (interpret); to 'translate' (Ferraris 1997: 6). We can express (describe) and explain texts, but also feelings or the signs of nature. Is a text tantamount to nature? Obviously yes, insofar as for the philosophical tradition of the West, and of Islam as well, nature is an open book wherein the signs of God are written. The Qur'ānic word *āya* is particularly interesting here (and I will discuss it at length below): it means both the verses – that are the signs making up the Book – and the tokens of nature pointing to God. Semiotics is a peculiar hermeneutical science then: through the decoding of signs we are able to go back to the things of which the signs are the translation/symbol. This resolves the difficulty of a merely subjective production of the world. As to feelings, they are too volatile and elusive to be grasped by hermeneutics.

---

7.   I postpone a systematic treatment of this issue to another book, *in sha'allah*. The same Muhammad Iqbāl, however, contended that the three main demonstrations of God's existence (the ontological, the teleological and the cosmological) are at the end inconsistent or even *petitiones principii* (Iqbāl 2013: 28–31.

There is an existential hermeneutics of feelings, of course, of the human *Da-sein* that is the object of phenomenological psychology and psychiatry, but textual hermeneutics, especially hermeneutics of the holy texts, requires the transcending of psychology in favour of history.

# 2

## THE QUR'ĀN AS EVENT

Martin Heidegger wrote once that '*Hemeneuèin* is that kind of exposition that puts forth an announcement in so far as it is able to listen to a message [...] *Hermeneuèin* does not mean primarily "to interpret", but, before this, to convey a message and an announcement' (Heidegger 1959: 105). Heidegger's position is somewhat original. Modern Christian hermeneutics of the Sacred Texts started at the beginning of the sixteenth century both in Catholic (Erasmus from Rotterdam) and Protestant world (Luther) developing a historical besides the philological or theological approach to revelation. By now it is universally performed, despite Christian fundamentalist's and litteralists' resistence and the major difficulties to accept the authenticity, say, of the Gospels *as such as they have been transmitted.* The Gospels' inner contradictions and the non-omogeneous picture they offer of Jesus lead to exegetical problems involving the very likelihood of the Messiah's figure – did Jesus, the Messiah, really say what the evangelists attributed to him? Did he really behave as the evangelists say he did? And so on.

After the beginning of modern hermeneutics on the Holy texts, the perspective of historicity was no longer abandoned. All hermeneuts applied a historical analysis of the texts – an approach the Muslim mind is as yet reluctant to carry on, often frightened by the risk of downplaying the sacredness of the Holy Text and jeopardizing the immutability of God's will. If Friedrich Schleiermacher (1768–1834) elaborated the meaning of hermeneutics as communication; if Wilhelm Dilthey (1833–1911) suggested that hermeneutics is comprehension and understanding; if Friedrich Nietzsche (1844–1900) saw in hermeneutics the way to unmask the negativities of present time – Hans Georg Gadamer has been probably the thinker who productively intertwined the look of the interpreter with the objective datum of the text through a keen use of language which is the tool by which Being can be understood (Gadamer 1960; Bleicher 1986; Ferraris 1997; Weinsheiner 1985).

In the light of these remarks (useful also in all the following arguments), we are able to read Abrahamic revelations as 'messages' and 'announcements'. In this sense, the prophets are 'hermeneuts' in the clearest sense. In Hebrew, the prophet is a *nabi'* (pronounce:*navi*), that is a messenger: he communicates to humans what God reveals to him. In Arabic, the 'prophet' (again *nabī*) is a 'warner' and a bringer of 'good tidings'. Muhammad in particular in the Qur'ān is exhorted to say: 'Really, I was sent to you from [God] as a warner (*nadhīr*) and a bringer of good tidings (*bashīr*)' (Q. 11:2). The *nubuwwa*, or 'prophecy' is first of all 'to make someone acquainted with God's message'. The term appears six times in the Qur'ān and is almost always (Q. 3:79; Q. 6:89; etc.) connected with Scripture (*kitāb*) and wisdom (*hikma*). *Nubuwwa* seems something different from 'Scripture' then, although Scripture encapsulates the contents of prophecy. The prophet brings the Scripture with wisdom. *Nabī* (Arabic) is obviously strictly linked to *nabi'* (Hebrew) and probably derives from the root n-b-', meaning exactly 'to announce' (see Nallino 1963; Penrice 2004; Abdel Haleem and Badawi 2008). To be a prophet means to be a 'messenger', to be an 'announcer'. In the Islamic tradition the prophet legislator (*rasūl*) conveys a message that builds up human society and politics through the application of the revealed Law of God. In Christianity, *euangèlion* means 'good news'. Announcing the 'happy tidings' of a renewal and rebirth of the world is Jesus' real mission: 'Now after that John was put in prison, Jesus came into Galilee, preaching the gospel of the kingdom of God, and saying, "The time is fulfilled, and the kingdom of God is at hand: repent ye, and believe the gospel"' (Mk 1:14–15). Obviously, being a saviour and a Messiah, Jesus is quite different from Muhammad (who is *not* mahdī, the word mahdī being entirely absent from the Qur'ān), whereas Jesus was primarily a prophet of the Jews bringing them a message of renewal in the imminent realization of God's kingdom.

Thus hermeneutics is also a kind of announcement. Before discussing more thoroughly the event of the Qur'ān, it is important to evaluate the exegetical outcomes involved in the hermeneutical 'announcement'. For example, if the revealed messages are announcements both in Jewish, Christian and Islamic traditions, do Biblical and Qur'ānic exegeses have the same characteristics? Baruch Spinoza's hermeneutics of the Holy Scripture in the *Tractatus theologico-politicus* gave rise to fierce hostility in the Jewish conservative milieu of the seventeenth-century Netherlands and deserve scrutiny (Spinoza 2004: 276–327, chapter VII). His argument develops following three main steps:

1. The interpretative method of the Scripture is tantamount to the interpretative method of nature (*dico methodum interpretandi Scripturam haud differre a methodo interpretandi naturam*) as far as it is a rational method grounded in history (*sinceram historiam*);
2. Knowledge of the contents of the Scripture must be derived from the same Scripture (*cognitio horum omnium rerum quae in Scriptura continentur, ab ipsa Scriptura sola peti debet*);
3. The teachings of the Scripture must be completely related to its history (*regula universalis interpretandi Scripturam est nihil Scripturae tanquam eius documentum tribuere, quod ex ipsius historia quam maxime perspectum non habeamus*).

Spinoza's analysis identifies two well-defined questions: on the one hand, the necessity to explain or interpret the holy texts by themselves;on the other the necessity to historicize and contextualize both the literal evidence of the text and the reliability of the stories contained therein. The first necessity is openly recognized in Islam. A great number of commentators, like Tabarī in the so-called Middle Ages down to contemporary female exegetes like 'Ā'isha 'Abd al-Rahmān Bint al-Shāti' and Amina Wadud, underlined the duty to understand and explain the Qur'ān by the Qur'ān. The internal coherence of the Qur'ān, both regarding the content and the language, would be proof of its authenticity and of the manifestation of the divine personality within it.

The second necessity is a troubling leit-motive in the confrontation between contemporary Islam and (Western) modernity: Muslim traditionalist thinkers shrink from the possibility of questioning the meta-historical universality of revealed commands and the absolute veracity of the transmitted stories of revelation; reformist thinkers argue boldly that without historicization and contextualization the message will remain mute in the face of the provocations and challenges of modernity. As I have said before, in the Christian tradition no serious scholar today challenges the historical approach to the Bible, one that became standard for every researcher. In the Jewish tradition, the hostility reserved for Spinoza has not completely disappeared but the mainstream of Judaism is today firmly rooted in the Western tradition, assuming largely the same intellectual framework. In Islam, a real historical method in interpreting the Holy Book has not yet been applied. A critical edition of the Qur'ān is 'unthinkable', in Arkoun's terms (Arkoun 2002). On the contrary, the Gospels have been submitted to critical inquiry since the time of Erasmus of Rotterdam. Although critical editions are not always particularly useful to the understanding of the true meaning of a text, the problem lies in the emergence of a *mentality*. Nasr Abū Zayd (1943–2010) argued strongly that hermeneutics does not compromise the sacredness of the Qur'ān, but traditional conservative Muslims charged him with apostasy.

However, we must strongly emphasize that the Hebrew Bible and the Gospels, on the one hand, and the Qur'ān, on the other, have a very different inspiration.[1] The Qur'ān is both an *event* and a *discrimination (furqān)*. It takes place in disclosure and cuts off the path of revelation.

---

1.    The most perceptive Muslims grasped this very clearly. For example, discussing the tales of the Fall in the Bible and the Qur'ān, Muhammad Iqbāl wrote:

> 'The remarkable points of difference between the Qur'ānic and the Biblical narrations suggest unmistakably the purpose of the Qur'ānic narration. The Qur'ān omits the serpent and the rib story altogether. The former omission is obviously meant to free the story from its phallic

What does it mean that the Qur'ān is an *event*? Kenneth Cragg called his most famous book 'The *event* of the Qur'ān' (Cragg 1971) meaning that the descent (*tanzīl*) of the Qur'ān was 'eventful', a total event within history. Even more clearly, Cantwell Smith said that the Qur'ān represents 'the eternal breaking through time; the knowable disclosed; the transcendent entering history and remaining here, available to mortals to handle and to appropriate; the divine become apparent' (Cantwell Smith 1980 quoted in Shah 2013, vol. IV: 379). I largely agree with these definitions, but a more refined analysis is in order.

It is in Heidegger's philosophical system that the 'event' became meaningful as 'disclosure' – an idea that we can perhaps express in Arabic with the term '*kashf*', a term loaded with metaphysical and mystical implications as well. In Heidegger's terminology, the *event (Ereignis)* presupposes that the original existential dimension of *Da-sein* must be re-interpreted epistemologically as the place (*Lichtung*) wherein the truth of Being is disclosed. This happens at two levels: the level of language, and the level of 'disclosure of truth' (*a-letheia*). On the one hand, 'Thinking brings this relation to being solely as something handed over to thought itself from being. Such offering consists in the fact that in thinking being comes to language. Language is the house of being. In its home human beings dwell. Those who think and those who create with words are the guardians of this home. Their guardianship accomplishes the manifestation of being insofar as they bring this manifestation to language' (Heidegger 1998: 239). On the other hand, *a-letheia* or 'Truth' is 'unhiddenness' or 'disclosure', which designates 'what is present and manifest in the region where human beings happen to dwell' (Heidegger 1998: 168).

I believe that Heidegger's proposal is useful to better define the role of the Qur'ān. The Qur'ān is both a linguistic system where the Being (that is God) shows Himself, and the 'disclosure of truth' through the words of God conveyed by the Prophet. The truth has been hidden in past times, and the Qur'ān comes to 'disclose' it again with a new language in the house (world and society) where human beings dwell. In the paragraphs below, we will

setting and its original suggestion of a pessimistic view of life. The latter omission is meant to suggest that the purpose of Quranic narration is not historical, as in the case of the Old Testament, which gives us an account of the origin of the first human couple by way of a prelude to the history of Israel. Indeed, in the verses which deal with the origin of man as a living being, the Qur'ān uses the words "bashar" or "insan", not "Adam", which it reserves for man in his capacity of God's vicegerent on earth. The purpose of the Qur'ān is further secured by the omission of proper names mentioned in the Biblical narration – Adam and Eve. The word Adam is retained and used more as a concept than as the name of a concrete human individual' (Iqbal 2013: 83).

define more precisely what these elements mean. It is important firstly to apply Cragg's, Cantwell Smith's and Heidegger's remarks to the Qur'ān.

As in the case of the Gospels and Jesus, the Qur'ān's authenticity has been questioned and the deep meaning of Muhammad's message has been scrutinized. I have no room here to discuss thoroughly the huge Orientalist literature about the historicity of the Qur'ān and of the Prophet's figure or the reliability of the traditional Islamic sources – and the counter-attack of Muslims (see for e.g. Donner 1998; Berg 2000; Motzki 2000 and my discussions in Campanini 2007, 2016a, 2016b). Matters of faith are obviously often at odds with the historian's shrewdness. I believe however that in order to place the Qur'ān and the Islamic revelation in their proper historical contexts, especially as reference points in the troubled times of radical Islamism, we must emphasize the *Muslim* approach to such burning issues. Even if Muhammad did not utter exactly *those* words (even if Jesus did not utter exactly the words the evangelists put in his mouth), the really important thing is that they became the leading guides for believers and their praxis.

According to the Muslim creed, just from the start, Muhammad's message appears not simply as an evolution of previous steps in revelation history, but as a break with regard to the polytheistic Arab religion as well as the monotheistic – Jewish and Christian – religions. Actually, it disputes against *jāhiliyya* (the pre-Islamic ignorance) as well as against Jewish-Christian tradition.

First of all, in regard to *jāhiliyya*, Muhammad's message struggled against a 'pagan' *Weltanschauung* from a number of points of view; the two most important are the following:

- The uncompromising affirmation of God's oneness (*tawhīd*): 'Say: He (*huwa*), God, is One; God the unknowable (*samad*). He did not beget nor He was begotten and nobody is equal to Him' (Q. 112). God's oneness involves many theological and political outcomes. The *rabbaniyya* means the sovereignty of God in the universe: He is the Unique One who gave the universe its performative laws; and He is the Unique One who holds up its functioning, and, if He wants, He can change the natural laws as He pleases. The *ulūhiyya* is the acknowledgment that only God is worthy of adoration (*'ubūdiyya*). The *hākimiyya* means the sovereignty of God in human society and political organization. *Hākimiyya* took on a particular meaning in Sayyid Qutb's (1906–1966) theory of Islamic government, for example, where God would be the only one who has the right to legislate. But, apart from that, *hākimiyya* implies the fundamental recognition that Islam is *dīn wa dunyā*, religion and worldly dimension. This theocentrism (not theocracy!) led to the overcoming of Meccan monolatry. Seemingly, Meccan paganism allowed the prevalence of a supreme god over other lesser gods: 'They worship alongside God things that can neither harm nor benefit them, and say: "These are our intercessors with God"' (Q. 10:18, trans. Abdel Haleem); '[there are] those who choose other protectors beside Him, saying: "We only worship them because they bring us nearer to God"' (Q. 39:3; trans. Abdel Haleem). Against this synchretical attitude, Muhammad's message emphasizes the uniqueness of God both as a legislator and as a *cible* of adoration.

- The promotion of social justice was a part of Muhammad's message that particularly worried Meccan (Qurayshite) aristocracy, eager to keep unchanged the social structure of the city. Obviously, Muhammad was not a revolutionary who sought to stir up class struggle; but his moral call to relieve the poor or the conversion to Islam of slaves like Bilāl involved a *bouleversement* of social relations (see for e.g. Marlow 1997; Hallaq 2009a, 2009b; Ramadan 2009). The critique of old traditions and practices threatened the very identity of the Qurayshites. Of this there is clear evidence in the Qur'ān itself: 'Whenever We sent a messenger before you to warn a township, those corrupted by wealth said, in the same way, "We saw our fathers following this tradition, we are only following in their footsteps". The messenger said: "Even though I bring you a truer religion than what you saw your fathers following?", and they replied: "But we do not believe the message you bring"' (Q. 43:23–24) (trans. Abdel Haleem).

Moreover, Muhammad's message argued against Judaism and Christianity in a number of ways. The question of the relationship between the Muslim community and the other communities 'of the Book' is a delicate one.[2] It involves the related questions of tolerance (is Islam 'tolerant' towards other religions? Does Islam admit other religions near itself?),

2. There is a wide literature on the subject. See Emon (2012) who argues that 'the pursuit of pluralism through the institutions of law and governance is a messy business'. However, the Qur'an contains many verses which acknowledge pluralism like the celebrated and much quoted Q. 49:13: 'O mankind, indeed We have created you male and female and We have made of you peoples and tribes, so that you may know each other (*ta'ārafū*)'. Reza Shah-Kazemi argued that mutual knowledge and reconnaissance (*ta'āruf*) is the epistemological fundament of diversity. As to the famous *āya* Q. 2:256 ('There is no compulsion in religion'), Shah-Kazemi emphasizes the necessity to understand it through its second part: '*the right path is well distinguished from error*', meaning that tolerance is strictly bound with knowledge: reciprocal knowledge of course, but also mainly the capacity to distinguish truth from false (Shah-Kazemi 2012).

freedom of expression and political outcomes in specific historical situa-
tions (the living together of Jews and Arabs in Palestine after the foundation of Israel, for example). The Qur'ān alternates ecumenical openings (Q.
2:62: 'The believers, be they Jews, Christians or Sabians, who believe in
God and in the Last Day and do good actions, they will have their reward
with their Lord, and no fear nor sorrow will befall on them') with aggressive closures (Q. 9:29: 'Fight those of the People of the Book who do not
[truly] believe in God and the Last Day, who do not forbid what God and
His Messenger have forbidden, who do not obey the rule of justice, until
they pay the tax and agree to submit', trans. Abdel Haleem).

Although the order to 'fight' seems to be addressed *only* to those among
the People of the Book who do not *truly* believe, Nasr Abū Zayd was perfectly aware of the potential difficulty inherent in the harmonization of
these two odd propositions, and suggested that the Qur'ān be read as a set
of 'dialogues'. In the first phase of his thought, Abū Zayd argued that the
Qur'ān is a *text* (Abū Zayd 2000a). Later he had a major change of mind
(Abū Zayd 2004, 2010): the Qur'ān is no more considered as a text (*nass*),
but as a set of dialogues (*discourses, khitāb*). In point of fact, the perspective is turned completely upside down. The Qur'ān as text must have a
settled structure (*tartīb*), from many points of view unchangeable, because
fixed, as it were, in a 'physical form', containing 114 chapters, arranged in
a precise order, an equally fixed number of verses, Meccan or Medinese,
sentences and words that cannot change their place or meaning, nor their
number, without upsetting the whole, and so on. Such a Qur'ān is called by
Muslims the *mushaf*, that is the 'book' proper, handwritten or printed on
'pages' that are in turn bound up in a cover. The *mushaf* is different from
the dogmatic, historical, spiritual contents of the book, which properly
represents the 'Qur'ān'. Having confused the *mushaf* with the Qur'ān, the
outward and literal aspect (what Abū Zayd calls the 'sense') with the living
and moving aspect of the content (what Abū Zayd calls the 'meaning'),
the Qur'ān was transformed into a closed and silent body, embalmed in its
objectivity, even silencing God himself.

In order to avoid this danger, the Egyptian philosopher put forward the
proposal that the Qur'ān be read as a set of dialogues. Dialogues between
God and his Prophet, between the Prophet and his companions or enemies,
between Muslims and Jews or Christians and so on. As a set of dialogues,
the Qur'ānic structure is open; it is possible to discover in it many parallel
threads of reasoning. Moreover, the Qur'ān now no longer displays only
one end and direction, as was the case if considered merely as a text. The
Qur'ān suggests different options according to the different contingencies in
which it was revealed. Thus, it keeps its historical character. For example,
we find in the Qur'ān incitements to war and incitements to peace; but it
does not mean that the Qur'ān is a wholly pacific or a wholly warlike text.

It depends on the circumstances. The verses referring to war or peace (for instance regarding the Jews) were revealed in response to particular historical occurrences during the Prophetic experience of Muhammad or the ongoing events of Islam as religion.

Abū Zayd's *volte-face* is clever but does not remove the fact that some Qur'ānic passages suggest:

- that Islam is the last religion of humankind, abrogating the previous religions: 'Today I [God speaking, not Muhammad!] perfected for you your religion and I completed upon you my bounty and I am satisfied to give you Islām as [your] religion (*dīn*)' (Q. 5:3). Admittedly, 'Islām' possibly does not mean in this context the *historical* religion of Islam, with its rituals, laws and beliefs, but the primitive, universal and natural religion 'to surrender oneself to God', that is *islām*. The historical religion of Islam, with its rituals, laws and beliefs, developed later in precise historical circumstances – becoming what Marshall Hodgson would call perhaps 'Islamdom'. Nevertheless, there is a break with the previous Jewish religion. Abraham was neither a Jew nor a Christian, but a monotheist, a *hanīf* (Q. 6, 79: 'Abraham in truth was not a Jew neither a Christian, but he was a Muslim [i.e "one who surrenders himself to God'], and one of pure faith [*hanīf*, i.e. a 'monotheist']"). Islam is the *natural* religion of humankind (Q. 30:30: 'Turn your face to religion (*dīn*) as a pure monotheist (*hanīf*), the nature (*fitrat*) in which God created humanity'): all human beings are born in the natural religion and only education transforms them into believers of a *historical* religion.[3] Islamic revelation came down in order to 'correct' the misinterpretation of the Scripture by Jews and Christians, the so-called *tahrīf.* Judaism and Christianity having betrayed the original message of God, He sent Muhammad to show the misguided the path of righteousness.
- Thus, the relationship with Jews and Christians is problematic. In the Qur'ān, there are ecumenical verses, as we said above, but there is also the admonition: 'O believers, do not take Jews and Christians as friends (*awliyā'*)' (Q. 5:51).[4]

3.   This is a common refrain in the texts of the theologians. For instance, al-Ghazālī in the *Munqidh min al-dalāl* says explicitly that 'everybody is born in the natural religion (*islām*) while through education he/she becomes a Jew, a Christian or a Zoroastrian'.
4.   It is true that, if we translate *awliyā'* as 'supporters' rather than 'friends', the admonition is weakened and can be contextualized in the struggle of the Muslims against the Qurayshites.

In general terms, Islamic interpretation of prophetic history through the ages highlights the break suggested by these assertions. A number of scholars (starting from John Wansbrough 1977–1978) have questioned the reliability of the 'Islamic salvation history', but, noted above, the real issue is the functionality of religious ideology in the believers' life. Thus, from an Islamic perspective, there is certainly a continuity from Abraham (or even from Adam and Noah) to Moses to Jesus to Muhammad. But there is also a change of direction. Muhammad is more than a new Moses or a new Jesus: he starts a new epoch. The Qur'ān became part of this prophetic history and acquired full historical reality: Muhammad is a full historical character (albeit somewhat doubtful in some of the details).[5] Muhammad's life is *by itself* a historical narration of facts and has its rationale purely in the historical occurrence of the events. As a consequence, since the life of Muhammad is also the history of revelation, revelation has its rationale in its own history.

This is clearly demonstrated by Ibn Ishāq and Ibn Hishām's *Sīra* and in general by the other 'Biographies' of the Prophet. From the point of view of Islam, Muhammad's message marks a break with the previous religious (even monotheistic) traditions. For, although Waraqa Ibn Nawfal, the cousin of Khadīja, is said to have asked the Prophet:

> "O son of my brother, tell me what thou hast seen and heard". The apostle told him and Waraqa said: "Surely, by Him in whose hand is Waraqa's soul, thou art the prophet of this people. There hath come unto thee the greatest Nāmūs, who came unto Moses" (Guillaume 1982: 107).

Emphasizing the continuity between the prophecies, the Qur'ān stresses the rupture:

> The apostle of God began to receive revelations in the month of Ramadān. In the words of God: "The month of Ramadān in which the Qur'ān was brought down as a guidance for men, and proofs of guidance and a decisive criterion (*furqān*)" [Q. 2:185]. And again, "Verily We have sent it down on the night of destiny (*qadr*), and what has shown you what the night of destiny is?" [Q. 97. The rendering of the verses is obviously by Guillaume] (Guillaume 1982: 111).

Martin Lings's biography of Muhammad is similarly a fully historical narration (at odds with the Gospels and also, partially, with the Bible) and his choice to narrate the life of Muhammad through the Qur'ān links together the two historical dimensions (Lings 1988). Obviously, Lings read Muhammad's life through the eyes of the believer, and clearly he considered the tra-

---

5.    There is no longer a place – I believe – for a radical sceptical and revisionist critique that disputes *a-priori* the reliability of Muslim sources in relation to Muhammad's life and to the Qur'ān's composition.

ditional Islamic sources reliable. Andrew Rippin called Ling's work 'utter mythology', but Rippin belongs to the sceptical school of Wansbrough. Any exaggeration must be avoided. Traditional 'Islamic history of revelation' presents many faults, traditional Islamic sources like Ibn Isḥāq and Ibn Hishām's *Sīra* are late (but why *ipso facto* 'mythological'? A prejudice is at work in my view): this is undoubtedly true, but it does not mean that a whole library of witnesses and documents are liars and lies.

Lings' biography is important because it connects Muhammad's life and message with the historical context and grounds them in revelation. Thus, Ling's biography clearly pointed out the difference between the Gospels and the Qur'ān. Muhammad's life is marked by revelation: the narration of Muhammad's life unfolds the steps of revelation. Jesus's life in the Gospels is itself revelation and consequently transcends history, is *out* of history. Muhammad's decisions can be explained by history (and reason); Jesus's decisions are a matter of faith.

This does not mean that Qur'ānic stories are real historical facts, however. Khalafallāh taught us to understand better the symbolic value of the Qur'ānic stories as we will see extensively below. Rather, the history of prophecy is completely merged in the history of humanity and the ancient data of the stories of Adam, Abraham, Moses, Jesus and Muhammad have the indubitable features of a reality based on human consciousness if not on human factual behaviours and factual action in history. The Qur'ān is fully in time but it does not in any way lose its universal value.

We must stress again, then, and perhaps with better understanding, the fact that the Qur'ān is an *event*. The Hebrew Bible is the retrospective reconstruction of a concluded and finished historical evolution; *the Bible arose from history, it is the history of the Jewish people, but now is by itself out of history*. On the contrary, being not the retrospective reconstruction of the past but the present and factual narration of the ongoing process of revelation, the Qur'ān opens a new history, starts a new epoch.[6] It is the *furqān*, that

6.   Northrop Frye's argument is summarized by El-Desouky as follows: 'The narrative unity of the Bible, which is there in spite of the miscellaneous nature of its content, was something that I stressed. And that concern for the narrative seems to me to be distinctive of the Bible among other sacred books. In the Koran, for example, the revelations of Mohammed were gathered up after his death and arranged in order of length, which suggests that revelation in the Koran pays no attention to narrative continuity – that's not what it is interested in' […] 'Crucially, the Qur'an is not about narrative or story in the same way the Bible is. In notebook two, Frye writes: "The history of the Bible is story: the Koran has shape (at least the individual suras have) but it does not tell a story. Story is connected with the fact that the heart of the Bible is ritual drama, not teaching"' (Frye 2000, quoted in El-Desouky 2014: 12–13). There are obvious analogies with, but also differences from, my position. In my view, first of all, the Bible is the conscious narrative of

is the discriminating event between two phases of history, before and after revelation. Besides the previously quoted Q. 2:185, we can recall Q. 25:1: 'Exalted be Him who revealed to his servant [Muhammad] the discriminating [event] (*furqān*) as a warning to all the universe'; but even clearer in Q. 3:3–4, where it is said that God revealed the Torah and the Gospel and then the *furqān*: Torah, Gospel and Qur'ān are in continuity, but the Qur'ān *now* is a 'discrimination', a *furqān*.[7] Many Qur'ānic passages (for example Q. 10:32: 'This God, your Lord, is the Truth (*haqq*) and what there is after the Truth (*haqq*) save error (*dalāl*)?'), discriminate between the true (*haqq*) and the false (*bātil*). This Qur'ānic awareness (see also Q. 21:18: 'God hurls Truth (*haqq*) against falsehood (*bātil*)') is something more than a question of knowledge; it is an ontological question. Islam distinguishes itself from other ideologies and religions both from the point of view of belief and from the point of view of history and even of essence. This is patently demonstrated by the clear-cut opposition Muhammad drew between his religion and the pagans' religion. Remember the Qur'an's declaration:

> Say: O deniers/disbelievers! I do not worship what you worship; neither do you worship what I worship. I do not venerate what you venerate; neither do you venerate what I venerate. You have your religion and I have mine (Q. 109).

From the same point of view (as a *furqān*), we must understand the clearcut contrast between Islam on one hand; and Judaism and Christianity on the other.[8] Two (or more) phases of history, I stress, and not of a mythologi-

---

the history and destiny of the Jewish people; the Arabs, by contrast, are not the center of Qur'ānic outlook. The Bible is the Book of an elected people; the Qur'ān is the book of a people, the Arab people, but later and progressively acquired the awareness of having been revealed for all humanity. Moreover, in my view, the Qur'ān is a *furqān*, while the Bible emphasizes the continuity of history from creation to the final triumph of the Jews with the manifestation of the Messiah.

7.   The translation of *furqān* as 'salvation' (by many commentators including Arberry and Bausani) is, in my view, misleading. Scarcia Amoretti (2009: 54–55) discussed the issue in depth, concluding that 'salvation' is the most comprehensive meaning of *furqān* (perhaps derived from the Aramaic *purqān*). It is true that the word has been interpreted in many ways (as Scarcia Amoretti recalls): as distinction between what is true and what is false by Zamakhsharī, as the totality of 'solid' (*muhkamāt*) verses by Qummī, as the totality of the revealed Books by Tabātabā'ī, and so on. But I believe that the Qur'ān's awareness of itself to be a 'discriminating event', strongly supports the translation I chose.

8.   This presupposition is obviously at odds with a long-standing scholarly tradition. From Goldziher to Fahd, from Kister to Lecker (not forgetting Claudio Lo Jacono), many scholars have emphasized the continuity and permanence of the 'pagan' pre-Islamic culture – with its beliefs and practices – in Islam. I have no reason to dispute the well-grounded results of such scholarly research. However,

cal past (Judaism) or of a mythological contemporaneity (Christianity). In conclusion, *God is Himself history* and history is 'the days of God'.

Muhammad Iqbāl (1873–1938) argued that: God is time; history is time; then God is history. Progressively, his reasoning unfolds as follows:

> "God causeth the day and the night to take their turn. Verily in this is teaching for men of insight" (Q. 24:44). This is why the Prophet said: "Do not vilify time [*dahr*] for time is God". [...] Time regarded as destiny forms the very essence of things. As the Qur'ān says: "God created all things and assigned to each its destiny". [...] The Ultimate Ego [God] exists in pure duration wherein change ceases to be a succession of varying attitudes, and reveals its true character as continuous creation, "untouched by weariness" and unseizable "by slumber or sleep" [hint to Q. 2:255]. [...] Divine Time is what the Qur'ān described as the "Mother of Books" in which the whole of history, freed from the net of causal sequence, is gathered up in a single super-eternal "now". [...] History or, in the language of the Qur'ān, the "days of God", is the third source of human knowledge according to the Qur'ān (Iqbal 2013: 11, 50, 60, 76, 138 respectively).

Islamic monotheism represents a break for while Jewish religion was strictly identified with the Jewish people so that God manifested Himself in Israel as well as Israel acquiring its identity in God,[9] Islam is the univer-

---

a hermeneutical analysis of the Holy Book, attentive to its deep spirit, cannot but acknowledge that the Qur'an's self-awareness represents a radical change and innovation: Qur'ānic revelation definitively breaks the course of history.

9. From the Islamic point of view, the Jews did not comprehend Moses' mission and, in spite of God's warnings, persevered in their mistakes (see for example Q. 2:47–71). The Jews broke the covenant attributing to themselves the qualification of 'elect people'. As we read in the Bible: 'for you are a people holy to the LORD your God. Out of all the peoples on the face of the earth, the LORD has chosen you to be his treasured possession' (Deut. 14:2). The Qur'ān says: 'Say [Prophet]: You who follow the Jewish faith, if you truly claim that out of all people you alone are the friends of God, then you should be hoping for death' (Q. 62:6; trans. Abdel Haleem). Judaism is, in fact, the religion of a particular people only much later extended to embrace all humanity. Islam, by contrast, claims to be the only true monotheism – a monotheism that, on the one hand, emphasizes the unity of God (*tawhīd*), while, on the other, it fosters the universal unity of the human community (often the Qur'ān says: *ya ayyuhā al-nās*... 'o you people...'). Patriarch Joseph's tale in the Bible (Genesis 37–50) highlights this perspective. In my view it is not merely a folk tale as Liverani suggests (Liverani 2003). Particularly through Joseph, and long before the systematization of the stories of Moses and the Exodus, Israel discovered its identity and its favoured status. Israel was chosen by God to dominate foreign countries and peoples. Israel was granted authority from the Nile to the Euphrates. Possibly, the very roots of the contemporary myth of the Great Israel (nurtured by Jewish fundamentalism even now) can be detected here. Israeli people *acknowledge themselves in God*, and because of this

sal religion connecting all peoples and races: 'O mankind, indeed We have created you male and female and We have made of you peoples and tribes, so that you may know each other. Surely the noblest among you in the sight of God is the most godfearing' (Q. 49:13).

This is 'eventful' as Cragg and Cantwell Smith put it.[10] But the Qur'ān is also a 'disclosure' (*a-letheia*) of the Truth. In this context, 'truth' (*haqq*) is 'disclosure' (*kashf*), that is *a-letheia*. *A-letheia* is not simply removal of the veil, but phenomenological 'putting down' and disclosure of the essence. This is particularly important for the Qur'ān not only because it is a revelation, that is, a manifestation of the hidden (*ghā'ib*), but also because the same Qur'ān is truth (*haqq*) spoken by God and speaking to humans. 'We shall show them (*sanuriyhim*) Our signs in the material world and within themselves, until it becomes manifest (*yatabayyana*) to them that He is the Truth' (Q. 41:53). Truth is 'manifestation' and 'showing', particularly of the 'signs' of God. We will discuss more thoroughly the meaning of *haqq* ('truth' and 'reality') in the second part of this book. But 'disclosure' involves a perceptive hermeneutical activity. Literalism and literal adherence to the text are no more satisfying. We cannot grasp by literalism the multifarious appearances of Truth (*haqq*): if facts are all interpretations, because we look at them through our own eyes and prejudices, Truth is equally interpretative in itself.

acknowledgment Israel lays claim to the Promised Land. Everything is designed to stress the ethnic and religious pre-eminence of the elected people. Thomas Mann illustrated all this very well in his four-part novel, *Joseph and His Brothers*. For in Mann's mythical-ironical reconstruction, the discovery of monotheism is nothing but the ongoing self-identification of God through humanity. The history of the patriarchs, from Abraham to Jacob to Joseph, is the same history of God's self-identification.

10. In the perspective of 'eventfulness' we can understand Paul Ricoeur's position: 'Ricoeur arrives at narrative as a possibility of experiencing the word by experiencing the events recounted directly, and not dwelling on questions of the narrator or author, that is, on the idea of a direct speaking voice. While this may come across as a counterintuitive move, he succeeds hermeneutically in arguing for the "character" of an event as the vehicle of the proclamation, or what we may call the image of the speaking voice. The examples Ricoeur offers of the election of Abraham or the anointing of David or the resurrection of the Christ are interpreted as not simply passing events but events that transcendentally mark a rupture in history and a new epoch. It is within the story itself that Yahweh is designated in the third person as the ultimate *actant*' (Ricoeur 1980, quoted in El-Desouky 2014: 27–28). In Ricoeur, the 'event' is something happening in history, and undoubtedly Christ's 'event' changed the world and began a new epoch'. But the Qur'ān unites 'eventfulness' with 'discrimination' (*furqān*) and '*a-letheia*', and it claims to be more than an 'eventful' happening, rather a switch.

# 3

## TAFSĪR AND TA'WĪL

Qur'ānic hermeneutics began very early in the history of Islamic culture, possibly even before the ultimate and complete edition of the *mushaf*. It assumed the two well-known forms of *tafsīr* and *ta'wīl*. There is no need here to explain what *tafsīr* and *ta'wīl* are or to sketch out a short history of these hermeneutical genres. Rather, it is useful to note that the word *tafsīr* appears only once in the Qur'ān (Q. 25:33): 'They do not bring you any example (*mathal*) but that We give you the Truth (*haqq*) and the best interpretation/explanation (*tafsīr*)', apparently meaning that God Himself will interpret/explain His Scripture (but where? And how?). In any case, *tafsīr* seems to have precisely the meaning later attributed to it. As to the word *mathal*, I will discuss it in Chapter 4. *Ta'wīl* appears 17 times, eight of which in *sūra Yūsuf* (Q. 12), where it means interpretation of dreams and not 'hermeneutics'. The most important occurrence of the word is obviously Q. 3:7, but I will discuss this too in Chapter 4.

The question in point here is that the genre *tafsīr* in Muslim literature cannot be considered a real 'hermeneutics'. Neither the *tafsīr bi'l-ma'thūr* (the *tafsīr* based on prophetic traditions) nor the *tafsīr bi'l-ra'y* (the *tafsīr* based on free personal judgement) satisfy the conditions of interpretation arising from the previous stated characteristics of the Qur'ān as *a-letheia*. Grammatical analysis or historical surveys of prophets and kings do not 'disclose' any inner meaning of the text.

Undoubtedly, *ta'wīl* involves a hermeneutical approach of 'disclosure', that can be literary or philosophical, or religious and spiritual. Literature and philosophy, on the one hand, and spirituality and Gnosticism, on the other, do not always perform on a homologous level, however, as far as method and contents are concerned. I profess here my intention to exclude from my analysis the esoteric level, because spirit is not definable and quantifiable, while literature and philosophy are, and can be systematized, or better, rationalized within well-defined boundaries. This may imply a painful renunciation: i.e. giving up mysticism (*tasawwuf*) as an interpretation mode – an interpretation mode repeated evidence for which is well-known within the history of Islamic thought: yet here we must leave the field free for a future exegesis that (to paraphrase Kant) will present itself as a Science.[1] Liter-

1.  At least two great Islamic *sūfī* thinkers conceived their major works as Qur'ānic

ary hermeneutics will be discussed in depth, however, because literature is particularly fitted for both linguistic and symbolic hermeneutics which are absolutely central for a holy text like the Qur'ān.

The Arabic word *ta'wīl* indicates the attempt to go back to 'sources', to the original foundation of language, so it represents the process by which the exegete tries to seize the deep, innermost meaning of a verse without abdicating to literality. This *ta'wīl* discipline is of venerable antiquity in Islamic religious literature, particularly Shiite but also present in Sunnism. Contemporary hermeneutics, though, goes widely beyond the limits of classicism, updating or even reversing them. Thus *ta'wīl* assumes a philosophical declination that tries to harmonize the results of theoretical and intellectual research with the appearance (*zāhir*) of a text such as the Qur'ān, which articulates, beyond all interpretative doubt, God's very word uttered in clear Arabic so that it is immediately understood by everybody. 'Ali Merad wrote that:

> *Grosso modo*, the couple *tafsīr/ta'wīl* is equivalent to the couple exegesis/hermeneutics. While *tafsīr* makes use of all the language resources in order to understand objectively the revealed text, *ta'wīl* means an effort of interpretation aiming to make all the semantic and symbolic values of the text apparent. In the Qur'ānic lexicon, the term is used either to indicate the interpretation of dreams, or the interpretation of the Book itself. The etymology of *ta'wīl* suggests the idea of "bringing back to" or "making something arriving at", that is to *direct* the meaning. In exegesis, *ta'wīl* consists not simply in *saying* what the revealed datum means, but in *suggesting* (or even *deciding* arbitrarily) what must be understood (Merad 1998: 47).

Unfortunately, Islamic thought did not problematize *ta'wīl* enough. The science of *ta'wīl* remained within the limits of 'thinkable' and 'thought' – again in Arkoun's terms.[2] On the other hand, philology is a special kind of hermeneutics, very important as far as it is applied to the Holy Texts.

---

commentaries: Abū Hāmid al-Ghazālī with his *Ihyā 'ulūm al-dīn* (*The Revival of Religious Sciences*); and Muhy al-Dīn Ibn 'Arabī with his *Futūhāt Makkiyya* (*The Openings of Mecca*) and *Fusūs al-hikam* (*The Bezels of Wisdom*). The approaches taken by Al-Ghazālī and Ibn 'Arabī are utterly different however. The former was very careful to avoid any compromising with theopathical excesses. The latter was deeply esoteric. Al-Ghazālī's commentary aimed at reconciling mystical experience with the Law; Ibn 'Arabī's commentary aimed to set out a new framework of thought, potentially antinomic. Al-Ghazālī's path is useful to my argument; that of Ibn 'Arabī is not.

2.    Mohammed Arkoun (1928–2010) was an Algerian who taught for 40 years at the Sorbonne in Paris. He was one of the first Muslim modern intellectuals to claim the application of sociological, historical, humanistic sciences to Qur'ānic exegesis.

The case of the Christian Reformation is particularly telling. Unfortunately, in Islamic *tafsīr* there is a lot of philology, but only rarely does philology become hermeneutics.

To enable the reader to better understand which kind of *ta'wil* we are speaking of, we have to distinguish our position from that of Seyyed Hossein Nasr, perhaps the most prominent contemporary metaphysician moving in a traditional, esoteric framework (see for example, Nasr 1966). For while he maintained that Islamic philosophy is essentially a philosophical herme-neutics of the sacred text, he meant 'prophetic philosophy' grounded upon 'spiritual hermeneutics' (*ta'wīl*) (Nasr 2006). This perspective is discarded here as was explained earlier.

A Qur'ānic verse that is worth quoting again is: 'We shall show them (*sanuriyhim*) Our signs in the material world and within themselves, until it becomes manifest (*yatabayyana*) to them that He is the Truth' (Q. 41:53). 'We shall show', that is 'We will make them see', the verb is *arā* involving the idea 'to make something clear and apparent'. 'To become manifest', that is *tabayyana* or 'to make something clear and intelligible' through an *osten-sio* – in Latin *ostendere* means both 'to move towards' and 'to show' and 'to manifest/demonstrate'. The Truth becomes apparent through an act of 'showing' (*ostensio*). This Qur'ānic utterance does not mean only that there is a connection between the external and internal dimensions of human beings, but also that knowledge emerges from a disclosure of Truth. More-over, this does not merely mean removing the veil that conceals the nucleus of truth, but rather, using Heidegger-derived terms, the phenomenological showing and disclosing itself of the Being (in this case God). The statement by Mahmūd Muhammad Tāhā (1909–1985), who is considered a martyr by many, must be understood in this sense: the process leading the individual to transform from 'believer' (*mu'min*) into 'Muslim' (*muslim*) is based on a ' truth of certainty' (*'ilm haqq al-yaqīn*) which moves/points to God as the goal of our progress:

> The truth of the matter is that *al-islam*, as conveyed in the Qur'an, comes in two stages: the stage of dogma (*al-'aqida*) and the stage of the truth (*al-haqiqa*) or knowledge. Each of these two stages has three levels. The levels of dogma are *al-islam, al-iman* and *al-ihsan*, while the levels of knowledge are *'ilm al-yaqin, 'ilm 'ayn al-yaqin* and *'ilm haqq al-yaqin*. Finally there is a seventh stage in the ladder of evolution, which is *islam*, which completes the cycle. The end of religious evolution resembles the beginning, yet they are not identical. The beginning is *al-islam* and the end is *al-islam*, but there is vast difference between *al-islam* at the beginning of religious evolution and *al-islam* at the end. The stage of *al-'aqida* is the stage of the nation of Mu'minin, which is the nation of the First Message of Islam. The stage of knowledge is the stage of the nation of Muslimin, which is the nation of the Second Message of Islam. This nation has not come yet. [...] The coming nation is a nation of both

> Muslimin as well as Mu'minin at one and the same time, while the first
> nation was one of Mu'minin (believers) and not of Muslimin (submit-
> ters) in the final sense of *al-islam* as total and intelligent surrender to
> God (Taha 1996: 46–47).

Tāhā's argument is grounded on specific *hadīths* and Qur'ānic verses. The distinction between *islām*, *īmān* and *ihsān* is clearly articulated in the well-known and widely transmitted '*hadīth* of Gabriel' which is no matter to quote extensively here. While the three stages of knowledge are alluded in Q. 102:5–7: 'No indeed, if you know it with certain science [or "science of certainty", *'ilm al-yaqīn*], you would see Hell! But later you will see it with a certain eye [or "eye of certainty", *'ayn al-yaqīn*]'.

Being certain that Truth (*haqq*) has come and has defeated falseness (*bātil*) (cf. Q. 21:18) implies the fact that God displayed some signs (*āyāt*) that reveal Him in the cosmos, in the soul and in Scripture. In this way, the veil of appearance is actually removed to show Truth. 'Signs' clearly refer to a world of symbols that must be decoded, i.e. interpreted.

# 4

## SYMBOLISM

Decodifying symbols is obviously a hermeneutical activity. Is Islam a symbolic culture? In order to answer this question, it is necessary to define the meaning of 'symbol'. Now, symbol has at least three main meanings: (a) what is representative of another thing in virtue of an analogical correspondence; (b) as a synonym of 'sign'; (c) as something that reveals the secret, being in this way a path to the comprehension of the sacred (see Ries 1994). Moreover, as Ernest Cassirer put it (Cassirer 1985), symbol is a sensible 'sign' bringing a meaning: the same language is a 'symbolic form' through which man not only communicates with other human beings, but builds up a whole *Weltanschauung* (and a whole ontology).

If we understand 'symbol' both as a 'sign' referring to an underlying reality, and as a representation of another thing *via* their analogy and as a key to unlocking the sacred through a meaningful language, undoubtedly Islam is a highly symbolic culture. Maybe it is not by chance that Qur'ānic verses as well as natural signs are both called *āyāt*. Interpreting the *āyāt* of nature is the straight path to the knowledge of God, because they are symbols of God's omnipotence and creative activity. Interpreting the *āyāt* of the Qur'ān is the straight path to a thorough knowledge of the secrets of God's project ('habits' or *sunna*), because God's plans and will are 'disclosed' in the Book. Once more, Nasr Abū Zayd grasped the kernel of the issue:

> The special linguistic dynamics through which the Qur'ānic language influenced Arabic have transformed the linguistic signs, vocabulary, into semiotic signs. In other words, the Qur'ānic language transfers a lot of Arabic vocabulary to the sphere of semiotics where they refer only to one absolute reality which is God. The function of such transformation is to evade the seen reality in order to establish the unseen divine reality of God; that is why everything in the whole seen reality, according to the Qur'ān, is nothing but "signs", *āyāt*, referring to God. Not only natural phenomena, animated and non-animated, are semiotic signs but human history is also presented in the Qur'ān as a series of "signs". The everlasting struggle between "truth" and "non-truth", *al-ḥaqq wa'l-bāṭil*, or between the oppressed and the oppressor, *al-mustaḍ'afīn wa'l-mustakbirīn*, is presented in the Qur'ān as signs of God's sunna (Abū Zayd 2000b: 8).

Semiotics is hermeneutics. A symbol is something that 'takes the place of' another thing. It is vital to go beyond the literal.

We have now to distinguish between metaphor and symbol. Metaphor means 'transfer of meaning from a thing to another'. As Aristotle put it: '*metaphorà* consists in giving a thing a name that belongs to another thing: this transfer may be done from the genus to the species, from the species to the genus, from a species to another species or by analogy' (*Poetics*, 21, 1457b 7). There is an obvious common ground between symbol and metaphor. However, the symbol keeps and perhaps enhances the direct connection (and sometimes the resemblance) between the symbol and the symbolized thing: the *āyāt* of nature are the symbols of God's creative activity; the *āyāt* of the Qur'ān refer symbolically to the eternal decrees of God written in the Preserved Tablet (*lawh mahfūz*) or Mother of the Book (*umm al-kitāb*). On the other hand, a metaphor is an allegorization of the metaphoricized thing: their underlying meanings can be somewhat different.

From a philosophical point of view, the outcome of symbolization, and particularly metaphoricization, is that 'reality', 'certainty' and 'truth' do not correspond to one another. A thing can be certain and/or true, but not real (for example, a geometrical figure). A thing can be epistemologically (scientifically) 'true', but not 'real' (for example, in quantum mechanics, the reality and the position of a subatomic particle). We will deal extensively with truth and reality in Part II of this book. For the present, we have to emphasize the necessity of a hermeneutics that decodes the symbolism of the message, of the alleged utter clarity of the text. To this end, I will examine the Qur'ān itself, the figure of the Prophet Muhammad and the Ka'ba as the symbolic 'house of God'. We will try to understand how this decodification of symbols is helpful in going beyond what is literally apparent.

## THE QUR'ĀN

In Arabic, there are two main roots expressing the concept of 'symbol': r-m-z and m-th-l. *Ramz-rumūz* and *mathal-amthāl* are the Arabic words translating 'symbol(s)'. The first root (r-m-z) appears in the Qur'ān only once (Q. 3:41), but it does not seem to convey the meaning of 'symbol': while, for example, *ramz* is rendered by Arberry in his interpretation of the Qur'ān with 'tokens', Abdel Haleem has 'gestures' and, similarly, the Italian translator Alessandro Bausani has 'gesti'. On the contrary, the second root (m-th-l) occurs frequently. The form *mathal/amthāl* alone appears more than 40 times. The most meaningful occurrences for our purpose are perhaps the following:

- Q. 13:17: '*kadhālika yadribu Allāhu al-amthāl*': 'this is how God makes illustrations' (Abdel Haleem; Arberry: 'similitudes'; in Italian, Bausani: *parabole* = parables). The *mathal alluded to* is the 'symbolic' image referring to a hidden meaning and explaining it, is the following: 'He sends water from the sky that fills riverbeds to overflowing, each according to its measure. The stream carries on its surface a growing layer of froth, like the froth that appears when people melt metals in the fire to make ornaments and tools: in this way God illustrates truth and falsehood (*mithluhu kadhālika yadribu Allāhu al-haqq wa'l-bātil*) – the froth disappears, but what is of benefit to man stays behind' (trans. Abdel Haleem).

The declensions of 'm-th-l' comprise: 'comparisons' (Q. 29:43: 'Such are the comparisons (*al-amthāl*) We [God speaking] draw for people', trans. Abdel Haleem [Arberry: 'similitudes'; Bausani alike: 'similitudini']); 'examples' (Q. 17:89: 'In this Qur'an We have set out all kinds of examples (*min kulli mathal*) for people', trans. Abdel Haleem [Arberry: 'similitude'; Bausani: 'esempi', examples]); 'description' (Q. 18:54: 'In this Qur'an We have presented every kind of description (*min kulli mathal*) for people', trans. Abdel Haleem [Arberry: 'similitude'; Bausani: 'esempi' again]); and so on. However *mathal* is translated – 'similitude', as coherently[1] rendered by Arberry, or 'illustration'/'explanation'/'example' for 'explaining' and 'illustrating' a concept, a secret, another 'thing' through a symbol of it – it is a key hermeneutical word involving 'disclosure' and the subsequent necessity of interpretation, i.e. of going beyond literality.

- Particularly important, for its ontological implications, is the passage Q. 30:27: *lahu al-mathal al-a'là fī'l-samawāt wa'l-ard*, that is literally: 'To Him the supreme similitude in the heavens and

---

1. The question of coherence in rendering the same word in different contexts is crucial in translation (and then in interpretation), especially of a Holy text. In the case of the Qur'an, the alleged change of meaning of many words, for example from the Meccan to the Medinan period of revelation (and the word *jihād* is a substantial case in point), can give rise to difficulties, because orientalists and critics will suggest that the words changed their meaning in relation to changed historical circumstances. But what about the 'intentions' of God? Did they change accordingly? Or when God revealed the Qur'an, did He *always* use a word with the same meaning, despite the period of revelation? From an Islamic point of view, this is an intricate problem, because it is not simple to justify theologically a change in God's intentions. Hermeneutics would need flexibility in meaning, but the coherence of revelation would need a univocal approach to meaning. The issue is tantamount to that of *zāhir* and *bātin*, but here there is the additional issue of communication – from God to humans, and among the humans from one man/woman to another – especially for non-Arabic-speaking Muslims.

the earth', or hermeneutically '*He is the supreme symbol of the heavens and the earth*'. Quite an odd expression, certainly. A very interesting comment is that of the Jalālayn (whose famous commentary was composed in Mamluk Egypt in the fifteenth century): 'This attribute of sublimity is that there is no god but God (*lā ilāh illā allāh*)'.[2] However, the rendering of the translators is sensibly different: 'He is above all *comparison* in the heavens and earth' (Abdel Haleem); 'His is the loftiest *likeness* in the heavens and the earth' (Arberry); 'His is the most exalted *attribute* in heaven and earth' (Dawood); 'Sua è solo la *somiglianza* più eccelsa nei cieli e sulla terra [only His is the loftiest *resemblance/likeness* in the heavens and the earth]' (Bausani). Notwithstanding the differences of rendering, apparently the term *mathal* hints here at the substantial heterogeneity in essence between God and the creatures. None of them 'resembles' Him, there is no 'comparison' with Him, because God is a symbol of Himself, He explains Himself by the affirmation of ipseity *huwa huwa*, 'He is Himself' while things are other than Him. Again, we will discuss this point at greater length in Part II of the book. Now, we have to remember first of all Q. 42:11: '*laysa ka-mithlihi shayy'un*', that is 'nothing has resemblance with Him' ('There is nothing like Him', Abdel Haleem). Secondly, that the universe is a *āya* of God, one of His 'signs'. Particularly meaningful is Q. 45:3–6: 'There are signs (*āyāt*) in the heavens and the earth for those who believe: in the creation of you, in the creatures God scattered on earth, these are signs (*āyāt*) for people of sure faith; in the alternation of night and day, in the rain God provides, sending it down from the sky and reviving the dead earth with it, and in the shifting of the winds there are signs (*āyāt*) for those who use their reason (*ya'qilūna*). These are God's signs (*āyāt*) that We recount to you [Prophet, to show] the Truth (*haqq*)' (trans. Abdel Haleem). Through the 'signs' God makes the Truth 'manifest'. The signs stimulate rational (hermeneutical?) activity in human beings. Moreover, the Jalālayn glosses the word *āyāt* as follows: 'A demonstration of the omnipotence and Unicity of God Most High' (*dālla 'alā qudrati Allāh wa wahdāniyyatihi ta'ālā*). Thus, the universe is a symbol of God's activity, but God Himself is in a sense a 'symbol' of the universe's complex structure. God and the universe are utterly different, but God is the rationale of the universe. Fazlur Rahman wrote: 'This gigantic machine, the universe, with all its causal processes, is the prime "sign" (*āya*) or proof of its Maker. Who else but an infinitely powerful, merciful and purposeful Being

---

2.    See any edition of *Tafsīr al-Jalālayn, ad locum.*

could have brought into existence something with dimensions so vast and an order and design so complex and minute? […] The universe as a sign vanishes into nothing when "put beside" God, for beside God nothing at all has any inherent warrant to exist. That the earth supports people and does not sink, and the heavens holding this immense space do not shred is itself a miracle (Q. 34:9; 50:6ff.; 51:47ff.; also 13:2ff. and all verses that speak of the heavens and the earth having been firmly built and well-knit). Indeed, there could have been just empty nothingness instead of this *plenitude of being*' (Rahman 1989: 68–69; my emphasis).

- Last, but not least, there is obviously the critical verse of the Light, Q. 24:35. As is well-known, the verse says that God is the 'Light' of heavens and earth (*Allāh nūr al-samawāt wa'l-ard*) and that His Light 'resembles' a niche, etc. (*mathalu nūrihi ka-mishkātin...*). There is a double symbolism: the Light of God is the symbol of the well-knitted structure of the universe; and the niche is the symbol of the same God's Light. Thus, Light, universe and niche recall each other by subtle analogy and explain one another. The esoteric, psychological, philosophical hermeneutics of the verse involves a homogeneous explanation. Many interpretations of the verse have been put forward. We will refer here to only five of them, perhaps the most pertinent: (a) Abū Ya'qūb al-Sijistānī, a prominent Ismaili theologian who lived in the tenth century CE, interpreted the niche, glass, tree, oil and so on as referring to the hierarchy of Shiite *imāms*; (b) Abū Hāmid al-Ghazālī (d. 1111, perhaps the greatest 'Muslim intellectual' [see Watt 1962] of all times), to the hierarchy and functions of human intellect from the bottom up to its utmost perfection; (c) the great Aristotelian philosopher Ibn Sīnā (Avicenna [980–1037]), to the hierarchy and structure of the cosmic intellects; (d) Shihāb al-Dīn Suhrawārdī (d. 1191), the master of Illuminativism, an esoteric philosophy based on the metaphysics of light, to the hierarchy of the metaphysical Lights ordained by God who is the Light of Lights (*nūr 'alā nūr*); (e) Mullā Sadrā Shirāzī (an Iranian theosopher, heir of Avicenna, died 1640), as the graded modulation of Being (*tashkīk*). All these interpretations would imply a correspondence and thus an analogy among their components. God (*Allāh*) is always above and beyond the hierarchical structures, however (He is *nūr 'alā nūr*). The niche, glass, tree and oil as symbols of His Light have a purely formal analogy with His essence that is *over* (*'alā*) the hierarchies.

In order to better understand the philosophical hermeneutics of symbolism, it is important to consider the problems of the famous verse Q. 3:7:

> It is He who sent down upon you the Book (*kitāb*), wherein are verses/
> signs (*āyāt*) clear/solid (*muhkamāt*) that are the Mother of the Book
> (*umm al-kitāb*), and verses *mutashābihāt* [see below for the rendering].
> As for those in whose hearts there is deviation (*zaygh*), they follow what
> is *shābih*, wishing for dissension (*fitna*), and wishing for its interpreta-
> tion (*ta'wīl*), but none knows its interpretation save God and those firmly
> rooted in knowledge (*al-rāsikhūn fī'l-'ilm*) say: "We believe in it; all is
> from our Lord".

The clear/solid verses or signs (I stress again that Qur'ānic verses are
'signs' and symbols of supreme reality) in the Mother of the Book seems
beyond interpretation, because they are the eternal archetypes of God's
Word and so outside human fallible interpretation. But the destiny of the
*mutashābihāt* seems different. In Q. 3:7 *mutashābihāt* verses are clearly
verses to be subjected to hermeneutics and interpretation (condemned by the
Qur'ān? This is a hermeneutical open question). What does *mutashābihāt*
mean exactly, however? (see Kinberg 1988). The root sh-b-h in the Qur'ān
has almost always the sense of 'resemble', 'look like'. For example: the
mysterious verse Q. 4:157, referring to the alleged 'double' of the cruci-
fied Jesus, is translated by Abdel Haleem as follows: 'They [the Jews] did
not kill him [Jesus], nor did they crucify him, though it [*hu* referring to
whom?] was made to appear like (*shubbiha*) that to them'; or Q. 6:99 (and
other similar expressions): '…olives and pomegranates, alike yet different
(*mutashābihan wa ghayr mutashābihin*)' (on the debated issue of Jesus'
crucifixion in the Qur'ān see for example, Lawson 2009 and Saeed 2014).

A significant occurrence of *mutashābih* is Q. 39:23 – another difficult *āya*:
'God sent down the most beautiful of all communications/tales (*hadīth*), a
Book/Scripture *mutashābihan mathānī*'. Abdel Haleem translated: '[Scrip-
ture] that is consistent and draws *comparisons*'; Arberry: '*consimilar* in
its oft-repeated'; Bausani: 'Libro di allegorie [Book of *allegories*]'. The
verse seems to say that in the Scripture there are a number of often repeated
*āyāt* similar to one another; but it is not clear if this similitude involves the
*necessity* of esoteric (symbolic or allegorical) interpretation (as Bausani's
translation implies). For just three verses below, Q. 39:27–28 says: 'In this
Qur'ān We have put forward all kinds of illustration for people, so that
they may take heed, an Arabic Qur'ān free from any distortion – so that
people may be mindful' (Abdel Haleem) (see also Q. 41:3). Abdel Haleem's
'illustration' is in the Arabic text the word *mathal* (!): can we render it as
'symbol'? Are these symbols 'free of any distortion' (*ghayr dhī 'iwāj*), that
is absolutely clear and beyond any interpretation? Is it possible for a symbol
to have no need of interpretation?

Consequently, we understand why al-Tabarī (tenth century), a very distinguished Qur'ānic commentator who made wide use in his work of the
Prophetic traditions, commenting the first verses of *sūra Yūsuf* (Q. 12:1–2:

'These are the signs of a clear Scripture. Indeed, We revealed an Arabic Qur'ān so that maybe you will understand' (*tilka āyātu'l-kitābi'l-mubīni inna anzalnahu qur'ānan 'arabiyyan la'allakum ta'qīluna*) writes that:

> "Clear Scripture" [means] that: These verses of the Book are clear for those who recite it and meditate on it, with regard to [what is prescribed in it] of licit or illicit and prohibited, or to all kinds of meanings contained therein. For God Most High defined it "clear" and made no distinction between the part and the whole with regard to its clarification. [The expression we are dealing with] refers to the whole [Qur'ān], because all its content is clear' (al-Tabarī 1957).

Actually, al-Tabarī refuses in general the idea that the Qur'ān contains 'solid' (*muhkamāt*) or *mutashābihāt* (allegorical, symbolic) verses: for him, *all* verses are clear.

Another outstanding *mufassir*, al-Baydāwī, commenting the same verses Q. 12:1–3, wrote:

> By the "Book" here is meant the *sūra* itself. The meaning is (therefore): These verses constitute the verses of the *sūra* which presents itself clearly as inimitability; or, as that of which the meanings are clear; or, as that which makes clear (*bayyana*) to anyone who reflects upon it that it comes from God; or, that which makes clear to the Jews what they have asked about. [...] *As an Arabic Qur'ān*: This part (of the whole revelation) is designated here as *qur'ān*. In origin, this word is a generic noun which is applicable to the whole (of the class) as well as to a part of it. It then became predominant as a proper name referring to the whole... *Perhaps you will understand*: This is the reason why God sent down the Book in this (Arabic) form. The meaning is (therefore): We [God] have sent it down to you [Muhammad] as something that is composed in your own language or can be recited in your own language, so that you will be able to understand it and grasp its meanings; or, that you will employ your intellect and (through it) discover that the account, out of the mouth of a man like this who could not produce a (comparable) account (previously), is a matchless miracle (*mu'jiz*) which one can conceive only as having been revealed (quoted in Gätje 1976: 53).

Clarity and perfection of Qur'ānic Arabic (*i'jāz*) is a pre-condition/consequence of the clarity and un-ambiguousness of the *muhkamāt* verses. Qur'ānic inimitability (*i'jāz*), which became a dogma of the Islamic faith but is far from undisputed,[3] can be a hindrance to translation and interpretation as we shall see in Chapter 9.

3.  Perhaps the most important classical theologian who dealt with *i'jāz* was al-Baqillānī (d. 1013). He underlined that the unique character of the Qur'ān resides in three main features: it contains information about the invisible (*ghā'ib*); it has been uttered by an illiterate Prophet keeping notwithstanding all its literary qualities; it is wonderfully organized and composed, bringing divine inspiration

To sum up, although it can sound quite paradoxical, *mutashābihāt* in Q. 3:7 would not mean 'ambiguous' (Abdel Haleem; Arberry) or 'allegorical' (Bausani) verses, but *symbolic*. There is a measure of ambiguity in symbolism, and allegory is a form of symbolism. But can we say that *mutashābihāt/ symbolic āyāt* (verses) *must* necessarily be interpreted? Are they not analogical with the symbolized and so reflecting exactly the characteristics of the symbolized? Is al-Tabarī right then in looking often with suspect allegorization/interpretation? The Qur'ān itself states that the *mutashābihāt* can be 'interpreted' (submitted to *ta'wīl*), although he who does it risks divine condemnation (as told in Q. 3:7); moreover, God as symbol *must* be interpreted, otherwise there is the risk of anthropomorphization.

Moreover, the very distinction between *zāhir* and *bātin*, two key terms in Islamic theology and philosophy, compels interpretation. The text can be obvious-clear-manifest-patent, that is *zāhir*, or secret–inward-hidden, that is *bātin*. But the hidden must be drawn out of the secretness and showed; and this is possible only through interpretation. For something hidden sunk in secretness is of no use: it must be 'disclosed' in openness to be suitable for action. The *zāhir* dimension represents the 'sense' of the text; the *bātin* dimension the 'meaning'. As suggested above, Abū Zayd distinguished keenly between 'sense' and 'meaning': the 'sense' of a text is the cultural product of a particular linguistic context (the 'sense' of the Qur'ān is the cultural product of the Arab environment of the seventh century); the 'meaning' of a text is the sense's outcome in an interpretive framework (Abū Zayd 2002: 48. The *zāhir* is immutable, codified. The *bātin* is changeable, interpretative. Nobody can stop at the *zāhir*. Not everybody is capable of grasping the *bātin*. Ismaili and *sūfī* hermeneutics are largely grounded on these presuppositions.

There are intriguing social and political implications in this outlook. The interpretation of *bātin* is reserved to an élite (*khāssa*) that can be also a political élite governing the state (the *'ulamā'*, for instance). The requirement that the masses (*'āmma*) submit to *zāhir* forces them to obey the élite. Hermeneutics can be a powerful tool of dominion.

---

to a level of exquisite literary sensibility and yet rescuing it from the 'poetry' of human beings and the ravings of charlatans. There is something sublime in its literary elegance which makes it accessible to everyone. The debate on this topic developed throughout the Islamic thought and, among others, the Mu'tazilite al-Nazzām (living in the ninth century) argued that the Qur'ān is inimitable with respect to its Arabic language because God brought about the miracle of preventing human beings from producing anything similar. The superiority of the Book consists then in its content, not in its form. See for example, Martin 1980, Mir 1990, Campanini 2016a. I shall return to this issue later discussing the translation of the Qur'ān.

## MUHAMMAD

In Islamic tradition, the Prophet Muhammad is the symbol of the 'perfect human being' (*insān kāmil*). He is the archetype of humans, both from the practical and the cosmological point of view.

On the one hand, the *imitatio muhammadis* is compelling for every believer. Abū Hāmid al-Ghazālī (c. 1056–1111) synthetized this attitude:

> Know then that the key to happiness is to follow the *sunna* and take as a model the example of God's messenger – on whom may God's blessings fall! – in all that which he has done and said, even to the smallest details: how he moved and how he stood still, how he ate and how he behaved, how he slept and how he talked. And I do not mean only in relation to behaviour in worship (*'ibādāt*), since, as far as that is concerned, it is inconceivable that this be ignored when following the *sunna*, but in relation to all the everyday gestures of life, for from them comes the perfect model (in the ways of the Prophet). God – praise be upon Him! – said: "If you truly love God, follow me [i.e. the Prophet] and God will love you" (Q. 3:31); and again: "Whatever the Messenger gives you, accept it; and whatever he forbids you, forbear from it" (Q. 59:7) (Al-Ghazālī 1974: 102–103).

The imitation of the Prophet is the right path (*sirāt mustaqīm* or *sharī'a*)[4] to balance the inner and outer dimensions of human beings: perfecting the person in this world, it sets out the way to the next world.

On the other hand, Muhammad is the juncture connecting the microcosm and the macrocosm. Let me quote Annemarie Schimmel:

> As the *insān kāmil*, the Perfect Man, Muhammad is as it were the suture between the Divine and the created world; he is, so to speak, the *barzakh*, the isthmus between the Necessary and contingent existence. This role of the Prophet as the intermediate principle is found, according to the school of Ibn 'Arabī, in the very words of the profession of faith, *Muhammad rasūl Allāh*: Muhammad is the "manifested principle", *rasūl*, the messenger, is the "manifesting principle", and Allah is the "Principle in Itself". It is the element *rasūl* that relates the Principle in Itself to the manifested principle. [...] Muhammad, the prototype of the universe as well as of the individual, "the pupil in the eye of humanity", the Perfect Man who is necessary for God as the medium through which He can manifest Himself to be known and loved – all these ideas have been theologically elaborated after Ibn 'Arabī by his followers, among whom 'Abdul Karim al-Jili (Schimmel 1985: 134, 137).

---

4.  *Sharī'a* is obviously the commonest name for 'Islamic (revealed) Law', but its first meaning is 'way', 'path' (leading to water). Consequently, it has a function that is more ethical than normative.

Last but not least, Muhammad with his very person – and more, with his very *body* – embodies the interpretation of the Qur'ān. Muhammad's life is a living hermeneutics of the Qur'ān (see Ramadan 2006). A prophet is not a mere passive receptor of revelation. Muhammad *lived* the revelation into himself and the word of God led and enlightened his actions. His personality and character were molded by revelation, just as revelation was manifested through the actions and the words of the prophet. This is the reason why the *person* of the prophet represents a living hermeneutical key to the holy text. The Qur'ān itself emphasizes the hermeneutical (explicative) function of Muhammad (such as other prophets), a function that distinguishes him in regard to other prophets and makes him more excellent than them:

> We do not send before you men but those whom We inspired [revelation]. You [people] can ask those who own knowledge, if you really do not know it. We [always God speaking] [sent them] with clear signs (*āyāt*) and Scriptures (*zubūr*). Upon you [Muhammad] We sent down the remembrance (*dhikr*) so that you can explain to people what has been sent for them. Maybe, they will reflect (Q. 16:43–44).

Montgomery Watt argued that Muhammad's experience was real and sincere (see for example, Watt 1991), but Muhammad transferred upon the revelation his own psychological troubles and found in revelation the necessary support to solve his practical problems. Thus, the Qur'ān represents the contents of prophecy, while the prophet, and especially Muhammad, hands the message on to human beings interpreting it through his very person and activity.

The hermeneutical importance of Muhammad's life and person in interpreting the Qur'ān can be appreciated considering the long-standing discussion between historians as to whether we have to study the Book in order to know Muhammad's life or *vice versa* whether Muhammad's life is a guide to understand the Book. Arguing that the Qur'ān has been 'constructed' *a-posteriori* in a 'sectarian milieu', John Wansbrough contended that the Holy Book contains only vague and approximate informations on the Prophet's life: rather, it is the Prophet's life that constitutes a commentary of the Qur'ān, as it were, because both where 'invented' and elaborated together (Wansbrough 1978). Angelika Neuwirth and Nicolai Sinai (Neuwirth and Sinai 2011) argued that the Qur'ān – more than following step by step the Prophet's life through the development of revelation – evolved in accordance with the evolution of the believers community's needs. Be that as it may, it is apparent that Muhammad's life and the Qur'ān are strictly intertwined and that we cannot understand the former without the latter, and *vice versa*.

The inseparability of the message from the messenger is fully established and represents a cornerstone of Islam. The prophet conveys the message and, at the same time, the message substantiates the person of the prophet. When 'Ā'isha, the most beloved wife of Muhammad (after Khadīja's death), said that 'Muhammad's character was the Qur'ān', she meant exactly this. Accordingly, the Prophet Muhammad has been able to say in a famous *hadīth*: 'I am the house of knowledge'.

As Fazlur Rahman put it:

> Muhammad, like all other prophets, is a "warner and a giver of good tidings" and his mission is to preach – constantly and unflinchingly. Since this message is from God and is direly needed by men for survival and success, it has to be accepted by man and implemented. His preaching, therefore, is not conventional speech-making but has to "bring home" the crucial message. If the message is not accepted and the mission does not succeed, then the preacher may have discharged his duty, but God has definitely failed and humanity is doomed. But if God's purposes are frustrated and humanity doomed, has the preacher "discharged his duty"? His duty is to *succeed* in implementing the message in order "to reform the earth and remove corruption therefrom", and to institute an ethically-based social order wherein "good shall be commanded and evil prohibited" and "God's sovereignty shall be upheld" (Rahman 1989: 83).

Succeeding in implementing the message, the prophet interprets practically – historically – the Qur'ān. His *ta'wīl* is an 'active *cogito*', as Hasan Hanafī would say. The subjective thoughtful experience of the Prophet goes to the origins (*awwala* then *ta'wīl*) of the message, to the inner meaning of revelation. This is why it is so important to study Muhammad's life along with the Qur'ān.

The difference from Christianity is striking. Jesus Christ does not interpret the Scripture: he is *himself* Scripture. The Qur'ān is the Word of God. Jesus Christ is himself God. Muhammad interprets the Qur'ān. Jesus Christ interprets himself, so to speak.

## THE TEMPLE

In all religions, the temple plays a central role: it is the house of God, the place where believers pray to their God, the gathering place of men and women seeking the sacred and mutual cooperation, but also the symbol of universal order and of the very presence of God on earth. In this latter sense especially, it is a highly hermeneutical key. It is not a literary or formal hermeneutics, but a 'concrete', 'physical' hermeneutics, so to speak.

In Islam, the temple *par excellence* is obviously the mosque (*masjid* in Arabic, plural *masājid*) (AA.VV. 1991). Its meaning is purely exoteric, for the mosque is first of all the *place* where worshippers *prostrate* themselves (*sajada* then *sujūd*) before God. The 'great' mosque is a gathering place, a *jāmi'*. The mosques – *masājid* – are 'houses' established for the service of God prescribed by the Law, for the ceremonies of worship and for the celebration of other religious duties. The first building established by Muhammad after the Hegira to Medina was a mosque. The first building established by Muslims after the conquest of a territory was a mosque, a place where people could come together and pray.

In the Qur'ān, the word *masjid* with its plural *masājid* occurs 28 times, and the neatly prevailing qualification is spatial. The many occurrences of *al-masjid al-harām*, the 'Sacred Mosque', pointing to the holy enclosure of Mecca where the Ka'ba stands, clearly hint at a physical place. For example, Q. 2:191: 'Kill them who fight you everywhere you find them… but do not fight them near the Sacred Mosque (Holy Temple) (*al-masjid al-harām*)'. Or in Q. 22:40, where *masjid* is cited alongside 'monasteries, churches, synagogues…where God's name is much mentioned'. The cited temples are evidently the places where due worship and rituals are given to God. The same spatial qualification, on the subject of *masjid al-harām*, prevails also when the *qibla*, the direction of prayer, is mentioned. For example in Q. 2:144, 149–50: 'Many a time We [God] have seen you [Prophet] turn your face towards Heaven, so We are turning you towards a prayer direction (*qibla*) that pleases you. Turn your face in the direction of the Sacred Mosque (*al-masjid al-harām*): wherever you [believers] may be, turn your faces to it. […] [Prophet], wherever you may have started out, turn your face in the direction of the Sacred Mosque' (trans. Abdel Haleem).

Therefore, the *qibla* direction towards Mecca does not have a purely spatial meaning, but also an important historical and allegorical meaning. Historically, it marks one of the clearest breaks with Judaism: turning the direction of prayer, *qibla*, from Jerusalem to Mecca meant the acquired awareness of being a Muslim. When Muhammad broke with the Medinese Jews who did not want to acknowledge him as a Prophet, God changed the direction of prayer in order to emphasize the identity of the *Muslim* community (*umma*), as distinguished and different from the other communities 'of the Book'.[5] Allegorically, the *qibla* is the symbol of the believer's spiri-

---

5.   Fred Donner (Donner 2010) argued that the awareness of the 'believers' (*mu'minūn*) of being 'Muslims' (*muslimūn*) grew up progressively over time. The first community was a blend of Christians, Jews and new followers of Muhammad who shared a common yearning for religious reform inspired by strict monotheism. Only a century or so later, a proper *Muslim umma* was born, with a full awareness of being a separate community from Judaism and Christianity. Donner's thesis is obviously more historical and acceptable than John Wansbrough's nihilism. That a proper 'Islamic' consciousness developed slowly is also acknowledged by Asma Afsaruddin (Afsaruddin 2008) among others. Muhammad Mahmūd Tāhā contended that the only 'Muslim' of his epoch was the Prophet Muhammad, while other people were mere 'believers', not yet sufficiently mature for deep faith and spiritual per-

tual and even mystical tension in relation to God. The believer turns his/her attentions, thoughts and single-minded adoration to God (cf Q. 6:162–63: 'Say: My prayer, my devotion, my life and my death are for God, master of the universe'). In this sense, all the world can be a *qibla*: 'Wherever you turn, there is God's face (*wajh*), for God is Wide (*wāsi'*) Knowing' (Q. 2:115). The switch from a 'place' to an intentional 'direction' is highly hermeneutical (see Part II, introduction).

The symbolic and hermeneutical value of the Islamic temple becomes overwhelming with the Ka'ba. The Ka'ba stands in *al-masjid al-ḥarām*. Originally, only the Ka'ba had the honour of being considered *bayt Allāh*, 'house of God', although later on the *masjid* in general also came to be viewed as 'house of God'. This holy cubic building, standing at the centre of the *masjid al-ḥarām*, represents not only the spatial heart of the Sacred Mosque, but also its spiritual symbolization/sublimation. The Ka'ba is at one and the same time a place and a symbol. Outstanding mystics such as Abū Yazīd al-Bisṭāmī (tenth century) and Ibn 'Arabī (d. 1240) made the Ka'ba a symbol for transcending (sometimes antinomically) space and corporeity/corporality (see the texts quoted in Wensinck and Jomier 1978). Al-Bisṭāmī asserted that: 'In my first pilgrimage, I saw but the temple; the second time, I saw both the temple and the temple's Lord; finally, I saw only the Lord. No sanctuary exists without mortification. Sanctuary is only where there is contemplation. The whole universe is His sanctuary'. For Ibn 'Arabī, the Ka'ba is our very being: in other words, there is no need to reach the *physical* place of the Ka'ba to achieve perfection; perfection can be achieved *within* our soul.

The Qur'ān describes the Ka'ba simply as '*bayt*', literally 'house', of God. For example, in Q. 3:96: 'The first house [of worship] (*awwal bayt*)

fection (Taha 1996). However, the Qur'ān suggests that God, through his Messenger, decided when the 'believers'' community would become a *new* 'Muslim' community – that is, when the *qibla* was changed. Fazlur Rahman (Rahman 1989: 133) argued that there was a smooth transition between the two phases, Meccan and Medinan, of revelation. He then places (Rahman 1989: 165). Muslim awareness of being a separate community early in the Medinan period: 'In Madina, the terms "sectarians" and "partisans" are dropped, and Jews and Christians are recognized as "communities", although, of course, they continued to be invited to Islam. As we noted earlier, the Qur'ān, in the early stages in Mecca, does not speak at all in terms of communities and certainly not in terms of exclusivist communities (and probably equally exclusivist subgroups in Christianity) that led the Qur'ān first to call them "sectarians" and "partisans" and subsequently to recognize them (in Madina) as communities. It was the solidification of these communities that led to the announcement of Muslims as a separate community'. The awareness of being Muslim went in parallel with the 'creation' of Jewish and Christian communities (an idea possibly supporting Donner's thesis, although he extended it over too long a period).

[less meaningful is here Bausani's translation: 'the first Temple'] to be established for people was the one at Bakka [= Mecca]. It is a blessed place; a source of guidance for all people; there are clear signs in it; it is the place where Abraham stood to pray; whoever enters it is safe' (trans. Abdel Haleem). The Ka'ba is both a place and a symbol. It is, as a building, the house of God, but it has been established to be a sign and a presence for humans' benefit. Perhaps more clearly in Q. 22:26: 'We showed Abraham the site of the House, saying "Do not assign partners to Me. Purify my House for those who circle around it, those who stand to pray, and those who bow and prostrate themselves"' (trans. Abdel Haleem). Once more, the privileged role of the Ka'ba is acknowledged, but always with an anthropological end. Moreover, the Ka'ba claims a remote and mythical origin: it was built by Abraham and Ishmael (Q. 2:127) and enjoys a *physical* spatiality. The Qur'ān refers to the Ka'ba by name in Q. 5:97: 'God has made the Ka'ba – the Sacred House – a means of support for people, and the Sacred Months, the animals for sacrifice and their garlands: all this' (trans. Abdel Haleem). In this passage, the *physical* character of the building as a place of worship is recognized along with its function as a 'support for people', who draw from it many religious benefits.

The Ka'ba is obviously linked to the pilgrimage (*hajj*). One of the main rites of the pilgrimage is *tawāf*, that is the circumambulation ( seven times anticlockwise) around the Ka'ba. The circumambulation opens and closes the pilgrimage, both in major pilgrimage (*hajj*) and in lesser ('*umra*). Pilgrimage, however, is not a mere exoteric act, but may have an esoteric meaning. In this case, the Ka'ba is no longer just a building, but a spiritual temple, a symbol of the reached/achieved divine presence. A few *sūfī* mystics connected *tawāf* with God's vision. Other antinomistic mystics dismiss the outer acts of worship, focusing on the inner practice. One of these is al-Hallāj (d. 922) who identifies the Ka'ba with the heart:

> The pilgrims go to Mecca, while I [go] to Him who dwells into my soul.
> The pilgrims offer [sacrificed] victims; I offer my blood and my life.
> Somebody turns around His [God's] temple without her body,
> Because she turns around God Himself who releases her from the rites
> (al-Hallāj 2007: 74).

God dwells in the believer's heart, and the heart is the temple substituting the Ka'ba: thus, the mystic (the spiritually realized person) is released from the obedience to outward rites.

The celebrated mystical poet Jalāl al-Dīn Rūmī (d. 1273) expresses a similar view of the utility of pilgrimage:

> O people performing the pilgrimage, where are you, where are you!
> The Beloved is here, come back, come back!
> The Beloved is neighbor to you, you live very close to him:

what a strange idea wandering in the Arabia's deserts!
The form without the form of the Beloved,
The master, the House and the Ka'ba – all is yourselves! (Rūmī, 1980: 93).

The spatiality of the temple is denied here: the temple is within the soul, and the heart is the true house of God. The heart is the symbol of God's House, it is no less than the Ka'ba. Rūmī praises 'the heart purified by long seeking and long religious exercise' – a heart finally worthy to become the true 'house of God'. He refers to his own experience, writing:

> I surveyed all over the Cross, from one side to another,
>     And knew all the Nazarenes: He was not on the Cross!
> I entered the pagoda, the ancient monks' temple:
>     Nowhere did I see His color.
> I turned my research to the Ka'ba, but nobody I found
>     in that destination of young and old people!
>
> [...]
> Finally, I looked within my own heart, and here I saw Him!
>     Nowhere He was but there!
> Really, I was much perplexed, astonished and drunk
>     That not even an atom of my being was left. I existed no more!
> (Quoted in Bausani, 1959: 285–86).

The same metaphysical function of the heart is assigned to the cosmos. The Ka'ba is the metaphysical centre of the cosmos. The cosmos, as discussed above, is the 'sign' (*āya*) of God's omnipotence for those who are able to reflect and use their reason along with (or maybe beyond) their heart and spirit. The Qur'ān indicates that meditation on the cosmos acknowledges, *through reason*, the divine activity and Providence, as can be seen in Q. 13:2–4 (trans. Abdel Haleem):

> It is God who raised up the heavens with no visible supports and then established Himself on the Throne; He has subjected the Sun and the Moon each to pursue its course for an appointed time; He regulates all things and makes the revelations clear so that you may be certain of meeting your Lord; it is He who spread out the earth, placed firm mountains and rivers on it, and made two of every kind of fruit; He draws the veil of night over the day. There truly are signs (*āyāt*) in this for people who reflect (*yatafakkarūna*). There are, in the land, neighbouring plots, gardens of vineyards, cornfields, palm trees in clusters or otherwise, all watered with the same water, yet We make some of them taste better than others: there truly are signs (*āyāt*) in this for people who reason (*ya'qilūna*).

This is why the mystical poet 'Attār (d. bef. 1300) describes the universe like a 'Inhabited Temple', a Ka'ba, filled with God's Light and full of Love for Him ('Attār 1990: 58): reason and mystical intuition converge towards a shared perception that the universe is the symbol of God's *plenitudo [plenitude]* (a meaningful Latin word), and so we must read in it the (to be interpreted) signs of His loftiness. In the *sūfī* language, the body is a 'temple' (in this case the most commonly used Arab word is *haykal*) 'summarizing' (a compendium of) the cosmos.[6]

In Shiite thought, the 'house of God', the symbolic temple where God dwells, is the *imām*. Henry Corbin, a keen scholar and interpreter of Shiism, perceived that, insofar as 'it is necessary to God that His presence dwells in the Temple' (Corbin 1971–1972, vol. IV: 428), the most suitable image and translation of the Temple we can find is the very person of the *imām*. The *imām* displays God, reveals Him, like a 'disclosure' (*a-letheia*) for, without the imamate, only an apophatic theology would be possible – a strictly negative theology (*tanzīh*). On the contrary, through the *imām*'s person, the believer has a glimpse *within* God, as it were. *Imāms* interpret the Scripture with their very body (think of the bloody corpse of the martyr Husayn, killed by the Umayyads), just as Muhammad did.

Although Corbin's reconstruction is, as always, fascinating if possibly extending the limits of the texts too far, in his analysis the symbolism and the pre-eternal archetype of the Imamate take precedence over the individual person of the *imām*. The Imamate in itself, beyond the individual *imām*, is the symbol of the esoteric cipher of the cosmos and constitutes the hermeneutical key disclosing God's secrets. Equally, the symbolism and the pre-eternal archetype of the Ka'ba point directly to the pilgrimage's eso-

---

6.    Titus Burckhardt (Burckhardt 1979: 69–70) wrote: 'We can say that man, who is a micro-cosmos, and the universe, which is a macro-cosmos, are two mirrors reflecting one another: on the one hand, man exists only in relation to the macro-cosmos containing and determining him; on the other, man knows the macro-cosmos and this means that all the possibilities displayed in the world are contained originally in the intellectual essence of man'. Nasr Abū Zayd went further, connecting the micro-cosmic man with the Qur'ānic 'logo-cosmos': 'According to [Ibn 'Arabī] the Qur'an is a "logo-cosmos", *kawn mastūr*, that manifests both man (the micro-cosmos) and the universe (the macro-cosmos), which in turn are different manifestations of the divine Reality (*al-haqq*). Thus the truth contained in the Qur'an expresses all the facts about the universe from top to bottom. Deciphering these facts is only possible by the mystic who attains the vision of Reality through himself, discovering his nature as the micro-cosmos representing the macro-cosmos. Such an accomplishment leads to the realization of the divine manifestation reflected in man, i.e. realizing himself as the mirror that reflects Reality in a more comprehensive mode than the universe. This is the state of perfection, and the Perfect Man is the real representative (*khalīfa*), of Reality, who is able to decipher all the cosmic facts in the logo-cosmos, the Qur'ān' (Abū Zayd 2000b: 22–23 referring to Abū Zayd 1998). Thus the Qur'ān becomes the hermeneutical structure allowing man to understand (interpret) the universe.

teric and inner secret. The Shiite theologian Qāzī Sa'īd Qommī (d. 1691) said that 'the temple's cubic structure shows why the Imamate is limited to only twelve *imāms*, not one more. Moreover, this form of the Temple, by now only spiritual without any matter in it, discloses itself as the very secret of the spiritual man, the interior man, and, at the same time, reveals us the secret (*sirr*), the esoteric (*bātin*) of the pilgrimage as act and rite' (Corbin 1971–1972, vol. IV, 148).

Although going far beyond the anti-classical concreteness (in Iqbāl's words) of the Qur'ān that is directed towards ethical action and social cohesion (see Rahman 1989) rather than pure speculation, Corbin's interpretation and key to the analysis of the idea of the temple in Shiism is useful, however, in the understanding of the 'natural' Shiite inclination to hermeneutics.

# 5

## BEING AND LANGUAGE

As I have suggested, Qur'ānic hermeneutics is strictly linked to the use and implications of language. Language is the 'house' (as Heidegger would put it) in which the Being (God) shows Himself. The great Andalusian philosopher Ibn Rushd (Averroes, 1126–1198) and his hermeneutical proposal in the *Fasl al-maqāl (Decisive Treatise)* constitute one of the most interesting experiments in Islamic thought pointing in this direction: moving towards a hermeneutics of Being as language. As Gadamer put it: 'Being that can be understood is, insofar as it can be understood, language'.[1] Ibn Rushd's thought deserves particular attention for a contemporary hermeneutics of the Qur'ān too, not only because his ideas are very topical, but also because he has recently become one of the authorities most quoted by contemporary Muslim reformers and innovators (von Kuegelgen 1994). Suffice it to mention the Moroccan Muhammad 'Ābid al-Jābrī (1936–2010).

In al-Jābrī's opinion, Ibn Rushd

> [elaborated] a methodology allowing a conformation [of inner] with the "apparent sense" of the text. Here, Ibn Rushd is indebted to Ibn Hazm. [...] Like Ibn Hazm's method, that of Ibn Rushd consists in keeping close to the apparent sense (*zāhir*) of the revealed Text without driving

---

1.  This assertion is so important that it is worthy of being quoted in German: 'Daß die Sprache eine Mitte ist, in der sich Ich und Welt zusammenschließen oder besser: in ihrer ursprünglichen Zusammengehörigkeit darstellen, hatte unsere Ueberlegungen geleitet. [...] Wir erkennen jetzt, daß diese Wendung vom Tun der Sache selbst, vom Zur-Sprache-kommen des Sinns, auf eine universal-ontologische Struktur hinweist, nämlich auf die Grundverfassung von allem, auf das sich überhaupt Verstehen richten kann. *Sein, das verstanden werden kann, ist Sprache*' (Gadamer 1960: 478, author's emphasis). Gadamer implies a congruity between the knowing 'Ego' (very important also in Muhammad Iqbāl's elaboration) and the known world. Interpretation is comprehension through language. In a sense, the identity between being and language could seem a simplistic assertion insofar as it seems boldly sure to be able to define *what* Being is. Ontology is a very intricate issue however, although many philosophers – and particularly analytical philosophers – have suggested that the key of access to the understanding of our beliefs is linguistic (Varzi 2005). Language is indispensable when speaking of the world even if it does not grasp *essentially* what Being is.

hermeneutics (*ta'wīl*) – where it is necessary – far beyond the "exten-sion" of the particular connotations of a term from its real meaning to the figurative meaning. Obviously without departing from the rules of the Arabic language. When one is not able to grasp a meaning, it is nec-essary that he/she turns to the inductive examination of the revealed text as a whole's wholeness. Moreover, Ibn Rushd stresses the necessity of considering the "intention" of the revealed text. Following this meth-odology, Ibn Rushd is able to point out that the truths achieved by the "indicational" way of revelation and those proved by the "demonstra-tive" method of the philosophers are in correspondence and harmony with one another (al-Jabri 1994a: 120).

Al-Jābrī praised the rupture of (Islamic) 'Western' rationalism with the (Islamic) 'Oriental' Gnosticism that took place in medieval Anda-lusian philosophy. The former school of philosophy, whose most distin-guished representatives were the Zāhirī jurist and philosopher, Ibn Hazm of Cordoba (d. 1064), and Ibn Rushd, rejected any confusion of the field of science and human knowledge (the 'known') with the transcenden-tal level of revealed religion (the 'unknown'). Ibn Rushd declined to interpret religion with philosophical instruments (and philosophy with religious instruments), thus opening the way to the independence and autonomy of science. The latter school, whose main representative was Ibn Sīnā (Avicenna, 980–1037), cultivated a dangerous and compromis-ing syncretism, setting aside reason in favour of a hybrid mixture of logic and mysticism.

This outlook – albeit not historically accurate (possibly Avicenna cul-tivated esotericism, but considering him as 'a thinker of the darkness' as al-Jābrī does (al-Jābrī 1994a) is frankly exaggerated) – has significant her-meneutical outcomes. Ibn Hazm, in al-Jābrī's interpretation, argued, consis-tent with his Zāhirī viewpoint, that:

> Everything that is Qur'ānic is understandable, and everything under-standable is Qur'ānic. The Qur'ān is a clear book...and its clarity appears...to everyone who knows the [Arabic] language through which we have been informed [by God about religious truths]. The Arabic words, whose meaning is explicit in the language in which the Qur'ān was revealed...cannot be deprived of the meaning they have in the language through which God Most High spoke to us in the Qur'ān, translating them in a meaning different from that prescribed (al-Jābrī 1994b: 304–305).

As we can see Ibn Hazm appears to anticipate the pacific co-existence of religion and reason *via* the linguistic mediation of a wholly meaningful lexicon: the same as that later posited by Ibn Rushd in *Fasl al-maqāl*. Both Ibn Hazm and Ibn Rushd elaborated their theories on the basis of linguistic coherence.

As to Ibn Rushd, al-Jābrī wrote,

> the method [he] proposes in order to deal with the religious discourse in such a manner that it keeps its autonomy, is grounded on three principles: the first states that religious discourse is strictly coherent with what intellect has determined, either through evident demonstration or allegorical exegesis. The second principle is that the Qur'ān must be explained by the Qur'ān itself: this means that, while there are verses whose literal meaning diverges from the intellect's conclusions, there are also verses whose literal meaning explains what is the *real* meaning of the previous [ambiguous] verses –, a meaning which is perfectly coherent with the conclusions of the intellect. The third principle consists in differentiating what it is licit to allegorize and what is not. To this end, Ibn Rushd emphasizes that there are three fundamentals of religion that cannot be allegorized: God's existence, prophecy and the Last Day. All the remaining can be allegorized, obeying furthermore three conditions. First, the compliance with the rules of the Arabic language is mandatory, because to allegorize means "the extension of the significance of an expression from a real to a metaphorical significance, without abandoning the standard metaphorical practices of Arabic" [Ibn Rushd 1976: 50]. Second, the internal coherence and unity of the religious discourse must be respected, and we cannot permit the entry of things alien from its characteristic milieu, as it was defined during the Prophet's time; thus, it is mandatory that no hermetic concepts or philosophical speculations are introduced forcibly into the Islamic religious framework. [...] Third, it is mandatory to respect the knowledgeable and cultural capacities of those for whom it is appropriate to allegorize [the philosopher] [...]. Consequently, for Ibn Rushd the distinction between *zāhir* and *bātin* in religious discourse is simply the distinction between reality (*haqīqa*) and metaphor (*majāz*) (al-Jābrī 1994b: 320–21).

Ibn Rushd aimed to revive the clarity (*bayān*) of exposition-interpretation, confining himself to the evidence (*zāhir*) of the text and referring to it by demonstration (al-Jābrī 1994b: 531). The Moroccan philosopher put forward a reading of Ibn Rushd that emphasizes the contemporary value and usefulness of his exegetical method.

Before continuing, it is useful, I believe, to recall the central features of Ibn Rushd's theory of truth. Religious truth and philosophical truth are not in contradiction: 'truth does not oppose truth (*al-haqq lā yudadd al-haqq*) but accords with it and bear witness to it' (Averroes 1976: 50). Truth is one but is predicated on different linguistic levels: rhetorical for the masses; dialectical for the theologians; apodictic and demonstrative for the philosophers. Ibn Rushd declares in the *Fasl* that there are three classes of human people: the masses, the theologians and the philosophers,[2] but all of these

---

2.   Ibn Rushd makes this distinction in many places. For example: 'People in relation to Scripture fall into three classes: One class is those who are not people of interpretation at all: these are the rhetorical class. They are the overwhelming mass, for

will assent (*tasdīq*) to truth through language. Thus it is possible to harmonize very odd propositions – like 'the world is created' and 'the world is eternal' – by having recourse to linguistic subtleties and refinements. But how (if so) can we move from the level of semantics to the level of ontology/metaphysics? How can Ibn Rushd's theory of truth be applicable to Qur'ānic hermeneutics?

Let us consider the hermeneutical circle which is formed between the interpreters (be they common people, theologians or philosophers) and the interpreted text (the Qur'ān). As to the interpreter, Ibn Rushd argues that, if the masses are the interpreters, the hermeneutical circle does not work. For the language of the masses is not fitted for interpretation: they are either confined to the literality of the text or remain satisfied with rhetorical images that are very far from attaining true being. The language of the masses does not express false propositions, because they predicate being to a degree through rhetorical images; but their comprehension is only apparent rather than genuine. Thus, the masses believe that Paradise is a luxuriant garden with rivers and beautiful girls. If the theologians are the interpreters, the hermeneutical circle works only partially. For the theologians try to interpret, but the inaccuracy of their language leads them to erroneous and ungrounded conclusions, so that the risk of *kufr* is always at hand. Only with the philosophers does the hermeneutical circle work properly. For interpretation is a duty for the philosophers and the accuracy and exactness of their demonstrative language leads to a real and conclusive definition of being with a perfect correspondence between being and language – a correspondence the masses and the theologians only touch upon.

Now, we have to consider the characteristics of what is to be interpreted, the Qur'ān, and with this end in mind, we must come back to the topical verse Q. 3:7 and to the distinction between *muhkamāt* and *mutashābihāt* verses. Undoubtedly, Ibn Rushd considered verses that are free of any interpretative uncertainty to be clear and firm. For instance, the verses declaring the Oneness or the existence of God, or the verses attesting to the existence of Paradise and Hell, and so on. Their literal meaning cannot be subject to any allegorical interpretation because they express truths that must be accepted by all humanity. Generally speaking, Averroes shares the well-known principle in the history of hermeneutics that *in claris non fit inter-*

no man of sound intellect is exempted from this kind of assent. Another class is the people of dialectical interpretation: these are the dialecticians, either by nature alone or by nature and habit. Another class is the people of certain interpretation: these are the demonstrative class, by nature and training, i.e. in the art of philosophy. This interpretation ought not to be expressed to the dialectical class, let alone to the masses' (Averroes 1976: 65).

*pretatio* ('no interpretation is allowed in clear and explicit utterances'). If the text is ostensive and obvious, the text itself attests its meaning in the light of the rules of grammar and language. The texts speak straightforwardly to the interpreter. This is the reason why the philosopher must accept literally, like the masses, the expressions of the Qur'ān that do not lead to any interpretative issues: for instance, as we saw, that God is unique, that He has attributes, that He will judge on the Last Day, that Paradise and Hell exist.

But a large number of verses remain to be interpreted. For example, Ibn Rushd considered 'ambiguous' the verses describing God in an anthropomorphic way or the verses describing Paradise as a 'physical' garden with rivers and *hūrīs*, or the verses regarding theodicy. Hermeneutical inquiry (*ta'wīl*) must be applied by philosophers only to these ambiguous expressions. All men and women have to give their assent to the truths of faith, the masses, theologians and philosophers alike; the real meaning of the ambiguous verses have to be explained by philosophical hermeneutics only, because rhetoric and dialectic leave their followers open to the danger of *kufr* (unbelief).

If the text is ambiguous, the *ta'wīl* begins to work and the hermeneutical circle goes into operation. In this case, it is the interpreter who attests and justifies the meaning of the text by his/her independent reasoning (*ijtihād*). This is the reason why the philosopher must allegorize the ambiguous expressions of the Qur'ān, for instance concerning the face or the hands of God, the justice of God, the real nature of Paradise and Hell, and whether they are, respectively, a garden and a furnace or whether they are spiritual abodes. We can reach *ijmā'* on practical issues, Ibn Rushd says, but not on theoretical issues. And this is because men have at their disposal the Law and the Qur'ān whose moral and ethical verses are clear and firm and beyond any possible allegory. On the contrary, *ijmā'* is not viable in theoretical issues because, on the one hand, the languages (rhetorical, dialectical and demonstrative) expressing the unique truth have different degrees of obligation; and, on the other hand, because often the Qur'ān conceals those deep metaphysical truths only the philosophers are able to unveil through hermeneutics and demonstration beneath ambiguous images.

As to the obscure expression concluding the verse Q. 3:7 'firmly rooted in knowledge' – it is well known that a different reading of it is possible. A fideistic reading is possible if we mean that only God is in possession of the true interpretation; a rationalistic reading is possible if we mean that those firmly rooted in knowledge are in possession of the true interpretation along with God. 'Orthodox' Muslim theology accepted the first reading: the already quoted great Qur'ānic commentator al-Tabarī denied absolutely that human beings can share the knowledge of God. The second reading is taken up by Shiite theology where at least 'Alī and the *imāms* are able to interpret the hidden meaning of religion and religious sciences.[3]

While he was not a Shiite, Ibn Rushd supported the second reading of the verse. In the *Fasl*, for instance, he writes: 'Many of the early believers of the first generation as well as others, have said that there are allegorical interpretations which ought not to be expressed except to those who are qualified to receive allegories. These are "those who are well grounded in science"; for we prefer to place the stop after the words of God the Exalted "and those who Allah grounded in science"' (Averroes 1976: 53–54).

For the philosophers are inheritors of the prophets: as Galileo Galilei would say, philosophers do not know all the propositions that are infinite and only God has infinite knowledge, but they know the propositions they are able to understand with the same clarity and exactness of God.

Philosophers can carry on the duties and tasks they are obliged to comply by reason through the 'allegorical interpretation' (*ta'wīl*) of the Holy Text. Ibn Rushd's idea of *ta'wīl* is completely different from the Shiite view, however. Although both aim to go beyond the literal meaning of the text, the Shiite *ta'wīl* is a 'spiritual hermeneutics', as Henry Corbin put it, linked to an esoteric perception of religion and of the same structure of the universe. By contrast, Ibn Rushd thinks that *ta'wīl* is an 'extension of the significance of an expression from real to metaphorical significance (*min al-dalāla al-haqīqiyya ilà al-dalāla al-majāziyya*), without forsaking therein the standard metaphorical practices of Arabic, such as calling a thing by the name of something resembling it or a cause or consequence or accompaniment of it, or other things such as are enumerated in accounts of the kinds of metaphorical speech' (Averroes 1976: 50). The linguistic and semiotic character of the interpretation is predominant in Averroes, while the spiritual and esoteric character is characteristic of the Shiites.

Now, Ibn Rushd, through the hermeneutics of the Qur'ān, the *ta'wīl*, decides to direct, to *orient* the meaning of the text in harmony with what has been stated about the exegetical science of the Holy Book (see above Ali Merad's similar observation). The Holy Book has many meanings that must be grasped beyond the literality of the text. But now it seems mandatory to go further: the consequence we can apparently draw from the previous analysis is that the connection between philosophy and religion is pursued on the linguistic level through the reduction of the metaphysical problem to a simple linguistic problem. The ambiguous expressions of the text are *oriented* by hermeneutics (*ta'wīl*). This is not to say that for Ibn Rushd, Being *is* language; rather that, as we have said before quoting

---

3.    See the articles of J. McAuliffe (Quranic Hermeneutics: the Views of al-Tabarī and Ibn Kathīr) and of M. Ayoub (The Speaking Qur'ān and the Silent Qur'ān: a Study of the Principles and Development of Imāmī Shī'ī Tafsīr), in Rippin 1988.

Gadamer, 'Being, as far as can be *understood*, is language'. If comprehension in hermeneutics implies that the truth of a proposition does not express Being in itself, but that the truth of a proposition must be judged in relation to the historical and linguistic referentiality of the discourse, it is clear that for Ibn Rushd comprehension does mean to convey linguistically the metaphysical content of a proposition. Ibn Rushd is persuaded that the flexibility of language adheres perfectly to the different phenomenologies of Being (see also Leaman 1988). The language displays Being, *puts* it *forth (ostensio)*. A perfect identity is supposed to exist between thought, being and language: thought thinks being and language displays correctly being in different forms along with the different kinds of languages used by individuals. Every time we speak significantly, we speak of Being and consequently of truth; and we have to be silent on everything we are not able to speak of (to paraphrase Wittgenstein's famous comment).

Now, the language of philosophy is more coherent and compelling than theological or juridical language, so that, if two propositions contrast, it is the weakest formulation (the theological-juridical) that needs interpretation in order to come nearer to the stronger formulation (the philosophical). Despite this process, Being does not depart from its ontological necessity; simply, Being unveils itself in language and we can have, literally, *a-letheia* of it, i.e. *unhiddenness* or disclosure. Thus, if we recognize – hermeneutically – that any knowledge of the truth has an essentially interpretative character (see Vattimo 2002), Ibn Rushd's doctrine enables us to attain a plurality of approaches to Being through language without Being losing its ontological basis. This happens because truth does not contradict truth, that is there exists a common ground for truths, a noumenon of truth, as it were, although we do not know its essence.

An argument that appeals to the flexibility of language in order to prove the more binding character of the philosophical demonstration on the eternity of the world in respect to the theological, is contained also in the *Fasl al-maqāl* (Averroes 1976: 55–57). Here, Averroes puts forward the contemporaneous validity of two opposed propositions ($p_1$) the world is created and ($p_2$) the world is eternal. The first proposition is normally maintained by theologians; the second is normally maintained by philosophers, even though Averroes is careful to distinguish between Platonists and Aristotelians. For the Platonists substantially share the idea that the world is created; rather, the Aristotelians are open supporters of eternity. This assumption is aimed at shortening the difference between theology and philosophy, one of the objectives of the *Fasl*. Now, Averroes contends that three kinds of beings exist: an eternal uncaused being, i.e. God; many contingent created and caused beings, that is, all the substances, human beings, animals, plants and minerals living in the sphere under the Moon; and a being that is properly neither eternal nor caused and created, that is the universe on the whole.

The universe is eternal by comparison with God, but created in comparison with the substances of the sphere under the Moon. Thus, the issue of the eternity or creation of the world is merely semantic and, in any case, needs a hermeneutical application (*ta'wīl*) to the Holy Text. Both philosophers and theologians allegorize the literal meaning of the text and, when dealing with such a sensitive topic as the eternity of the world, they are obliged to resort to hermeneutics. If we consider the literal expressions of the Qur'ān, however, hinting at primordial smoke or a Throne on which God is seated, we realize that the philosophers and not the theologians mostly approximate the truth. Averroes does stop here.

We realize moreover that the main question – central both to philosophy and to theology – remained unsolved: is the universe eternal or created? The question has no answer either on the metaphysical or on the physical level: the universe is eternal if predicated analogically to God, but it is created if predicated analogically to the contingent beings. The universe does not possess its own metaphysical and physical essence: its physics and metaphysics are solved in language. The two propositions $(p_1)$ and $(p_2)$ are not divergent and contradictory, rather they live together (truth is one) because of that conjunction or connession (*ittisāl*) between philosophy and religion guaranteed by language. Ibn Rushd's comprehension does mean to convey linguistically the metaphysical content of a proposition. Ibn Rushd is persuaded that the flexibility of language adheres perfectly to the different phenomenologies of Being.

As to the Qur'ān, Ibn Rushd settles carefully the rules of *ta'wīl*. First of all, he obviously maintains that, if philosophical propositions are not provided in Scripture or the theological propositions are not provided in philosophy, no contradiction is possible. But, 'If Scripture speaks of [something], the apparent meaning of the words inevitably either accords or conflicts with the conclusion of the demonstration about it. If this [apparent meaning] accords, there is no argument. If it conflicts there is a call for allegorical interpretation of it' (Averroes 1976: 50). Put differently, if the simple reading of the text does not accord with the philosophical conclusions, the religious text ought to be subjected to allegorization. This claim can convey the false presupposition that for Ibn Rushd in philosophy there is more truth than in religion and that philosophy can do without religion, while religion cannot do without philosophy. Surely, Ibn Rushd's idea was different: the statement that truth does not contradict truth was absolutely sincere. The point is that the concept of truth consists in the reciprocal congruence of the manifold ways by which our languages describe reality. Being, therefore, is shown by language and understood through language.

What are the consequences of Ibn Rushd's approach to *ta'wīl* on the Qur'ān? It is not trivial to wonder whether Ibn Rushd's doctrine of truth and of Qur'ānic hermeneutics can be helpful for a modern reading of the Holy

Book. A positive answer seems unavoidable just starting from the basic conclusion we reached in the analysis of the *Fasl*, that is the criterion of truth lies in the reciprocal congruence of languages.

For, if the juridical and the philosophical languages, when interpreting the Qur'ān, do not express different religious truths but agree in explaining the unique truth, we can argue that the Qur'ānic language is essentially a language *of signs* and not of *metaphysical* content. I mean that the reduction of truth and metaphysics to the level of language excludes the possibility that the contents of the Qur'ān have a metaphysical existence tantamount to the existence of Platonic ideas. The Qur'ānic concepts draw their only significance from the linguistic system of the Holy text. The Holy text is by itself a linguistic structure where the words are meaningful within a system constructed exclusively on semiotics. So, there is no more scope for a fundamentalist reading of the Text, because as a system of signs and as a linguistic structure, the Text becomes the object of hermeneutics, of an historical and philosophical hermeneutics. Starting from Ibn Rushd, we achieve the same goal of Nasr Abū Zayd (Abū Zayd 2002).

Moreover, we can achieve a very particular idea of God. In the *ostensive-obvious* language of the Qur'ān, the concept of God is *ostensive-obvious*. The Being of God does show himself, does *unveil* himself in the significant linguistic structure the Qur'ānic language builds up as an obvious reality, whose existence is beyond any perplexity. God is the obviousness of Being and the interpreter can look at Him without considering His metaphysical essence, but rather considering Him as a *telos* of human activity and social and political engagement, as we shall see in Part II of this book.

Finally, starting from the appreciation of Ibn Rushd's flexible utilization of language in describing metaphysical and ontological truth, we paved the way to the phenomenological approach to the Qur'ān. The manifold ways by which our languages describe reality allow a 'disclosure' of God on many levels of meaning: symbolic, linguistic and especially ontic.

# 6

## LITERARY HERMENEUTICS

Literary hermeneutics can hardly be considered as phenomenological. However, I believe a useful in-depth evaluation of literary hermeneutics is in order to show the philosophical and theological implications it can have.

Tāhā Husayn (1889–1973) contended that the Qur'ān is neither prose nor poetry; it is the Qur'ān, beyond any qualification. It is a narrative work, however, and hence worthy of literary attention. We cannot discard the literary hermeneutics of this text. It would seem that literary hermeneutics are ultimately to be connectable to the field of *tafsīr* rather than that of *ta'wīl*. Nevertheless, the Egyptian triad of famous literary hermeneuts – Amīn al-Khūlī (d. 1967), his wife 'Ā'isha 'Abd al-Rahmān Bint al-Shāti' (d. 1999) and his disciple Muhammad Ahmad Khalafallāh (1916–1998) – proposed an exegetic method that was extremely innovative for the time (the 1950s).

## HERMENEUTICAL PROBLEMS IN QUR'ĀNIC NARRATIONS

Muhammad Ahmad Khalafallāh's idea, that incorporated some methodological features of his teacher al-Khūlī's approach, was to consider the Qur'ān as a normal literary text, susceptible to critical analysis by the modern instruments of philology and literary criticism. In Europe, the tendency to 'secularize' the holy texts – meaning 'equalizing, from the point of view of hermeneutics, the Bible with other literary texts' (Ferraris 1997: 71) – began with the Reformation and flourished in the period of the Enlightenment when Biblical exegetes decided to submit the Old and the New Testaments to literary scrutiny. Obviously, this choice implied the liberation from dogma and the birth of a historical treatment of texts. As Hans Georg Gadamer explained:

> With [the] liberation of interpretation from dogmatism (Dilthey) the whole corpus of the Christian Holy Scriptures began to take the shape of a historical sources' collection, which, being literary works, ought to be submitted not only to a grammatical interpretation, but also to a historical interpretation. [...] And as today there is no more difference between the interpretation of holy or profane texts, so that it exists only *one* hermeneutics, this hermeneutics is definitely no more a function propaedeutical to any "Historical" [*Historik*] – insofar as it is the correct inter-

> pretation of written sources –, but comes to enclose the whole sphere of
> the same "Historical". For what is valid in regard to the written sources,
> i.e. that every proposition can be understood only on the basis of its
> context, is valid also in regard to the contents the proposition is speaking
> of (Gadamer 1960: 214–15).

In Islam much more time was needed to start this kind of hermeneutics. The fear of causing offence to the word of God acted as a barrier to any ambition to (re)read the Sacred text using new methods of inquiry. And this fear still exists today.

The possibility of a literary hermeneutics of the Qur'ān – considered as a normal text of literature – is highlighted in the prophetic tales and in their historicity. The Qur'ān contains a great number of narrations whose protagonists are the prophets. These narrations are attributed by scholars mainly to the so-called second and third Meccan periods of revelation. In this period (roughly 615–622 according to traditional chronology) the Prophet Muhammad acquires awareness of his divine mission, while he and his fellows are subjected to the violent hostility of the Qurayshites of Mecca. His protectors, his wife Khadīja and his uncle Abū Tālib die (c. 619). His clan is ostracized by the powerful masters of Mecca. His endeavours to get tribal support from outside the city fail. Everything seems to conspire to prevent the Prophet's mission. While Muhammad is troubled by these difficulties, revelation comforts and supports him through the example and the vicissitudes of the other prophets who often had to face similar obstacles. Faith in God and God's help strengthen rather than weaken God's messengers.

> When opposition starts against the Prophet's theses – that God is one,
> that the poor of society must not be allowed to flounder, and that there
> is a final Day of Judgment – numerous detailed stories about the earlier
> prophets are repeated in the Qur'ān. There can be little doubt that the
> Prophet heard these stories during discussions with certain unidenti-
> fied people, and the Meccans themselves were not slow to point this out
> (Q. 25:4–5; 16:103). Muhammad insisted, nevertheless, that they were
> revealed to him. He was, of course, right. For, under the impact of his
> direct religious experience, these stories became *revelations* and were no
> longer mere tales (Rahman 1989: 136).

Thus, in order to understand and explain revelations, a literary hermeneutics of the tales is needed.

Qur'ānic tales, especially the prophetic ones, have obviously raised questions about historicity: to what extent can they be considered as reproducing *actual* historical events? Research in Oriental studies is particularly sceptical about this matter. The first problem is that of the relationship between Qur'ānic tales and their alleged Old or New Testament Biblical matrix, or between the Qur'ānic tales and other archeological, epigraphical and historical sources belonging to the cultural environment where the Qur'ānic revelation bloomed. It is often the case that the events narrated in the Bible or in the Gospels differ markedly from those of the Qur'ānic tales. Which are the 'true' ones? The problem is a hermeneutical one, involving both the contextualization of the texts and their 'political' use. The answer to this kind of question might seem justified in the light of an objective study of the sources and an objective comparison of the tales referring to the most modern historiographical and interpretative criteria. Yet the answer to such a question might also be strongly ideological and prejudiced: Jews and Christians consider Bible and Gospel stories as naturally 'true', and the Qur'ānic ones as false; Muslims believe it to be the contrary. Many Orientalists (like Wansbrough and his school or recently Luxenberg, Reynolds and others) argue for a strict dependence of the Qur'ān from Judeo-Christian sources, thus minimizing or rather denying Qur'ānic and Islamic 'originality'. A great ideological bias against Islam is at work here, I believe. An immeasurable space of research opens up which must attempt to mediate between the incontrovertible historical data and the ideological data, the latter being prejudiced of course, yet in its turn also a creator of history and an inspirer of praxis. The screen of the past, the distance from facts to the present, the unlikelihood of many circumstances force oriental studies to caution or even to a more or less radical scepticism. On the other hand, holy tales, Qur'ānic ones as well as Biblical ones, have a powerful role in shaping the believer's opinions and personality, in conducting his/her behaviour.

This is the methodological premise needed to approach Khalafallāh's famous book *The Art of Story-telling in the Qur'ān* (Khalafallāh 1999). The book raised a storm of controversy when it was first published in 1951. The title itself alludes to the two central terms on which the author's criticism will focus: namely *art* and *tale*. Both generate sensitive problems: is it at all possible to consider the Qur'ān as a work of 'art', as if it were the product of a human activity, against the very statements of the Holy Book which underline how the revelation is not 'poetry'? And in addition to that: in what sense does the Qur'ān 'narrate', in the style of a fable, when it is God's revelation and direct word? What is the relationship between this fabulation and the historical bases of the tales?

Khalafallāh writes that the Qur'ānic tales take their inspiration from real historical events and characters, but they transfigure them in a literary and artistic way which might appear as the result of a fantastic and creative imagination, which in fact they are not. He goes on to state that the Qur'ān's tales seek to admonish and induce meditation, and not to explain history or encourage belief in fragments of ancient tales. Through exhortation and reflection, the Qur'ān explains what is true and what is false in the principles of faith, what is correct and what is distorted in tradition, what is useful and what is harmful in the most consolidated habits. The Qur'an confines itself to being an example and a guide, and there is no doubt that its literal expressions, its contextualization and its arrangement prove how good can be sanctioned and evil rejected. Thus, according to Khalafallāh, the Qur'ān is neither a history book nor, evidently, a book of rules and norms: it is, on the contrary, a guide, an admonishment and a lesson.

Looking in more specific detail at Khalafallāh's exegetic proposal, we find that he subdivides Qur'ānic tales into three broad categories: historical, symbolic and fable-like. Several hermeneutical problems emerge from this: what narrative relationship is there between the tale and the real facts that are described in them? What is the relationship between objective knowledge and imagination, between objective knowledge and the symbols the tales convey? Is it possible to deduce, from a rhetorical study of the text, intellectual values and, so to speak, 'philosophical' indications? Up to what point is it necessary that the text symbolism corresponds to an objective reality? These are methodological and hermeneutical issues that both introduce the subject matter and inspire it.

Moving on to examples concerning the 'historical' tale, Khalafallāh discusses several Qur'ānic accounts. The historical tale certainly recounts events that have actually occurred, but the aim of the Qur'ān is not that of a history book. To give just one of the many examples he quotes, Khalafallāh states that the story of Lot included in the *sūra Hūd* (Q. 11, 77–83) has the primary objective of strengthening and comforting the prophet Muhammad's heart. The Qur'ān, in mentioning Lot's pain (v. 77), is concerned only to illustrate his psychological situation and, in this way, to make his emotions and reflections explicit. This is ultimately the *rationale* of the whole *sūra*, which also recounts how other prophets, including Arab prophets such as Hūd, Sālih and Shuʿāyb, experienced severe difficulties and problems when trying to cope with the populations among which they had been sent, just like Muhammad. The *sūra* speaks of their reactions and their thoughts. All this is made evident by the chapter *incipit* that directly analyses the Prophet's psychological situation on seeing his message being hindered. Thus, while this is not a historical tale in the scientific meaning of the term, it is a true story from a psychological-spiritual point of view.

As far as the symbolic and fable-like tales are concerned, Khalafallāh maintains that both enjoy an artistic and literary value. The author explicitly refers to many exegetes, both medieval and classic and contemporary, to prove how commentators have been content to admit that the Qur'ān contains symbolic tales founded on eloquence and rhetoric. This does not in any way imply that they have a 'real' content, since the feature of relating factual events belongs, as we have seen, to the historical tale. Khalafallāh does not seem to exclude that the prophets' imagination and mind have left a footprint, a specific 'coloring' to the symbolic tale, pouring into it their psychological and existential experience. The 'fable-like' tale question is a little more thorny, since the fable potentially implies invention or even lying. Khalafallāh admits that the classic commentators' opinions are vaguer than their ideas about symbolical tales. He nevertheless reminds us how the Mecca pagans often understood the Prophet's revelations as being the 'tales of the ancients'. This means that, to their ears, they sounded like *fairy tales*, and this cannot be without a reason. Khalafallāh comes to the conclusion that the Qur'ān includes 'fable-like' tales as well, even though they do not in any way affect the truth or the substance of the prophetic experience.

Khalafallāh's reasoning seizes a key point of the character of the Qur'ān's composition: namely, that the Qur'ān is completely different from the Torah, which has a systematic narrative course and may be considered a 'historical' book. The Qur'ān, by contrast, chooses to expose only some aspects of the prophets' and the messengers' stories; and beyond that does not deal with all of them. The vicissitudes of the various prophets, such as Abraham and Moses appear in several chapters and they do not make up a homogeneous tale. In particular, the Qur'ān emphasizes the Arab environment and so it is in the study of the Arab, Meccan and Medinan context that the 'sources' of the Holy Book must be investigated. In any case, as usual, Khalafallāh remarks that the Qur'ān does not intend to teach history to the people, but rather to spread its benevolent admonitions.

Khalafallāh's investigation opens up a very interesting aspect of analysis of Qur'ānic stories and it represents a critical reference point that we shall also take into account. The hermeneutical problems involved in his premises regard both the extent to which literary representations correspond to reality (or conceal reality), and the possibility of grasping a universal meaning in the story, useful in drawing out a general rule of behaviour or of interpretation. Thus, the analysis of prophetic stories that I will present below is an attempt to abstract symbolic teachings (i.e. to interpret the texts' literality) of theology and morals from the patriarchs' and the messengers' mythological vicissitudes, which might be useful to guide the reader's life and behaviour, be he/she a Muslim believer or not. I am not concerned, therefore, about either the historical likelihood of the tales or their literary origin, but only about their teaching.

Following the order of appearance in the Qur'ānic text, we will deal first with Joseph's story (*sūra* Q. 12), then with the eschatological stories in *sūra* 18 ('the Cave'), then with the vicissitudes of Solomon and the Queen of Sheba (Q. 27). We will deal with these episodes because they are particularly meaningful in what they tell us about the Qur'ān's content and its issues, even if they clearly do not exhaust the wealthy subject matter. They are prophetic stories belonging to the second and third Meccan period – close enough to each other from a chronological point of view – and thus illustrative in the view that we have seen, of divine aid and support to Muhammad who is in difficulty. It is immediately worthwhile noting that, in the Qur'ānic perspective, both Joseph and Solomon are prophets, whereas in the Hebrew biblical tradition they are simply a patriarch and a king: their religious standing, in the Qur'ān, is then particularly emphasized. This represents a further distinctive feature between the two holy books, and one that leads to a profound revision. Those orientalist scholars (numerous in the history of Qur'ānic studies and including Bell, Wansbrough and Luxenberg) who play down the originality of the Qur'ānic revelation if compared to the Hebrew-Christian ones, do not take into account the differences in inspiration, in addition to those in detail, that make the two holy books differ in their contents as well as differing in form. The discriminating criterion (the *furqān*) is here if we consider the religious experience of Muhammad true or false – a prejudice orienting the meaning and the direction of inquiry.

## JOSEPH'S STORY

It can be helpful to consider Joseph's story in the broad framework of the hermeneutical key I am proposing in this book. In my view, Joseph's story is intended to emphasize the Qur'ānic monotheism and God's omnipotence. Joseph's story in itself is but a pretext. Interpreting the pharaoh's dreams and the dreams of the pharaoh's dignitaries, Joseph 'discloses' the need that human beings have of God. The 'trust in God' (*tawakkul*) represents the theoretical nucleus of the *sūra*. In order to understand better my exegesis, I may resort to a bold comparison: An Italian historian of Greek ancient literature put forward the following statement about Homer's epic poem, the *Odyssey*: 'Reading *Odyssey* is not the same than reading a modern novel. Synthetically we can say that Homeric society was not interested in historical specificities, but in the structure of reality, that is in the paradigm. Homeric society was not interested in the description of a sea voyage or of a landing, but in a paradigmatic model of voyage or of landing showing every time the same features' (Privitera 2005: 47–48). If we change the essential terms we are able to rephrase the sentence as follows: 'The Qur'ān is not interested, like the Hebrew Bible is, in the historical specificities [of Muhammad's life and mission], but in the paradigmatic structure of the message. The Qur'ān is not interested in the description of a particular episode of the prophetic history, as for example that of Joseph, but in the description of the paradigm of prophecy. Joseph's story is a paradigmatic prophetic fact conveying a universal message always identical in itself'. The comparison with the *Odyssey* is interesting because it involves dealing with the Qur'ān both as a literary and as a paradigmatic prophetic text. Its interpretation therefore can, or must be both literary and (philosophical–)theological.

The story of Joseph, Jacob's son, occupies almost the entirety of *sūra* 12. The Qur'ān itself calls it 'the most beautiful story' (v. 3) narrated in an

'Arabic tongue' so clear that it must of necessity be understood by listeners (v. 2). Both definitions are significant. Joseph's is the most beautiful of stories since it represents a pregnant moment of divine revelation, meant to alert men on the best and most productive way by which they must follow their existential path. It is revealed in the Arabic tongue both because Arabic is a holy language since it is God's favorite, or even that spoken by Him, and because it is the language of those receiving the divine message and who are therefore supposed to understand it in its literal evidence as well as in its intimate and profoundest meaning. We could say that the content of the message and its linguistic form are tightly connected: the name and the named object refer to one another and correspond to each other, as both the Cordoban theologian we have already discussed, Ibn Hazm, and the great theologian and philosopher Abū Hāmid al-Ghazālī (c. 1056–1111) would have maintained.

In its fundamental structure, Joseph's story in the Qur'ān takes over and repeats the biblical story as in *Genesis* 37–50, even if in a much less elaborate and detailed manner. Although the biblical tale and the gist of the Qur'ānic one essentially correspond – from the brothers' hatred of Joseph to his kidnapping and sale in Egypt, from Potifar's wife's amorous allurement to the second imprisonment, from the interpretation of the pharaoh's dreams to the calling back to Egypt of Jacob and his tribe – differences are just as numerous. First, as we have noted, Jacob and particularly Joseph are merely patriarchs in the Bible, while in the Qur'ān they are prophets. Joseph's main prophetic feature is that of dreaming truthful dreams and knowing how to interpret not only his dreams but those of others. Beyond that, in the Bible, Jacob does not seem to be in any way aware that Joseph's brothers have betrayed him, whereas, in the Qur'ān, Jacob is from the outset alerted and aware that Joseph has been sacrificed on account of his brothers' hatred. Finally, the Qur'ānic tale ends with Jacob and his tribe's arrival to Egypt and the recognition of father and son, whereas *Genesis* goes on to tell of Jacob's death and burial, as well as of Joseph's wedding details, his fatherhood, his life as well as his death. Other less important questions, although rich in detail, could be mentioned. For example, although the Qur'ānic text is not entirely clear, it appears as if Joseph's mother is still alive at the time of these events, both when the boy dreams the dream of the sun, the moon and the stars which kneel down before him (a premonition that his father, mother and brothers will pay homage to him in the end as Lord of Egypt) (v. 4), and when Jacob and Joseph's brothers are summoned to the Nile valley. It is on the other hand well-known that, in the Bible's version, Rachel dies giving birth to Benjamin. The Bible recounts how Joseph, after being sent to jail by Potifar to avenge his wife's honour, prospers even in prison; a detail that the Qur'ān does not report, performing a narrative jump between the unfortunate incident at Potifar's house and the arrival of the pharaoh's dignitaries whose confused dreams will allow Joseph to show his talent for the first time (vv. 35–36).

The most important difference between the biblical and the Qur'ānic text, though, one that has obvious theological consequences, consists of the motivation of the story. In the Bible, Joseph's story has an eminently historical goal: he is one of God's instruments that will allow the people of Israel to go towards its destiny, walking the way of bliss and exaltation that will lead it to be the chosen people, favoured by God. In the Qur'ān, Joseph's story has a predominantly religious aim: the *leitmotiv* is the trust and surrender that the believer owes to God, to His providence and to His healing intervention, in one word the *Islam* (the trusting yielding to God's will) representing the sole religion pleasing the Almighty and accepted by Him. Joseph's story in the Bible has a hagiographical aim connecting the development of several historical events (without the arrival in Egypt, there would not have been the central, symbolic, even metaphysical fact of Israel's history which is Exodus). In the Qur'ān, Joseph's is a prophetic story that is useful for universal teaching of believers.

Certain specific episodes of Joseph's Qur'ānic story are particularly significant and gave rise to doctrinal elaborations, especially within Muslim mysticism or Sufism. We shall mention at least three.

First of all, while he is in prison with the pharaoh's dignitaries, Joseph invites them to embrace monotheism. 'Oh, my fellow prisoners, are distinguished lords better than the one victorious God? You adore in his place names that you have yourselves coined, you and your fathers [before you], for God has revealed no proof of them. Judgment rests solely with God, and he has commanded that you worship none but Him. Such is the true religion' (vv. 39–40). This is consistent with Joseph's prophetic function whereas it is more than natural that the Bible does not provide for religious implications in the relationship between the patriarch and Egyptians. The call to conversion is consistent with Islam's missionary spirit as a natural religion; in the Bible there is no interest in persuading non-believers, since the practice of the true religion is reserved for the chosen people.

Secondly, the Muslim interpretative tradition has embroidered the character and features of Potifar's alluring wife, giving her the name of Zulaykha. A misogynous interpretation has been developed besides a rather more interesting spiritual one. The misogynous interpretation sees in Zulaykha the archetype of the devious female, the one who, with her allure and her tricks, knows how to make man (the male) diverge from the right way. Notwithstanding this, the Qur'ān testifies that in the end the woman regrets having made an attempt on Joseph's virtue, recognizing the prophet's superior moral stature. Some have even gone as far as claiming that the literary origins of the dominating misogynism in traditional Islamic societies can be attributed to Joseph's story in the Qur'ān (Malti-Douglas 1991).

The spiritual interpretation, by contrast, sublimates Zulaykha's figure to a level equal to that of the *'donna gentile'* of Stil Novo poets like Dante. Zulaykha's love for Joseph is carnal and earthly but also spiritual. It is carnal insofar as the woman is charmed and troubled by the beauty of the loved object, with an erotic engagement that is explicit even in the very holy texts. Yet it is also a spiritual love since Joseph is nothing but a kind of mirror of divinity: Zulaykha's love for him corresponds to the mystic's and the believer's love for God. And it is precisely here that the material and the mystic-spiritual aspects come together. The believer, especially that love-drunk believer who is the mystic, sees in the world, and in woman in particular, the earthly symbolization of divine beauty, by whose light he is blinded. It is well-known how Islamic mystic poetry, from Ibn al-Fārid's in Arabic to that of Hāfez in Persian, often resorts to erotic and Baccha-nalian images to express the experience of God's love and ecstasy. Thus, Joseph's and Zulaykha's story is the subject of a mystic poem, deeply imbued with eroticism by the fifteenth-century Persian Jāmī (Giami 1980), a poem which, although it substantially abides by the Qur'ānic precepts, takes them very much further. The author actually imagines that in the end the prophet and the woman in love rightfully wed, until Joseph, tired of the world's allurements, asks God to be called by Him to Heaven. Zulaykha also draws her last breath on Joseph's body, in some way realizing herself and her passion. Jāmī comments that 'the lover walking sincerely down the way of love shall finally conquer the title of beloved': as Dante said, *amor che a nullo amato amar perdona...* ['Love that does not spare any beloved one from loving...'] (Dante 1991)

Finally, the episode contains an element of extraordinary symbolic impor-tance, absent in the Bible although present in Rabbinic tradition, according to which Zulaykha holds a feast to which she invites her female friends to present Joseph to them. The friends, astonished by such great beauty, cut their fingers with knives (vv. 30–31). Here, women represent theopathic mystics who, in their exaggerated love for God, no longer comply with daily and social conventions. According to the mystical poet Farīd al-Dīn 'Attār, Joseph's beauty symbolizes God's beauty, whose splendour has creation 'hurt its hand while cutting oranges': the universe, filled up with God's beauty, finds itself love-sick for him and the stars in the sky, at God's appearance, cut their hands with the knives used for peeling oranges, just as Zulaykha's friends hurt themselves staring at Joseph ('Attār 1990: 58).

All this pregnant symbolism has to be interpreted. A literalist approach would be completely misleading. The women cutting themselves is not a mere anecdotal incident that could be narrated as a funny story. It is a complex image of philosophical, mystical, even cosmic meaning. The dreams themselves are symbols to be decodified and the *ta'wīl* of dreams is a characteristic prophetical virtue.

Apart from the necessity of interpretation of the symbols, Joseph's story represents a lesson for Muhammad. Just as Joseph has experienced his brothers' persecutions, misery and jail, but is saved by his trust in God who allows him to acquire prosperity and joy; so Muhammad, who has suffered the Quraysh's wrongs and met with solitude and pain, shall rise and attain victory, putting his soul in God's service, trusting in His mercy. A *hadīth* of the Prophet Muhammad that Muslim mystics like repeating runs: 'the believer's heart is between the Merciful's two fingers'. Al-Ghazālī writes: 'Reflect on the words [of prophet Muhammad] – God bless and save him – : "The believer's heart is between the Merciful's two fingers". The meaning of the fingers is that [God] has the capacity to modify [anything] instantaneously. The believer's heart is tied up in a double grip: the Angel's and Satan's. The former guides him, the latter leads him astray: but God the Highest shapes the believer's heart with both fingers just like you shape any material with your fingers' (al-Ghazālī 2000: 128–29).

Divine presence is overwhelming. All Joseph's story is clearly projected and directed by God. God reveals Himself conducting Joseph toward his destiny (*Allāh ghālibu 'alā amrihi*). Therefore, as a prophet led to his destiny, Joseph has full confidence in God (*tawakkul*). *Tawakkul* is the pivotal theological concept in the *sūra*. Everywhere the characters of the story show *tawakkul*. Jacob is confident that his patience will be rewarded. The same (unnamed) Potifar accepts confidently God's decree. And this is obvious if he was a *muslim* as some traditions support: Muhammad Ibn Sa'd transmitted...that Ibn 'Abbās said: "the name of the man who bought Joseph was Potifar". [...] Muhammad Ibn 'Omar transmitted...from Mujāhid: "*malik* [litt. 'the king'] bought him, and *malik* was *muslim*". [...] Ibn Hamīd transmitted...from Ibn Ishāq: "He who bought him in Egypt was Mālik Ibn Dha'r... Ibn Madyān Ibn Ibrāhīm" [Tabarī 1956–57, commentary to the verse]', that is a scion of Abraham.

Joseph's destiny is the same as the Prophet Muhammad hinted at in a famous *hadīth* quoted by al-Ghazālī in the *Kitāb al-Arba'īn*: '*idhā ahabbu Allahu 'abdan ibtilāhu fa-in sabara ijtibāhu wa in radiya istifāhu*', that is: 'When God loves one of His servants He tries him, and if he [the servant] is forbearing, He [God] chooses him, and if he [the servant] is satisfied [of God's decree], He [God] elects him'. Joseph is tested and afflicted continuously, but he endures with patience so that God elects him and gives him authority over all the Egyptian land. In no way as happens in the Bible, does the Qur'ānic Joseph behave in a way that is proud and boastful about his earthly destiny. When he meets Jacob at the end of the *sūra*, he simply magnifies God's generosity and his condition of servant of God:

> Father, this is the interpretation of my vision of long ago; my Lord has
> made it true. He was good to me when He brought me forth from prison
> and again when He brought you out of the desert, after that Satan set at

variance me and my brethren. My Lord is gentle to what He will; He is the All-Knowing, the All-Wise. O my Lord, Thou hast given me to rule, and Thou hast taught me the interpretation of tales. O Thou, the Originator of the heavens and the Earth, Thou art my protector in this world and in the next [verses 100–101, trans. Arberry].

## THE SŪRA OF THE CAVE

The *sūra* of the Cave (*Al-Kahf*) is number 18 in the Qur'ānic ranking and contains four narrative nuclei, interrupted by digressions and reflections of various kinds. Among the most relevant of these digressions there is the firm condemnation of those (the Christians) who claim that God has had a son (vv. 4–5); the versions of Satan/Iblis's rebellion, who refuses to prostrate himself before Adam (v. 50); and a magnificent invocation to God, whose wealth and abundance are recognized beyond any countable quantity (v. 109). These digressions appear unconnected to the main narrative nuclei, whose content might be reduced to a lowest common denominator. They are as follows:

1. The story of the youths who fall asleep in the cave that gives the name to the *sūra*;
2. The parable of the two friends and the garden;
3. The story of Moses and the 'Green Man' (*al-Khidr*);
4. The epic of Dhū'l-Qarnayn, 'The man with two horns'.

Before identifying the main narrative thread of the stories, it is necessary to discuss their content briefly.

The story of the youths asleep in the cave (vv. 9–26) derives from the famous Christian legend of the so-called 'Seven Sleepers of Ephesus', of which we know several versions, Syriac, Copt and Arab. During Emperor Decius's anti-Christian persecutions, seven youths from Ephesus shut themselves up with their dog in a cave in the mountains close to the town. Here God let them fall into a miraculous sleep, waking them up again 309 years later, in the age of the Christian Emperor Theodosius. The Qur'ān obviously contains no references to Roman emperors, but speculates about the number of youths and the dog. Verse 22 asks if there were three, five or seven of them, but it underlines how it is a mystery known to God only and it seems to suggest the uselessness of speculating on the unknown and discussing a question whose secret it is not proper to clarify – that is to say that interpretation is pointless or even vain. Verse 9 seems perhaps (perhaps!) to indicate the dog's name, namely Raqīm (who else Raqīm might be remains otherwise undecided), and verse 18 grants the animal the function of ward and protector of the sleeping youths. Verse 25 resumes the 309 year-long miraculous sleep, but once again it reserves to God the knowledge of truth, the same God to whom belong the mystery of the earth and the sky (v. 26). Despite this apparent rejection of hermeneutics, it is important to remember how the Muslim exegetic tradition has discussed the number 309. The number is indeed the numeric anagram of the total of isolated, starting and suspended letters in the Qur'ān (i.e. 903), as well as of Jesus's name in Arabic, namely 'Isā being worth 390'.[1] There is, therefore, an esoteric exegesis of the Qur'ānic data, just as the esoteric allegorical interpretation of the Pythagoric Shiite, probably Ismailite, philosophical school of the Brethren of Purity (*Ikhwān al-Safā'*, flourishing in Iraq in the ninth and tenth centuries). According to this interpretation, the seven youths are bound to a complex heptadic celestial symbology which is related to the imamic succession to the prophet Muhammad foreseen by the Shiites.

In any case, in addition to all the details of the story as it is told in the Qur'ān, there are a couple of elements that must be pointed out. In the first place, the fact that the Qur'ānic tale is not systematic nor yet apparently fragmentary: the listener's knowledge of the development of the story seems to be taken for granted and, rather than narrating the events, the holy text seems to focus on moral and theological reflections. Secondly, and more importantly, the aim of the narrative seems to underline the features of God's role and essence. We have already mentioned the insistence with which God is acknowledged as the all knowing creator of all things in the universe. Moreover, he is the enactor of the miraculous sleep and awakening that teach men his might; the Merciful One provides for self-awareness; he is the one to whom men must look for shelter, the protective cave that welcomes peace seekers (vv. 10 and 16); finally, he is the one who truly knows the Time of Judgment Day (v. 21).

Linking ideally with the need to invoke the name of God before performing any act or deed (v. 23), the parable of the two men and the garden (vv. 32–44) stresses the true believer's obligation to rely on his/her Lord in order to be successful. Of the two men, the one who was proud of his wealth and the fruitfulness of his garden sees it become 'a desert land drowned in abundant water' (vv. 40–41) because he has raised God's wrath. Of the two men, the one who recognizes God's sovereign eminence, whom he knows cannot be associated with anything else (v. 38), also knows that God's reward is the best (v. 44) and can therefore hope for a better future and better destiny. Here, too, the narrative plot is very thin and directed solely at moral and theological reflection.

---

1.    In order to understand this we must here bear in mind the fact that in Arabic, as in Greek and Hebrew, the letters of the alphabet also possess a numeric value; and that a certain amount of Qur'ānic *sūras* start with 'suspended' letters, apparently disconnected from the text, whose meaning is ambiguous or frankly unknown.

Moses and al-Khidr's story probably represents the most central theme of this *sūra* (vv. 60–82). It is quite difficult to explain its contents in a perfectly consistent manner, for the same reasons that have already been mentioned concerning the seven sleepers and the two friends. The narrative structure, though, is somehow more solid. Moses may perhaps be the Biblical prophet, although not all commentators agree with this identification. Whatever the case, the name chosen for the protagonist evokes a figure of exceptional experience, potentially prophetic. Moses walks to where the two seas merge together, but when he gets there he loses a mysterious fish that finds a second life swimming in the sea waters (vv. 60–63). The symbology is patently linked with Semitic and Egyptian myths and legends about the waters of life. Both in the Sumeric and in the Egyptian world there are references to two oceans, a celestial and an underground one, which encircle the dry land. Is there a little bit of Gilgamesh in this Moses who travels towards a remote and fabulous horizon (in a quest for immortality)? Is there something of the Egyptian Sun God in this fish that dies and rises again, just as Ra' dies on his night journey in the underworld bringing back, in the morning – as he rises in the East – light, warmth and life to the worshipping humans? Water imagery is known to be Biblical too, consider *Genesis*: originally, God's spirit hovered over the waters and the waters may represent the primal substrate from which God produced Creation (interestingly, the Qur'ān speaks of prime matter in Q. 41:11 as 'smoke' and not as 'water').

Hints of the presence of ancient Middle Eastern religions give rise to the vexed problem of interpretation (just as the origin of the Jewish YHWH from the ancient Semitic pantheon [for example, among a huge literature, Xella 1982; Smith 2002]). Did 'pagan elements' infiltrate the Qur'ān? Was God admitting the existence of other 'gods'? Is there a common historical and cultural framework within which the Qur'ān grew up, thus losing a part of its 'originality' of revelation? Can the historical process of Qur'ānic composition help in a better explanation of its theological or religious content? The problem has its context in the wider debates about the construction, composition, inspiration of the Qur'ān. This is not the place to discuss these issues that, though chiefly Orientalist, have also been tackled by Muslims. The broad issue is whether these debates help the contemporary (philosophical) hermeneutics of the Qur'ān. In my opinion they do not. As mentioned earlier, we are dealing with a fixed, complete and, in a sense, closed corpus. Whether or not it derives from a Biblical subtext (Reynolds 2010), its availability for Muslim praxis is the same. Hermeneuts seek to uncover the symbols embedded in the text, and the human sciences are useful tools for this aim: history, philology, semiotics and so on. But knowing whether the Qur'ān is written in Syriac or in Arabic (see Christoph Luxenberg's provocative suggestion [Luxenberg 2007]), or if it was produced in Arabia

or in a sectarian milieu (see John Wansbrough's thought-provoking reconstruction [Wansbrough 1978]) does not greatly help in grasping Qur'ānic
theology or in setting a framework for action, because it does not change
the actual, apparent *thing-ness/what-ness* of the text. Angelika Neuwirth's
comments are insightful:

> How can Western Qur'ānic scholars produce knowledge that is both
> relevant and hermeneutically acceptable to their Muslim colleagues as
> well? One venue, already successfully tested in the Near East – by the
> Egyptian text linguist Nasr Abu Zayd – might be "semantic analysis"
> introduced by the Japanese scholar Toshihiko Izutsu. Another would
> be the investigation of Qur'ānic aesthetics as perceived by its readers,
> drawing on traditional Arabic rhetorics, such as has exemplarily been
> conducted by Navid Kermani; and recently Stefan Wild has proposed
> "mantic speech" as a further venue. These methodologies, however,
> avoid the crucial question of Qur'an's historicity and thus its relations
> to the traditions of the adjacent cultural groups. For both epistemologi-
> cal and political reasons, however, it seems indispensable to go beyond
> these post-canonical approaches and try to re-locate the Qur'ānic genesis
> in the context of Late Antique culture (Neuwirth 2007: 122–23).

Yes, it is true: maybe not only in the context of Late Antiquity, but also of
the ancient Middle East. But the existence of a pre-canonical Qur'ān or the
possibility of realizing a critical edition of the Qur'ān do not change the fact
that *this* is the (canonical) Qur'ān Muslims have to interpret. Its historicity
is a (necessary) tool, not an end. When Mahmūd Tāhā says that 'Islam, as
revealed in the Qur'ān, is not one message, but two: one at the beginning
closer to Judaism, the other at the end closer to Christianity' (Tāhā 1996:
123) – he resolves from a reformist (politically engaged) Muslim point of
view the Orientalist problem of the Biblical and/or Christian subtext of the
Qur'ān.

To return to Moses and the journey to where the two seas flow together,
here he meets al-Khidr. The Qur'ān does not actually state the name of
this character, merely defining him as a 'servant of Ours [of God] to whom
we granted the mercy that is with Us, and whom We let participate in a
part of our [it's always God speaking] knowledge' (v. 65). Al-Khidr is the
name attributed to him by the exegetic tradition and in Arabic it means
'the green one'. There is an evident allusion to the rebirth of nature in the
spring, maybe also still echoing ancient resurrection myths of Mesopota-
mic and Syriac origin. Al-Khidr is even more knowledgeable than Moses
and he is called on to teach him. In this way he stands out as the eminent
prophet among prophets. His teachings concern 'rightful actions' (v. 66)
since, in the context, Moses must draw a moral out of his mentor's baffling
actions. Al-Khidr actually commits some apparently evil and incomprehensible actions: he causes a ship to sink; he kills a youth with no evident

reason; he fixes a broken down wall without asking for a reward. All this has got an explanation, though: sinking the ship was to save those sailing it from an attack by pirates; he killed the youth because with his atheism he would have led his believing parents to perdition; fixing the wall was to keep a treasure hidden that would be discovered by a believer's two orphans as soon as they came of age. Moses at first does not understand the meaning of al-Khidr's behaviour and in fact the Qur'ānic text does not tell us whether he has drawn any moral from the received teachings. Yet the text makes us understand clearly the sense of the whole story. There is a logical answer to Moses' bewilderment: apparent evil has been committed for the sake of good; the far-sightedness of divine providence has provided for a longer-lasting good deriving from temporary misfortune. And al-Khidr has merely been an instrument in God's hands: 'What I did, I did not perform by myself' (v. 82). The origin of the deed, and even of the intention, is God.

The story of Dhū'l-Qarnayn, 'the two-horned one', deals explicitly with the end of the world (vv. 83–98). Who Dhū'l-Qarnayn might be is a question open to the widest speculation, but the majority of Muslim interpreters identify him with Alexander the Great. It is, of course, an Alexander outside history: not so much the Macedonian king and leader who subjected to his power all lands from the Mediterranean to India, but rather a mythical character, endowed with prophetic qualities, interpreting and acting out a divine decision. Certainly, Alexander's journey hit the imagination of Eastern countries and his story was perhaps the most widespread literary work in the popular tradition of Mediterranean Asia (Saccone 2008; Di Branco 2011). He is transfigured in the Qur'ān in order to convey an eschatological message. Like Moses, Dhū'l-Qarnayn is travelling. He is powerful and wise (v. 84). On his way he first meets an unnamed people where he is called on to do some good: in fact, he apparently accomplishes nothing; instead he exhorts them (v. 88) to do those good deeds which, as in the case of the best of the two men arguing in the garden, guarantee a large reward. The second time the two-horned man stops among a primitive people who know no shelter from the Sun, while God embraces everything with His science (vv. 90–91). The third and last stop is among a people fearing the invasion of the wild tribes of Gog and Magog, announcing the end of the world. Dhū'l-Qarnayn builds an iron and copper barrier against them (v. 96), so that they see their access hindered and hampered (v. 97). 'This is mercy from God' (v. 98): He has postponed the end of Time, of which one of the signs was the invasion by Gog and Magog, delaying the apocalypse to that day, whose date is known only to God, and on which trumpets will play and non-believers will find no one to intercede for them against God's wrath. In this context, Dhū'l-Qarnayn plays the role of the *Katechon*, the mysterious someone or something of Paul's second epistle to the Thessalonians, who precisely puts off and for a certain time prevents the last, supreme judgement from taking place.

The Qur'ān devotes some verses, after Dhū'l-Qarnayn's story (vv. 99–108) to an allusive description of the final Hour and the destiny awaiting the evil and the good (the former shall be thrown into hell, the latter shall be housed in the gardens of heaven).

I have tried, where possible, to highlight the internal links within the four stories of the Cave *sūra* in order to present a homogeneous interpretation. Many years ago, while analysing the legend of the seven sleepers of Ephesus, Louis Massignon spoke of an Islamic 'apocalypse' (Massignon 2012); and more recently, Paolo Dall'Oglio has – correctly – identified in the eschatological issue the *leitmotiv* of the *sūra* (Dall'Oglio 1991). The subject matter of death and resurrection runs through all four narrative themes in the chapter. The seven sleepers' slumber is like a sleep of death from which God awakes them so that they may be both witnesses and a miraculous sign of his might and his decision-making will: the awakening corresponds to a resurrection, both in spirit and in flesh, to a physical and spiritual renewal upon which believers must meditate. The garden blooming, dying and potentially being adorned again with flowers and fruit is an explicit sign proving God's reality: in the whole Qur'ān, God is praised as the one who extracts the living from the dead and makes the earth green after it has become dry and arid (e.g. Q. 16:65; 30:19, etc.), as the one renewing bones after they have become putrid dust (Q. 36:78–79), an enlivening power that alludes to the same divine power of making the dead alive again on resurrection day. We have already mentioned the symbolism of the fish and water in Moses and al-Khidr's story: whether or not this story echoes life cosmologies in the ancient Semitic or Egyptian East, its allusive function in relation to the process of renewal of nature's forces is undeniable. Finally, the Dhū'l-Qarnayn myth is explicitly eschatological both literally and metaphorically.

Eschatology, then. Yet it may be possible to identify a further element in the texture of the four Qur'ānic stories and that is theodicy. Theodicy is a term with multifarious meanings but which means, literally, God's justice and the justification of evil in relation to divine will and power. In a wider sense, though, it may also be used to refer to God's providence, his intervention to determine and manage nature's laws. The whole Cave *sūra* implies a reflection upon God's power and upon his decision-making will to determine good and evil. The fate of the seven sleepers is the result of God's discriminating intervention; he uses them to provide an example for human reflection. The story of the two men and the garden teaches that there is no hope and no salvation for those who do not place their complete trust in their Lord's benevolence (and this, as has already been said, is the profound meaning of *Islām*). Al-Khidr operates under the mysterious direction of divine will: his actions are not the result of the servant's will (i.e. the prophet's), but rather of the servant's obedience to his heavenly master. In addition to that, the supposed devil in the sinking of the ship or the killing of the youth is pure appearance: it hides the good that is the actual object and objective of the divine design. It would be interesting to compare this Qur'ānic principle with the reflection on evil by Augustine of Hippo. Evil is pure lack of good and good, the divine providence determined by his will, is the ultimate result of any decision, apparently absurd or incomprehensible, that God has made in ruling nature or human life. Dhū'l-Qarnayn is the one who announces the outcome that is absolutely reserved for the divine determination, which is the coming – when and how is unknown – of the final judgment.

Eschatology and theodicy are not alternatives, nor do they contradict one another. God's project has a clear direction and the *sūra* of the Cave, as a whole and in its inner coherence, constitutes both a warning and an example thereof. Without resorting to bizarre explanations of the Qur'ānic stories like those implicit, for example, in Wansbrough's or Luxenberg's analyses, we are able to interpret the stories as theological reflections and parenetic admonitions.

## SOLOMON AND THE QUEEN OF SHEBA

*Sūra* 27, the 'Ant', includes the story of Solomon and the Queen of Sheba (Q. 27:15–44). Once again, it is not systematically narrated according to a precise logical order but is more like a series of fast-moving film frames or rapidly changing theatrical scenes. As pointed out, in the Qur'ān Solomon is a prophet, as opposed to the Hebrew tradition, and he is acknowledged not only for the wisdom or learning that make him stand out among humans, but also for his supernatural ability to control men and spirits (*jinn*). Several passages of the Qur'ān allude to Solomon breeding horses; he controls the winds and the forces of nature; he commands the pearl-fishing demons and binds them to his will (Q. 38:30–40; and cfr. Q. 21:81–82); he speaks (here in *sūra* 27) the language of the beasts. In the *sūra* of the Ant he is first of all described as the leader of an army of men, *jinn* and birds (Q. 27:17). Among the strange soldiers of this composite army, particular attention is paid to the hoopoe (vv. 20–21) which, although it is nowhere else quoted in the Qur'ān and although it is not particularly active nor particularly gifted with extraordinary qualities, not even in this passage, in spite of its apparent ability for clairvoyance, has nevertheless become the object of philosophical-spiritual meditation by the *sūfīs* or Muslim mystics. To take just one of many examples one could choose, the poem by the already mentioned Farīd al-Dīn 'Attār *The birds' language* makes the hoopoe the leader of a flock of birds in quest of the mythical Simurgh, the fabulous king who lives at the world's edge. The metaphor is transparent and re-appears in many other mystical writings of Islam, from Abū Hāmid al-Ghazālī to Avicenna: birds are souls which, eager for fulfillment, set out to reach God, unaware of the toil and the dangers on their way. The hoopoe is not only the image of the spiritual teacher teaching the initiated how to purify their souls and prepare to meet God, but, according to some interpretations, it is also both the active intellect, as Avicenna has it, governing passions and ruling over the soul's inferior faculties, and the contemplative intellect aiming at speculation and transcendence of matter (Saccone's *Postscript* to 'Attār 1999: 383).

Once they get to the Simurgh, the birds/souls are shown a mysterious document, a parchment containing all the flaws and sins standing in the way of their spiritual development and the taste of the divine presence. It is curious to note how a similar event is related about Joseph and his brothers: when the latter get to Egypt and are welcomed by Joseph (whom they do not recognize), he gives them a document in Hebrew to read denouncing all their misdeeds ('Attār 1999: 328–29). The souls must purify themselves and become aware of their sinfulness so as to finally attain salvation and happiness.

Here it is the hoopoe (vv. 22–26) who draws Solomon's attention to the Queen of Sheba, once again unnamed in the Qur'ān (like al-Khidr and Zulaykha) but traditionally called Bilqīs. Bilqīs is clearly an authoritative woman: although she heeds her ministers' opinions, she makes decisions autonomously, showing care and wisdom (vv. 32–35). This incident is one of many that demonstrates that the idea of woman's inferiority in the culture inspired by Islam is not Qur'ānic, but is rather bound to the historical circumstances of the Arab expansion. Bilqīs reigns over an idolatrous people who worship the Sun instead of God. She possesses a wonderful throne, symbol of her power and a magical object that ensures her power. This throne is highly symbolic. Perhaps it alludes not only to the Queen's power, but also to God's Throne. Whatever the case, it must be interpreted in a political, theological or mystical way. Solomon first approaches her (v. 28), but she uses delaying tactics (v. 35), afraid of the Israelite king's army. Then, with the help of a *jinn* gifted with magic powers (vv. 38–41), Solomon seizes her throne to force her into visiting the court in Jerusalem. The *jinn* episode has been the object of several theological reflections. Of this character, it is said that he 'possessed the knowledge of the Scriptures' (v. 40); he was, like al-Khidr, someone who participated in divine knowledge. But there is more. According to traditional exegesis, this very knowledge that he possesses and which makes him capable of such a prodigy, is that of God's supreme Name, God's hundredth name which, in the Semitic theological vision, represents the name of power (remember that also the Jews do not call God's true name). Knowing this name, one can even magically 'force' God into operating in one's favour. We can thus surmise that the *jinn* knew God's secret name and made use of this extraordinary faculty to satisfy Solomon's wishes. 'As far as the character's identity goes, according to Muslim tradition, it is generally taken to be Asaf Ibn Barahiya, Solomon's *visir*. Some actually think, according to al-Baghdādī, that the above mentioned Asaf knew about the supreme Name simply because he had seen it inscribed on Solomon's famous seal, the magical ring where the secret of his power over all beings resided' (Gimaret 1988: 93).

Bilqīs comes before the king and at first does not recognize her throne since God reserved only to Solomon the true science (v. 42). The culminating point of the story, though, is Solomon's trick to force Bilqīs to surrender. Here it is worthwhile to quote the Qur'ānic verse directly (v. 44): 'She was told again: Come into the palace! And when she saw it, she believed it to be a great pool of water, and bared her legs. But Solomon told her: It is a palace paved with crystal! So the queen exclaimed: Lord! I have wronged myself, but now, like Solomon, I shall give myself to God [*aslamtu* in Arabic; that is 'I give myself up to God', 'I practice Islam – I become Muslim'], the Lord of Creation!'.

The story is interrupted here and there are no more developments narrated, yet its moral is evident. Bilqīs understands Solomon's deception and that she and her people had been worshipping false gods, deceiving in appearance just as the crystal floor of the king's palace appeared like water, and she converts to the true, natural religion, Islam, worshipping the one God. This was the same God that had granted to Solomon, as to al-Khidr and Dhū'l-Qarnayn, true learning and the authentic penetration of the secrets of knowledge; the Queen acknowledges her interlocutor's superiority. Bilqīs's action in raising her skirts is very feminine, yet symbolic: she bares herself before the truth. Oliver Leaman keenly identified a parallelism between the stories of Zulaykha and Bilqīs (Leaman 2004: 51–54): the apparently historical course of Solomon and Bilqīs's vicissitudes, just like those of Joseph and Zulaykha, refers then to a transcendental world of authentic truths of which our world – and the historical happening of facts – merely represents a symbol and a transfiguration that must be interpreted. The central role played by women in these stories is also notable: far from being the object of somebody else's decisions, Bilqīs and Zulaykha are masters of their own destinies and their decisions deeply affect those of Solomon and Joseph. The Qur'ān does not minimize the woman's role at all, as witnessed too in the stories of Mary (Maryam), Jesus' mother, included in the *sūras* 3 (*Āl 'Imrān*) and 19 (*Maryam*).

## SYNTHESIS

This exercise in hermeneutics demonstrates the utility of finding a philosophical pattern in order to understand apparently heterogeneous stories thematically. Despite the passage of time, and despite the methodological problems acompanying it, Khalafallāh's critique can be a useful starting point, insofar as literary hermeneutics is one of the main methodological keys for reconstructing the meaning of a text and its history. Perhaps it can be argued that my narration is not systematic, but it is more like a series of fast-moving film frames or rapidly changing theatrical scenes, but probably this is exactly the effect pursued by the Qur'ānic narration I wished to transmit through my exegesis. As Muhammad Abdel Haleem put it, regarding *sūra Yūsuf*, but actually we can detect the effect everywhere,

> The Qur'ān uses a different technique [from other narrative schemes] for telling the story, which has been called "dramatic". The story falls into 28 scenes structured on movement and dialogue; what little narrative there is serves mainly to introduce the characters by "he said", written as one word in Arabic and followed by the direct speech of the character. [...] As in a play, the curtain falls and rises between scenes with gaps left in time and action because they can be filled in from the remaining text [and] the whole text is clearly understood. [...] This technique, which relies on scenes (with gaps in between) and dialogue, is sufficient for the purpose of the story in the Qur'an and is by no means unique to the story of Joseph (Abdel Haleem 2011: 256–57).

The technique is particularly fitted to attract the listener's attention and it is 'dramatic' as like as the frequent change of the subject in Qur'ānic narration (*iltifāt*).

Moreover, we see again how the Holy Book of Islam has a very particular approach to history: it appears to contain historical facts and narratives, but it essentially conveys its message through a complex axiological symbolism. All this needs careful hermeneutical decoding of symbols.

Recently, a controversial Syrian exegete, Muhammad Shahrūr (b. 1938), set out a thorough examination of the stories in the Qur'an. Shahrūr has become famous for a book, *The Qur'ān and the Scripture (Al-Qur'ān wa'l-Kitāb)* (Shahrūr 1990), where he distinguished between the *Qur'ān*, that is the universal recipient of truth, and the Scripture (*kitāb*) whose message is contingent and imparts to human beings the appropriate rules of behaviour and legislation. Shahrūr suggested that the Qur'ānic tales be re-read from a contemporary perspective. He tried to go beyond Khalafallāh's literary approach, demonstrating that the tales of revelation (*al-qasas fī'l-tanzīl*) foreshadow in fact a philosophy of history (*falsafat al-ta'rīkh*). The hermeneutical distinction between the historical text (*al-nass al-ta'rīkhī*) and the historicity of the text (*tārīkhāniyyat al-nass*) is of vital importance in order to single out the epistemological, gnoseological and even political characters of a *philosophy* of the Qur'ānic tales. It involves a critique of the traditional intellect (*'aql salafī*) (Shahrūr 2012) that recalls al-Jābrī's critique of Arab intellect. It is a proposal worthy of development, insofar as it extends a philosophical hermeneutics to the Holy text. Shahrūr applies his method to a number of Qur'ānic stories, from Adam to Joseph *via* Noah, but fails perhaps to draw as many as he might of the conclusions present in the material.

A further hermeneutical point of view must be highlighted, however: whether *intertextuality* is a productive approach when seeking to penetrate beyond the outwardly apparent meaning of the text. I have tried to shed light, wherever possible, on the links and intersections, both formal and related to the subject matter, between apparently heterogeneous stories. These elements of continuity compel a *latitudinal* and *structural* reading of the Qur'ān, abandoning, if necessary, the *longitudinal*, chronological, reading restricted to a temporal ordering and collocation of the *sūras* and their themes.[2] This makes it possible to deal with the *sūras* not as a haphazard mixture of unrelated pieces devoid of logical sense, but as an intentional texture of communications between God and the believer. From this point of view, Nasr Ḥāmid Abū Zayd's exegetical proposal proves to be once more again highly effective: the Qur'ān is an open-textured dialogue, where the divine voice continues to speak to humanity, beyond the historical circumstances of revelation. The ongoing issues troubling believers will find a *contemporary* answer.

2.  Angelika Neuwirth is a well-known supporter of the intertextual approach, but she approaches the Qur'ānic text in a more chronological than thematic way. For a recent thorough discussion of Neuwirth's methodology and achievements (and those of her students) see Bori Caterina (2014: 33–41).

# 7

## STRUCTURE AND HISTORICITY

The previous discussions of symbolism (Chapter 4) and of literary hermeneutics (Chapter 6) suggest the possibility of a structural, thematic interpretation of the Qur'ān that requires further examination here. The issue is
whether the Qur'ān can be considered a structure whose extension is interpretation. By 'structure' I do not mean simply the 'order', *nazm*, of the text
and its potential coherence and well-constructed shape. I am thinking also
of the internal coherence and self-referentiality of the Qur'ānic language.
The problems of language and 'disclosure' surface again.

Now, the Qur'ān as a text has its own form resulting from impersonal
structures that seem to act independently of the subjective will of its Author,
i.e. God. Although it can sound highly paradoxical and provoking, I mean
that the text acquired through time an objective character with its own
clearly defined form. It is a closed corpus, although its readers interpreted
it in the light of their own particular social, practical and juridical aims.
These completely *human* aims are perhaps not the aims God intended for
the Book. The autonomous activity of human beings and their freedom of
judgement multiplied the meanings of the text. This is demonstrated by the
very different and multifarious ways in which the *mufassirūn* have interpreted the text in the past and are interpreting it in the present. Some read
the Qur'ān as a spiritual text only; some as a political text; some exalt its
inimitability; some deny its inimitability. Which was God's real intention?
To reveal truth in a spiritual and mystic way or to reveal truth in order
to change society through *jihād*? Or possibly both of them together? To
make the Qur'ān an inimitable text or not? When human beings act, do they
respect the intentions of God? Did God will that human beings wage war
in the name of religion or not? Is God freedom or coercion? I would hazard
the suggestion that the text, even a holy text like the Qur'ān, is whatever
human beings make of it, not what God decided it should be. But who is
able to claim to be right in interpreting the will of God? How can we know
what God's intentions really are?

Hasan Hanafī suggested that the author should be placed between brackets. This comes about as a result of the move of theology into anthropology. We have to pronounce the *epoché*: God is living but beyond our reach
(Hanafī 1972). This phenomenological idea (I will come back to it at the
very end of this book) might have an upsetting consequence: God, the

author of the Qur'ān, is, so to speak and using Roland Barthes' terminology, 'dead'. It means that the text is producing its effects without the intervention of its author who stands outside the sphere of any possible intervention. But human beings cannot be so arrogant as to claim to understand the intentions of God. Putting it simply, He let the text speak *within history*, at a human level. The text seems weakened. God is living but the text is working within the human sphere. When Nasr Abū Zayd proposed that the Qur'ān should no longer be considered as a text but as a collection of discourses, because Revelation is a dialogue between God and human beings (Abū Zayd 2004), he envisaged the possibility that God (the 'dead' author) can again change the text (and so still be 'living'). The Holy Book offers its readers many options of choice and so, being open to discussion and communication, may answer all the questions the historical contexts put to it.

See, for example, the *hudūd* penalties, such as whipping for adulterers or the cutting off of a hand for thieves. These penalties were effective, at the time when the Qur'ān was revealed, for a primitive society, an anarchic society where violence was endemic. God's revelation was contextualized.[1] It imposed the moral obligation to punish theft and condemn adultery – obligations we can still agree with today – and suggested penalties fitted for the period and for a particular society. Performed today, these penalties are absurd although the moral obligation is kept alive. It is obvious that if God were to prescribe the same moral obligation nowadays, He would change those penalties that, to contemporary sensibilities, are unacceptable. God has to speak the language humanity is able to understand at a particular period in time. Otherwise, God would be 'silent' forever. Otherwise, no human being would be able to understand the will of God or be able to act accordingly. The Islamists who nowadays seek to impose the *hudūd* penalties as they are *literally* prescribed in the Qur'ān in contemporary society could be said to be compelling the Qur'ān to speak independently from the will of God. They are closing the ways of communication between God and humans. Hermeneutics returns to God the freedom to legislate. It is necessary to read the text in the same spirit as that of he who produced it, as a divinatory act, so to speak, aimed at understanding the text even better than its Author. This is basically the suggestion of Schleiermacher's hermeneutics.

Clearly, the central hermeneutical problem of the circle between the 'reader' (the subject) and the 'read text' (the object) must be reconsidered. We have already discussed it in regard to Ibn Rushd. Here, it could be useful to recall an intriguing characteristic of Christian hermeneutics of the Bible. Pope Gregory the Great portrayed the image of the (Christian) Scripture as a wheel:

1.  For a new approach contextualizing the normative prescriptions of the Qur'ān, see Saeed 2006, discussed further in the Conclusion.

> [The image of] the wheel designates nothing less than the Holy Scripture, that turns in all directions from everywhere in order to adapt itself to the listener. Its message is not held back by any awkward corners and is not slowed down in its announcement by any angle, i.e. by any mistake. It turns in all directions from everywhere because it moves straight forward and close to the ground, passing through adversities and prosperities. The circle of its teachings can be found now upwards, now downwards. What is spiritually suitable for the perfect people, is suitable for the simple people only literally. What is understood in a literal sense by the simple people is raised up to a very high level by scholars through their spiritual intelligence (quoted in Bori Pier Cesare 1987: 31).

The path suggested by the Holy Scripture to those who meditate upon it, practice it and preach it moves not only upwards, raising the soul up to God through 'the divine machine of allegory', but also in a circular direction: after the elevation from history to contemplation, it is necessary 'to come back down'. The hermeneutical circle works only if the text is not closed and, as Pier Cesare Bori argues, interpreter and interpretation grow up together. As we have seen, the *mushaf* is closed. It is necessary to open it again. Paradoxically, once again it is an ancient Christian author, Vincent of Lerins, who provides the key. He wrote:

> Teach the things you learnt so that you do not say new things, but say the same things in a new mood (*cum dicas nove, non dicas nova*). If somebody asks: is there then any religious progress (*profectus religionis*) in Christ's church? – [we answer]: Certainly, there is and is very great [...], but in such a way that there is a real progress in faith but not a change [in dogma] (*permutatio*). It is characteristic of progress that a thing becomes larger; of the change, on the contrary, that a thing transforms itself (*transvertatur*) into another thing. (quoted in Bori Pier Cesare 1987: 61).

This formula would be satisfying either for the fundamentalist, conservative Muslim, or for the open-minded, progressive Muslim. The former would be reassured by the fact that revelation is settled and closed; the latter would find the fundamentals of knowledge developed and grown up pointing both to a re-reading of the sacred text and the transformation of society.

Considering the Qur'ān as a structure may lead us to escape from the trap of the objectivation and alienation of the text in respect of its Author. Here, we once again have to consider the matter of *language*. A major factor I am not able to deal with extensively here is that of the inner character of language. Is it a fixed system of rules and vocabulary or is it a work in progress? Obviously, languages change continuously over time: Shakespeare's English is different from Joyce's English; Dante's Italian is different from Carlo Emilio Gadda's Italian; Qur'ānic Arabic is different from modern standard Arabic. But it is precisely here that the problem lies. Qur'ānic Arabic is definitely fixed in time and cannot be changed any more. How can it reproduce the ever-changing meanings of a never-ending modifying reality?

In order to give a tentative answer to this troubling issue, I believe that an emerging question, in addition to discussing the Muslim dogma of the inimitability of the Qur'ān (*i'jāz*) and reaching far beyond the author's intentions, is the possibility of approaching the Qur'ān as a system of linguistic relations whose components do not exist by themselves but only in reciprocal connection. The text objectivizes the truth in a closed and interconnected linguistic system. In this sense, in Ferdinand de Saussure's terminology, the Qur'ān is not a *parole* but a *langue*, that is, a system whose single component keeps its specific value in relation to other components and in relation to the history of the text, i.e. the history of revelation itself. The first is a synchronic, the second a diachronic approach. These two perspectives may be combined in order to place the holy text within a time-frame perspective, which is an essential element of hermeneutics.

We need, consequently, to have a better understanding of the structuralist interpretation. In Jean Piaget's view, structure is a complex of transformations happening within a system without going beyond its boundaries and without any resort to external and exogenic elements. From this point of view, the structuralist distinction between the synchronic and the diachronic character of the language is of great importance. Synchrony is the simultaneous coexistence of linguistic facts; diachrony involves a change of the linguistic values and meanings from one to another phase of the language's history.

Now I believe that the Qur'ān is undoubtedly a diachronic *langue*. It is well-known that many linguistic items changed their meanings during the history of revelation, for instance the item *jihād* or even the same items *Qur'ān* and *Kitāb*.

The science of *naskh* (abrogation) is particularly telling from this point of view. The science of abrogation was developed by Muslim jurists in order to solve alleged contradictions within the text and contradictions between the Qur'ān and the *sunna*. The Qur'ānic verse apparently sanctioning abrogation is Q. 2:106: 'We [God speaking] will not abrogate (*nansakhu*) a verse or cause it to be forgotten without replacing it with a better or a similar (verse)', but it is controversial. Abdel Haleem even avoids using the verb 'abrogate': 'Any revelation We cause to be *superseded* or forgotten, We replace with *something* better or similar'. Arberry uses the verb 'abrogate and cast into oblivion'. 'To supersede' is much weaker than 'abrogate': it means that God 'substitutes' a verse with another, not 'deletes' it. Substitution does not imply the destruction of the substituted. Moreover, in Abdel Haleem's interpretation, the better is 'something' else, not necessarily another 'verse'. Potentially, abrogation could mean that God is contradicting Himself. We have to keep alive God's intentions.

Thus, the science of *naskh* can have a pivotal role in the interpretation of the text, especially from the point of view of practical issues. It is articulated in three ways (see Burton 1990, although my starting point is Burton's book, the elaboration is my own):

- *naskh al-hukm wa al-* tilāwa  that is the simultaneous abrogation of the rule enunciated by the text and of the Qur'ānic text itself. This first mode does not affect the internal coherence of the text, but keeps the text free from outside interpolations. For it consists of the forgetting of *sūras* or of parts of *sūras* in order to obliterate the ruling they conveyed, either because of human frailty or by a miraculous intervention by God. So, if parts of the historical revelation have been lost, all the parts that must be remembered have been preserved. This is an important definition of the actual structure and form of the surviving text. *All that which is useful to know, is included in the text*. This conclusion can be considered an interesting forerunner of the structuralistic approach.
- *naskh al-hukm* dūna al-tilāwa, that is the abrogation of the rule enunciated by the text while the literal expression of the text remains. When the rule is judged to be no longer useful by the *usūl* scholar, aware of the redundancy of some Qur'ānic verses, it is abrogated without any consequence for the integrity of the text. This second mode does not affect the internal coherence of the text altogether, essentially because the text's effectiveness is suspended. This is, rather, a clear practice by the *fuqahā'* to update inoperative Qur'ānic rulings. In this sense it can become very important for a historical reading of the text and secondly for the determination of juridical rules.
- *naskh* al-tilāwa dūna *al-hukm*, that is the abrogation of the literal text while the rule it contains is kept alive. This third mode can have a significant effect on the normative and practical value of the text, although not its internal coherence.

My aim here is not to discuss in depth the types and applications of *naskh* because I am not a jurist. It is important to stress, however, that the science of abrogation involves in some way a criterion of historicity and imposes the issue of the internal coherence of the text. Studying how abrogation works within the Qur'ān itself is even more important from a structuralist perspective, than is studying how the abrogation can modify the meaning of the text. In the evolution of juridical thought, the abrogation of the Qur'ān through the Qur'ān was limited to a very few cases. Yet, if the *naskh* doctrine was imposed on the Qur'ān from outside in order to smooth away the apparent contradictions of the text itself and of the text in relation to juridical practice, it acquired a high operative worth in fundamentalist and radical thought. Take for example the issue of war against the *kuffār* (unbe-lievers). In the Meccan Qur'ān, the attitude is that of dialogue, exhorta-tion and admonition: human beings must be converted by persuasion and good advice (Q. 16:125). In the Medinese Qur'ān the attitude changes and becomes more and more aggressive: the non-believers must be fought. So many Islamists contend that the so-called 'verse of the sword' (Q. 9, 5: 'when the sacred months are passed away, kill the idolaters whenever you find them, take them out, besiege them, make them fall in ambush') abro-gated all the previous more moderate verses, opening the door to merciless fighting.

In a sense, then, *naskh* has 'historicistic' implications, but with debat-able or even dangerous implications, permitting all-out war, instead of dialogue and polemic, against 'infidels'. The same dangerous and misun-derstood implications can derive from the alleged theorization of *naskh* in the Qur'ān:

> Q. 2:106, *For whatsoever verse we cancel or cause to forget, We bring a better or its like*, is repeatedly referenced as the Qur'ānic foundation of the exegetical theory of abrogation (*nāsikh wa mansūkh*) according to which one Qur'ānic verse can abrogate another which is supposed to be chronologically earlier. But if this verse is read in its literary context, it can immediately be seen that it is part of a long polemic with the Jews who refused to believe that God could send a Prophet and a revela-tion outside of the one chosen people, the Jewish people. Not only did Muhammad pretend to be a prophet, but he also claimed authority to quote the Torah and modify it. Thus it is that God in Q. 2:106 backs his Prophet by affirming that he can very well abrogate or ignore certain pas-sages of the Torah because something better will be sent down, i.e. the verses of the Qur'ān. The abrogation here does not, therefore, refer to the replacement of one verse of the Qur'ān by another verse of the Qur'ān, but rather the replacement of *certain* verses of the Torah by those of the Qur'ān. The other two verses (Q. 16:101; Q. 13:39) which are also invoked to justify the abrogation method, have a similar context: that of a polemic with the Jews regarding the Torah and do not refer to the Qur'ān. Several Muslim commentators of the late Nineteenth Century (Sayyid Ahmad Khan, 1817–98) and the Twentieth Century ('Abd Allah Yusuf 'Ali, 1872–1953; Abu'l-A'la al-Mawdudi, 1903–1979; Muham-mad Asad, 1900–1992) denounced the misinterpretation of Q. 2:106... but in vain. This doctrine continues to circulate as a quasi-dogmatic cer-titude. A Muslim researcher, Ahmad Hasan, in an article on the question of abrogation published in 1962, expresses his astonishment: "In view of the evident context of the verse under reference [Q. 2:106]... it looks strange that some of the most eminent authorities of *tafsīr* have missed the central point of this verse". We must conclude on this basis that the abrogation theory has no foundation in the Qur'ān; it is an innovation of the jurists (*fuqahā'*), belonging to *fiqh*, not to *tafsīr*. The example of Q. 2:106 demonstrates the danger of interpreting a verse in isolation,

without considering its literary context, and also the shortcomings of
many of the "occasions of revelation"; those invoked to explain Q. 2:106
are obviously artificial (Cuypers 2011: 6–7).

From the point of view of Nasr Abū Zayd, *naskh* must be obviously
rejected: if the Qur'ān is a set of dialogues, the longitudinal abrogation of
previous verses by the last is a mortal blow to dialogue. The Sudanese jurist
Abdullāhi al-Na'īm, pupil of Muhammad Mahmūd Tāhā, was another who
sought to pursue an in-depth revision of *naskh*. Quoting directly from his
master, al-Na'īm wrote:

> The main implication of *ustadh* Mahmoud's argument for the purposes
> of the present study is that the public law of *shari'a* was based on the
> Qur'an and related *sunna* of the Medina period rather than that of the
> Mecca stage. As will be explained in the next section of this chapter,
> this was done by the founding jurists through the process of *naskh*, by
> holding the subsequent texts of the Qur'an and the *sunna* of the Medina
> stage to have repealed or abrogated, for the purposes of the positive law
> of *shari'a*, all previously revealed inconsistent texts of the Mecca stage.
> The question that would then arise is whether such *naskh* is permanent,
> thereby rendering the earlier texts of Mecca inoperative for posterity.
> According to *ustadh* Mahmoud, this cannot possibly be so because if
> that were the case, there would have been no point in having revealed
> the earlier texts. He also argued that to deem *naskh* to be permanent is to
> deny the Muslims the best part of their religion. In other words he main-
> tained that *naskh* was an essentially logical and necessary process of
> implementing the appropriate texts and postponing the implementation
> of others until the right circumstances for their implementation should
> arise.

Al-Na'īm supports a real 'reversal' of *naskh*, and he quotes Tāhā directly:

> We consider the rationale beyond the text. If a subsidiary verse, which
> used to overrule the primary verse in the seventh century, has served its
> purpose completely and become irrelevant for the new era, the twen-
> tieth century, then the time has come for it to be abrogated and for the
> primary verse to be enacted. In this way, the primary verse has its turn
> as the operative text in the twentieth century and becomes the basis of
> the new legislation (al-Na'im 1990: 56, 60, quoting Taha 1996. See also
> 1990: 158–59).

While we are not concerned with the legal implications of these ideas as
drawn by al-Na'īm, it is clear that the reversal of *naskh* has decisive hermeneutical implications, for it assumes that a transversal and not longitudinal
reading of the texts is needed.

Thus, a structuralist attitude to history is critical as far as it envisages
a transversal and not longitudinal approach, considering reality as a relatively unchanging system of relations. For structuralism avoids the problem

of genesis, that is the problem of history. But the Qur'ān has at least a double genesis: God who revealed it and the *Ummu'l-kitāb*, the archetype that retains it from the very beginning of time. Now, the structuralist reading must choose a transversal hermeneutics, while the Islamist view with regard to verses Q. 9:5 and 2:106 is clearly the outcome of a longitudinal hermeneutics.

Hasan Hanafī correctly criticized the longitudinal commentary in the light of the 'thematic interpretation' of the Qur'ān that he espouses (Hanafī 1995: I, 407–28). I have discussed Hanafī's idea in an earlier work titled *'The Qur'ān: Modern Muslim Interpretations'* (Campanini 2011) and so will refrain from quoting his words again here. Instead, I should like to stress the consequences of thematic interpretation. First of all, it compels a systematic and compact treatment of the argument in order to give it its own thematic autonomy; for, from a hermeneutical point of view, the whole can only be understood if we start from its parts, but the single parts have a meaning only in relation to the whole. From this premise, it derives that the meaning of a text is not merely linguistic, but linked to motivations (inside the text) and interests or passions (outside the texts for the human beings). Elaboration of the text might produce a general pattern of interpretation of historical and/or psychological circumstances. In this sense, interpretation is a sort of 'ideology': involving the hermeneutical circle between the reader and the read, and provided that, in Gadamer's terms, the reader looks at the text through his/her pre-comprehension ('prejudices'), interpretation supplies the awareness that what lies beyond the literal meaning of the text activates the impulse to action accordingly. Thus, interpretation is a political fact. The unavoidable conclusion is that there are many meanings of the text and the plurality of meanings must be discovered by an interpretation going beyond the rigidity of literalism; structuralist analysis must be flexible.

Transversal, that is *thematic* interpretation, is particularly supported by Fazlur Rahman (1919–1988), one of the most prominent Islamic thinkers of the twentieth century, who may be considered as one of the first to develop a self-aware philosophical interpretation. Rahman challenges Gadamer directly, criticizing his theoretical attitude, saying that it is, in his opinion, conditioned by an excessive subjectivity. Instead, Rahman endorses Emilio Betti's hermeneutics, originally applied to case law but which the Muslim thinker claims he can extend to philosophy.

Fazlur Rahman begins by criticizing the 'atomistic' approach of many interpreters who failed 'to understand the underlying unity of the Qur'an, coupled with a practical insistence on fixing on the words of various verses in isolation'. This atomistic approach looks like the longitudinal commentary stigmatized by Hanafī. But Rahman also criticizes philosophers and mystics: 'The philosophers and often the Sufis did understand the Qur'ān as a unity, but this unity was imposed upon the Qur'ān (and Islam in

general) from without rather than derived from a study of the Qur'ān itself'
(Rahman 1984: 2–3). The necessity of studying the Qur'ān as a unity, that
is as a structure, leads Rahman to elaborate a two-step method. The first
stage consists of deriving the universal principles from the historical reality
of the Qur'ān; the second consists of applying the derived principles to
the practical level of praxis: it is a 'Galilean' method, as it were, inductive
(from particular to universal) and then deductive (from the universal to the
particular). The formulation of general laws or general rules of behaviour
provide the ethical principle from whose universality the contextualized
norms draw their inspiration. This is a very useful methodological suggestion, making it possible to escape the reification of the text (the Qur'ān) in
regards to the author (God), such as we have seen concerning the *hudūd*
penalties, for example. The text keeps its links with the intentions of the
author, albeit adhering to contextual reality. Returning to the examples
cited at the beginning of this paragraph, the issue we are concerned with is
to derive from the Qur'ān the moral and universal principle of the convic-
tion of adultery and theft and then punishment of the guilty with penalties
appropriate to the contemporary social context, rejecting sanctions such as
whipping the adulterer and mutilation of the thief's hand.

Rahman discussed Gadamer's method, seeing it as the unavoidable reference point for contemporary philosophical hermeneutics. He argues that
Gadamer undermines the objectivity of the text by an excess of subjectiv-
ism in the pre-comprehension generated by 'prejudices'. Yet, 'in the case
of the Qur'an, the objective situation is a *conditio sine qua non* for understanding, particularly since, in view of its absolute normativity for Muslims,
it is literally God's response through Muhammad's mind (this latter factor
has been radically underplayed by the Islamic orthodoxy) to a historic situation (a factor likewise drastically restricted by the Islamic orthodoxy in a
real understanding of the Qur'ān)' (Rahman 1984: 8). The relation between
the objectivity of the text and the objectivity of the historical context – the
contemporary age – when the text must be applied, led Rahman to an assertion that is hardly acceptable by a traditionalist Muslim: 'The contention that
certainty belongs not to the meanings of particular verses of the Qur'ān and
their content (by 'certainty' I mean not their revealed character for undoubtedly the Qur'ān is revealed in its entirety, but the certainty of our understanding of their true meaning and import) but to the Qur'ān as a whole, that is as
a set of coherent principles or values where the total teachings will converge,
might appear shocking to many Muslims' (Rahman 1984: 20).[2]

---

2.   This contention points to a structuralistic reading of the Qur'ān, although Rah-
     man's view can be considered very different from the usual structuralistic per-
     spective, insofar as he defends the historicity of the text. Such a defence, however,
     is highly important for the re-establishing of Islamic thought. The above quotation

Here again, we see how the central problem is that of the interaction between subjectivity (the interpreter's viewpoint) and objectivity (the scriptural data in its literality). Let us consider Rahman's belief that God's word, objectively revealed, unveils itself through the Prophet's subjective experience. The Qur'ān – Rahman states – is God's word, but it is so profoundly bound to the Prophet's personality that it may not have a purely mechanical relationship of communication and reception with it: the divine Word passes through the Prophet's heart. Rahman especially criticizes the 'atomistic' approach to the Qur'ān, putting forward instead the need to study the text transversally, not in a chronological sense but in a theme-based one. Moreover, Rahman does not consider the Qur'an as a book on theology, but a book on ethics, because it is the instrument that leads men in their behaviour and in the building of a fair and well-balanced society. The book *Major Themes of the Qur'an*, a text in which the Author puts his own method to the test, opens with the innovating acknowledgement that in Islam, God is the dimension that makes all other dimensions possible. God is the object of a diuturnal research and the demonstration of his existence is to be found in the continuous perception of his 'signs'. The issue, so important for Western philosophy, of the demonstration of God's existence, is bypassed in favour of a vision of divinity as a transcendental guarantee of all reality and its harmonious workings. The classic cosmological, ontological and intelligent design proofs, developed during the history of philosophy in the West (but the development of the *kalām* in the classical Muslim world, or at least in that part most strictly involved with the assimilation of the Greek rationalistic heritage, was quite similar) are no longer necessary: God's existence is obvious *a priori*.

is a clear condemnation of the stiffness of traditional interpretation and theology, too often confined to a blind repetition and imitation of the past. I believe that Rahman's criticism of Gadamer is too harsh, however. Gadamer's 'prejudices' are far from being inimicable to the text's significance and far from destroying the 'objectivity' of its meaning. Rather, it can be true that Gadamer did not provide for a practical and historically significant application of hermeneutical inquiry. The practical implications are, on the contrary, pivotal both in Hanafī and in Rahman. In the case of the latter, he argues that 'in Qur'ānic terms no real morality is possible without the regulative ideas of God and the Last Judgment. […] But the substantive or constitutive – as Kantian phraseology would have it – teaching of the Prophet and the Qur'ān is undoubtedly *for action in this world*' (Rahman 1984: 14). Contemporary Islam has indeed shown an enduring vocation to translate theoretical presuppositions into praxis (Campanini 2016a).

# 8

## SCIENTIFIC HERMENEUTICS

The scientific commentary (*tafsīr 'ilmī*) is one of the most curious outcomes of Qur'ānic exegesis (for an overview see Shalabī 1985; I discussed this issue also in 'Qur'ān and Science: a Hermeneutical Approach' [Campanini 2005b]). It deals with the problems of harmonization and coherence between the (especially natural) sciences and the Holy Book. Broadly speaking, in the history of Islamic thought, three main trends developed: one emphasizing the perfect concordance and harmony between the Qur'ān and physics or astronomy or biology; one emphasizing the complete impossibility of foreseeing in God's words anticipations of scientific achievements; the third seeking for a middle way. Given that no Islamic thinker has ever said that the Qur'ān is in contradiction with scientific research or rationality, the debate arose as far back as the so-called Middle Ages, which correspond to the classical phase of Islamic civilization, during which many (e.g. the great al-Ghazālī [c. 1056–1111]) claimed that the Qur'ān contains the key to all sciences, while others, as famous as al-Shatibī, underlined most of all the methodological impossibility of harmonizing science and Scripture. Maybe it is surprising that a 'fundamentalist' thinker like the Egyptian Sayyid Qutb (1906–1966) argued that a 'scientific commentary' of the Qur'ān is a surrender to the alien and imperialist outlook of the West and a betrayal of the true sources of the Islamic 'concept' (*tasawwur*), while the middle way, like that of 'Ā'isha Bint al-Shāti', argues that the Qur'ān can be opened up to modern material scientific discoveries without losing its 'divine' character.

'Ā'isha Bint al-Shāti' makes many references to Muhammad 'Abduh's methodology, and it is the case that 'Abduh maintains a balanced position between the necessity of adopting the results of modern science while retaining a respect for the literality of the Holy Book. The following long passage by Aziz al-Azmeh is worth quoting:

> What it is true of those verses that point to the existence of transcendental and invisible things is similarly true of matters about which certainty can be achieved, such as knowledge of history and nature. These are matters in which a contradiction appeared between the Koran and what the educated people of that age had learnt in the new and modern educational system.

A case in point is the story of Noah and the Flood. The examination of this story represented a transitional stage between *tafwīd* [fideistic attribution of all knowledge to God] and interpretation, it being open to the possibility of doubt and contestation and therefore to *tafwīd*. Muhammad 'Abduh considered that the tale of the flooding of the world is a narrative with no Qur'ānic authority, being based, rather, on an isolated *hadīth* which does not afford certainty. He then cited the arguments of some theologians and philosophers that the existence of shells and fossils of fish on the top of mountains proved that water rose up there, 'and this would never have happened unless it had covered the world'. He went on to cite the opinion of the majority of contemporary authorities, saying 'the flood was not universal, for reasons which would take too long to explain'. 'Abduh then concluded as follows:

> No Muslim may deny that the flood was universal merely because of the likelihood of such an interpretation of the verses of the Koran. On the contrary, no one who firmly believes in religion should reject something demonstrating by the literal meaning of the verses, and *hadīth* whose *isnads* are trustworthy in favour of this interpretation, except by rational evidence which positively shows that the literal meaning is not the one intended by the text. Arriving at this conclusion is a matter that requires deep study, great application and extensive knowledge of stratigraphy and geology. And this depends on various rational and traditional sciences. Whoever speculates irrationally without sure knowledge is reckless, should not be heard, and should not be permitted to propagate his ignorance.
>
> The fundamental points which this position affirms is the possibility of resorting to interpretation, indeed its necessity, when it is asserted that the literal meaning is "not the one intended". In this way the spirit of modernity is correlated with that of the text, and the definitive authority of the text entails endowing that authority with a meaning derived from modernity, which is incompatible with it on grounds of anachronism. Certainty and the text thus become counterparts (al-Azmeh 2009: 133–34).

The issue of a Qur'ānic literality in contradiction with scientific discoveries is overcome by 'Abduh through the acknowledgement that the text does not say what apparently it says. So, interpretation is needed in order to allegorize the crude expressions of the Book.

However, there are undoubtedly interpretations – *not* allegorical but deliberately involving a direct reproduction *in nature* of the Qur'ānic images (symbols) – that give rise to serious hermeneutical and epistemological problems. 'Abd al-Rahmān al-Kawākibī (d. 1903) suggested that the Qur'ānic Noah's Ark anticipated steamships; Ahmad Hanafī (d. 1940) suggested that the Qur'ān, when it says that the Sun and the Moon 'swim' (*yasbahūna*) each in its sphere (*falak*) (Q. 21:33), alludes to the Copernican cosmological model with planets revolving each in its own orbit. Many other such examples have been advanced. Here, I would argue, we face a real excess of interpretation. Every kind of meaning of the words is distorted, and the esoteric symbolism is over-stretched.

Scientific commentary is still widely practiced today, and there are numerous Muslim scientists and scholars who defend the idea that the Qur'ān contains precise biological, geological, astronomical and other information revealed in the remote past but confirmed by modern science. Theories like Darwinism, too, that sharply contradict religious convictions and are considered by traditionalists as the most dangerous attempt by 'atheists' to challenge the notion of Intelligent Design according to which God created the world and supports it, can be reduced to a level of dialogue with faith (see for e.g. Mehdī Golshani in Bigliardi 2014). Irrespective of the most reactionary and backward positions, for example those who still claim today that the Earth is flat because the Qur'ān says several times that God 'flattened' it, hermeneutics must find a way of reconciling science and revealed Scripture, preserving the former's autonomy and falsifiability, and the latter's feature as a divine message transmitted to mankind. The challenge is extremely open with many medical doctors, physicists and chemists attempting to understand the natural world while complying with religious tradition.

Discussing modern quantum theory, Muhammad Iqbāl wrote:

> I regard the Ashʿarite thought [of occasionalistic atomism] as a genuine effort to develop on the basis of an Ultimate Will or Energy a theory of creation which, with all its shortcomings, is far more true to the spirit of the Qur'ān than the Aristotelian idea of a fixed universe. The duty of the future theologians of Islam is to reconstruct this purely speculative theory and to bring it into closer contact with modern science which appears to be moving in the same direction (Iqbāl 2013: 70).

Einstein's relativity and Heisenberg's quantum mechanics are potentially at odds with the creative power of God and His providential Design, but Ashʿarite occasionalism foresaw those contemporary discoveries and paved the way to the harmonization between classical Islamic theology and modern science.

We take quantum theory as a meaningful example in understanding the relationship between revelation and science in contemporary Islamic progressive thought. Nidhal Guessoum, a physicist and professor at Sharja American University, stressed the harmonious correspondence between reason and revelation. His mentor is (again) Ibn Rushd:

> Ibn Rushd's modernity is not difficult to detect in his writings. But, above all, what makes him important is the flawless coherence and harmony he has achieved between his religious principles and his intellectual train-

ing. That is why I adopted him and will use him as a model for a harmonious fusion of science, philosophy and religion in Islam today. That
spirit of Ibn Rushd/Averroes is what this book will try to capture and
use to illuminate various topics of relevance (Guessoum 2011: XXIII).

The methodological spirit of Ibn Rushd/Averroes allows a balanced
approach. For although 'Quantum Mechanics cannot be explained simply
to a non-scientist, [because], as Richard Feynman famously put it: "nobody
understands QM"', on the one hand, 'various great scientists…adopted
various philosophical positions on the thorny question. Heisenberg, in particular, stressed that his uncertainty principle had allowed for a new acceptance of the "natural language" of religion' (Guessoum 2011: 40–41). On
the other hand, 'observers noted that the intrinsic indeterminism of QM
could be a doorway for God's action in nature, since one would normally
assume that God (the omniscient and omnipotent) is able to set the outcome
of the "wave function collapse process" to one particular choice among
those that the physics of situation allows. […] If God then can determine the
outcomes of any quantum mechanical process, which will always appear
indeterministic to us (according to standard Quantum Theory), then He can
"steer" events in a way that will be transparent to us. This invisible action or
intervention is not necessarily a source of unease, despite what non-theists
will say' (Guessoum 2011: 337).

A careful hermeneutics can lead to the realization of an epistemological harmonization between a text revealed 15 centuries ago in a (relatively)
primitive environment and a sophisticated modernity more and more sceptical about religious truths. The basis of discussion is *epistemological*, I
repeat, because it is objectively difficult to make a Qur'ānic *āya* correspond
to a mathematical equation. In this case, hermeneutics can profit from the
tools of linguistics and semiotics analysing the Qur'ānic terms involved in
(alleged) scientific utterances, but it has to work especially on the transcendent level of theory. Rather, Qur'ānic passages *symbolize* scientific achievements so that we may perceive the role of the Qur'ān as the metaphysical
foundation of science without arguing that it is a scientific text.

# 9

## THE TRANSLATION OF THE QUR'ĀN
## AS HERMENEUTICAL EXERCISE

Let us consider translation of the Qur'ān as a hermeneutical exercise. This involves making choices between one or more possible translations of a text, or one or more interpretations. Of course, translating is a highly hermeneutical activity. Translating is always interpreting. This is particularly true for poetry, novels and other literary texts. In Italian there is a saying: 'traduttore/traditore', that is 'translator/betrayer', because to translate is always to betray. When we are translating the Qur'ān, are we 'betraying' its meanings? This is a very worrying issue, because humans have the duty to comply with God's intentions and orders.

Discussing the topic of the Qur'ān's translation is then a very difficult task. On the one hand, the Qur'ān is not a normal literary text; and, on the other, Muslims do not accept the translation into another human language of the direct speech of God who spoke in Arabic. Actually, it is common knowledge that Muslims never speak of 'translation', but of rendering the approximate meanings of the text. Now, if the Qur'ān is written in Arabic to be comprehended by Arabs, it is obvious that it can be readily understood. But Islam is a universal religion and its message has been conveyed also to non-Arabs. Revelation is for all creatures, but God spoke in Arabic. How is it possible then to convey to all human beings, who speak many languages, the meaning of a message originally expressed in Arabic?

The problem of the Qur'ān's inimitability (*i'jāz*) is crucial here.[1] The issue has been partially discussed above in relation with the verse Q. 3:7.

---

1. The Arab term pointing to inimitability is not Qur'ānic and classical exegetes had to support inimitability resorting to the so-called 'Challenge Verses' (Q. 2:23–24; 10:38; 11:13; 17:88; 52:33–34) where Muhammad was commanded by God to ask his Meccan detractors to produce *sūras* like those of the Qur'ān. As they were not able to do so, the Qur'ān's perfection was established. Classical Muslim religious literature emphasized the *literary inimitability* of the Holy Book. Starting with al-Jāhiz and 'Abd al-Jabbār (both Mu'tazilites), for most exegetes the *i'jāz al-Qur'ān* rests on its linguistic purity (*fasāha*) and eloquence (*balāgha*) and Abū Bakr al-Baqillānī has been probably the standard supporter of this view. At least two other thinkers argued differently, however. Another Mu'tazilite, al-Nazzām, contended that the Qur'ān is inimitable for its *content* and not for its form, because the linguistic qualities of the Qur'ān were not superior to ordinary human abili-

Actually, inimitability could be placed either only on the formal level of the impossibility of the *literary* reproduction of the text or on the more substantial level of the content. As to the literary *i'jāz*, it is obvious that any kind of translation is impossible. For, if the text is inimitable in Arabic, it cannot be inimitable in other languages, like Italian or English. It could succeed as a beautiful text, an elegant and fascinating text with highly rhetorical effectiveness, but not inimitable. If we look at the content, we have to deal with the difficulty of distinguishing between the *zāhir* and the *bātin*, namely between the outward/exoteric and the inner/esoteric meaning. Does the inimitability of the Qur'ān pertain to the outward/exoteric or the inner/esoteric meaning? If we deal especially with the content, we are forced to agree that inimitability is limited to the inner meaning, not to the external meaning.

We need to examine this topic in greater depth. First, the linguistic-literary inimitability of the Arabic Qur'ān pertains to the outward/exoteric

---

ties 'in spite of God's saying so'. Rather, he took the position that the Qur'ān is a miracle only with respect to *sarfa*. The meaning of *sarfa* is that the Arabs were able to utter speech like that of the Qur'ān in terms of linguistic purity and eloquence (*al-fasāha wa al-balāgha*) until the Prophet was sent. When the Prophet was sent, this characteristic eloquence was taken away from them and they were deprived of their knowledge of it, and thus they were unable to produce speech like the Qur'ān. God's miracle was to *prevent* humans from speaking like Him in the Qur'ān, not to make the Qur'ān a piece of work beyond normal literary standards. For his part, 'Abd al-Qāhir al-Jurjānī argued that the overall composition of the Qur'ān, its meanings as well its wording, were the real miracle of inimitability; it was not only the structural composition of words and phrases that prove inimitability, but also the content and meanings. Al-Jurjānī's point is that of *nazm*, that is the 'order' of the Qur'ān, its well-knitted and well-established (by God) structure. The miracle of *nazm* has been studied in the past century by the *mufassir* al-Islāhī (see Mir 1986), but underpins also Abū'l-A'là Mawdūdī's reflections on the apparently haphazard structure of the Book. Given that:

> the different parts of the Qur'ān were revealed step by step according to the multifarious, changing needs and requirements of the Islamic movement during these stages; it therefore could not possibly possess the kind of coherence and systematic sequence expected of a doctoral dissertation.(Mawdūdī 1988, vol. I).

Mawdūdī continues, arguing that the Qur'ān's arrangement is altogether providential and was made by the Prophet under God's direction. Moreover, '[it] would have been quite contrary to God's purpose' if 'it had been supplemented with explanatory notes', for 'the main purpose [of] revelation was that all human beings should be able to refer to the Divine Guidance available to them in composite form and providentially secured against adulteration' (Mawdūdī 1988, vol. I: 18–20).

level of meaning alone.[2] The Arabic language displays images, concepts, ideas and tells stories that are unchangeable and unaltered in their outward/exoteric meaning. *Tafsīr* can be exclusively historical or literary and heavily dependent on *hadīth* and *sunna*. As Nasr Abū Zayd explained:

> efforts to reopen the meaning of the Qur'ān and addressing modern issues [must be done] by seeking to establish a new Qur'ānic exegesis without the usual heavy reliance on tradition in the classical commentaries of the Qur'ān. Put differently, the criticism of the *sunna* was basically one result of Muslim thinkers being involved in Qur'ānic exegesis in somewhat different way. The strong demand for a new approach to the Qur'ān that would open its meaning to new, challenging circumstances, made it essential to distance modern Qur'ānic exegesis from the traditional type heavily loaded with *hadith* quotations (Abū Zayd 2006: 27).

As we have seen, Muhammad Ibn Jarīr al-Tabarī argued that all the Qur'ānic verses are clear and that ambiguous or obscure verses do not exist, because the Arabic language is able to express them clearly. As a consequence, transferring the Qur'ān from Arabic to Italian or English does not seem unreasonable. From the point of view of outward/exoteric meaning the Qur'ān says in Italian or English the same things said in Arabic. The verse prescribing the possibility of marrying four wives if the husband is able to be equitable with them all (Q. 4:3) has the same meaning in Arabic, in English or in Italian. Thus, translation seems acceptable without particular problems.

As for the inner/esoteric level, if we assume that it is inimitable because no one except God is allowed to express the best, the deepest and the soundest utterances, the question becomes more complicated. The first key is linguistic however: we need to know Arabic. The second key is hermeneutical, but we have to understand what sort of hermeneutics is at issue here. Al-Shahrastānī, who was a crypto-Ismaili, maintained directly that the only viable hermeneutical key is the interpretation of the *imams*.[3] In any case, it

2.  The exoteric/outward level of comprehension is obviously linked with the clearness of the language in which a text is written (or spoken) – or revealed. The Qur'ān is written in *clear* Arabic: see for example Q. 16:103: 'This is clear Arab language (*hadhā lisān 'arabī mubīn*), a language accessible to everybody. The Qur'ān is written in (clear) Arabic so that everybody can understand' (Q. 12:2; 42:7); it 'makes the things clear' and everybody understands (Q. 43:2–3). Clearness of language helps interpretation. On the other hand, the Qur'ān is 'warning for all creatures' (*dhikr li'l-'ālamīna*, Q. 38:87), that is enjoys a universal character, not specifically 'Arab'.

3.  Al-Shahrastānī's theory is subtle. He points out that the *accomplished* dimension of the text, namely its literal dimension, is *ontologically* determined and closed, so to speak (see Mayer 2005): the text is a *thing*, or, better, a *mushaf* defined in its form; hence the meaning cannot be lost in translation. It goes without saying that

is clear that, if the literary-linguistic structure of Arabic conceals a hidden meaning, any kind of translation would make other linguistic keys useless so that no linguistic key would be suitable for opening the door of the hidden meaning. We would be unable to grasp the hidden meaning without Arabic. Moreover, anyone who is not Shiite or Ismaili is not bound by the *imam*'s interpretation. The text will continue to be closed in both cases.

The issue is how to keep alive the exegetical interpretation of a text originally written in Arabic and whose content (as opposed to form) is inimitable without resorting to Arabic which is deemed to be the only vehicle able to convey the inner meaning of the message. The shift from the literal level to the symbolic, semiotic or metaphorical levels seems to me unavoidable. From the point of view of symbols and metaphors, though, what reliance can we place upon a translation in a language other than Arabic? How can we be sure that an Italian or English translation respects the *true, inner* meaning of the text we are interpreting metaphorically? But other more serious problems arise. To what extent does the metaphor or the symbol contain precisely the cognitive value about which it is metaphorical or symbolic? Put differently: does the metaphor really say the same things as that of which it is a metaphor? What is the *real* meaning of the text? We are facing the previous dilemma: if the 'true' meaning of the text is the literal meaning, it can *only* be understood in the language in which it is written – in our case, in Arabic – and this conclusion prevents any kind of translation. On the other hand, the text would be merely obvious, superficial, unable to address modern issues.

If what we have said so far is true, namely that the translation of the Qur'ān in other languages does not change the literal meaning (although inimitability gets lost), no danger of going astray or *kufr* is incumbent, although the danger of a deep misunderstanding of the inner meaning of the text is almost inescapable. If we restrict ourselves to the literal meaning, the Qur'ān becomes an overwhelmingly normative and juridical text which imposes *hudūd* penalties and regards polygamy or slavery as lawful in any epoch or circumstances. But the normative verses of the Qur'ān are (relatively) few. Muhammad Mahmūd Tāhā argued that the first message of Islam encompassed in the Medinan revelation needs to be historically contextualized. Hence out-of-date customs, like polygamy, slavery, even military *jihād*, must be abandoned (Taha 1996). The universal message of Islam is encompassed in the Meccan revelation. But how are we able to perfectly

the 'accomplished' and outward dimension is scarcely meaningful from the point of view of axiology, theology or philosophy: it is meaningful from the point of view of narration or normativity alone. Moreover, al-Shahrastānī pointed out that the *inchoate* dimension of the text, namely that the text is 'in movement', remains unintelligible if human beings do not own the appropriate keys for disclosing the hidden meaning.

understand the universal Meccan message and through it address urgent contemporary issues if the symbolic-metaphorical 'translation' of the text is so difficult and we are bound by the original Arabic outward expression? If we are not able to understand the theological or philosophical or mystical meaning of the Qur'ān in a language other than Arabic, are we doomed to be silent? As we have seen, Ibn Rushd resolved the difficulty by distinguishing three different languages for people: rhetorical for the masses, dialectical for the theologians and demonstrative for the élite class of the philosophers. Thus, Paradise is literally a garden (*janna*) for the masses, but is metaphorically the intellectual and blissful vision of God for the philosophers – provided that *the rules of Arab language are respected* (see Chapter 5). Ibn Rushd tried to make consistent two very opposed propositions like 'the world is created' (the Qur'ānic view) and 'the world is eternal' (the philosophical view) through the linguistic tool of metaphor, but not everybody would be satisfied. After all, even though Ibn Rushd suggested a linguistic path to grasp the Being, concrete, material reality often stands as an insuperable obstacle for interpretation.

The *impasse* is serious and I do not have the final solution. Another possibility might be to move the issue to the ethical-political level. As Hasan Hanafī explained:

> The conflict of interpretations is essentially a socio-political conflict, not a theoretical one. Theory indeed is only an epistemological cover up. Each interpretation expresses the socio-political commitment of the interpreter. Interpretation is an ideological weapon used by different socio-political powers to maintain or to change the status quo, to maintain by the conservatives and to change by the revolutionaries (Hanafī 1995).

I am a long way from reaching a definite answer, however. I should like to quote from Nasr Abū Zayd who seems to me to be moving along the same path as Hasan Hanafī:

> Modern scholars of the Qur'ān share the concept of the Qur'ān as *text* despite the different interpretative strategies they employ in exploring its meaning. Dealing with the Qur'ān as only a text enhances the possibilities of interpretation and re-interpretation but allows as well the ideological manipulations not only of the meaning but also of the *structure*, following the pattern of the polemic interpretations of the theologians. I was one of the propagators of the textuality of the Qur'ān under the influence of the literary approach initiated by the modern and still appreciated literary approach. I recently started to realize how dealing with the Qur'ān solely as a *text* reduces its status and ignores the fact that it is still functioning as a *discourse* in everyday life. [...] Without re-thinking the Qur'ān, without re-invoking its living status as a *discourse*, no democratic and open hermeneutics can be achieved. But why should herme-

neutics be democratic and open? Because it is about the *meaning of life*. If we are serious about freeing religious thought from power manipulations, whether political, social or religious in order to empower the community of believers to formulate *meaning*, we need to construct open democratic hermeneutics (Abū Zayd 2004).

The Qur'ān as a simple *text* is scarcely translatable; the Qur'ān as *discourse(s)* is translatable so that it can be made available in different civilizational and political circumstances.

In any case, we cannot do without Arabic, especially if, as Fazlur Rahman contended, 'revelation [is] a unique form of cognition in the form of ideawords that are part of a creative divine act' (Moosa 2003: 14). Rahman stated clearly that:

> There is a vast literature in Islam known as *i'jāz al-Qur'ān* setting out the doctrine of the 'inimitability' of the Qur'ān. This doctrine takes its rise from the Qur'ān itself for the Qur'ān proffers itself as the unique miracle of Muhammad. No other revealed Book is described in the Qur'ān as a miracle in this way except the Qur'ān itself; it follows that not all the embodiments of revelations are miracles, even though the event of revelation itself is a kind of miracle. The Qur'ān emphatically challenges its opponents to "bring forth one *sura* like those of the Qur'ān" (Q. 2:23), and "to call upon anyone except God" to achieve this (Q. 10:38; cf. Q. 11:13, which is probably earlier). There is a consensus among those who know Arabic well, and who appreciate the genius of the language, that in the beauty of its language and the style and power of its expression the Qur'ān is a superb document. The linguistic nuances simply defy translation. Although all inspired language is untranslatable, this is even more the case with the Qur'ān.

> The Qur'ān is very much conscious it is an "Arabic Qur'ān" [cf. Madigan 2001] and, the question of ideas and doctrines apart, it appears certain that the claim of the miraculous nature of the Qur'ān is connected with its linguistic style and expression. Unfortunately, non–Arab Muslims do not realize this enough; while they correctly assume that the Qur'ān is a Book of guidance and hence may be understood in any language, they yet not only deprive themselves of the real taste and appreciation for the Qur'ānic expression but – since even a full understanding of the meaning depends upon the linguistic nuances – also cannot do full justice to the content of the Qur'ān. It is extremely desirable and important that as many as possible of the non–Arab educated and thinking Muslims equip themselves with the language of the Qur'ān (Rahman 1989: 104–105).

The same is argued by Toshihiko Izutsu:

> There are a variety of ways in which one gets to know the meaning of a foreign word. The simplest and commonest – but unfortunately the least reliable – is by being told an equivalent word in one's language: the

German word *Gatte* for example means the same as English "husband".
In this way, the Arabic *kufr* might be explained as meaning the same as
"misbeliever", *zālim* as "evil-doer", *dhanb* as "sin", and so on. There can
be no question that there is recognizably some sort of semantic equiva-
lence in each case; on the other hand, anyone acquainted with the Arabic
language will have to admit that these apparently nearest equivalents
are far from being able to do justice to the original words. A *zālim*, for
example, is not exactly an "evil-doer"; betweeen *kāfir* and "misbeliever"
there is a difference too important to be ignored. [...] The Arabic word
*kāfir*, to begin with, is an independent unit of structure which cannot be
further analyzed into component elements. Whichever English equiva-
lent we may choose clearly consists of two parts: an element implying a negative (mis-, dis-, un-) and another element representing what
may be called the material side of the meaning. This material part is, in
each case, "believer". That is to say that the semantic categories of the
English equivalents of *kāfir* are all based on the fundamental concept of
belief. There is, to be sure, no denying that the semantic category of the
Arabic word *kāfir* itself contains an important element of "belief". But
it must be remembered, this is not the only basic semantic constituent of
the word, nor is it the original one. An examination of pre-Islamic literature discloses that the real core of its semantic structure was by no means
"un-belief", but rather "ingratitude" or "unthankfulness". The word *kāfir*
was originally the contrary of *shākir*, "one who is thankful". [...] *Kāfir* is
a man who does not, would not show any sign of gratitude in his conduct
[towards God] (Izutsu 2004: 25–27).

Again, to understand the Qur'ān understanding Arabic is essential. It
means that the clear Arabic language discloses the truth of God in a dynamic
way. Arabic is more than a key of interpretation: it is the real structure of
*a-letheia* which paves the way for the connection linking man and God.[4]

4.    Emphasizing the versatility of the Arabic lexemes, Afnan Fatani points out the
      factual impossibility of 'translating' correctly the nuances of meaning of Qur'ānic
      Arabic into other languages. Moreover, quoting the Qur'ānic verse Q. 41:44 ('If
      We had made the Qu'ran in a foreign language, they would have said – assum-
      ing that its verses had not been made plainly clear – why [the Qur'ān has been
      revealed] in foreign language while [Muhammad] is Arab?' [*wa law jahalnāhu
      qur'ānan a'jamiyyan la-qalū law lā fussilat āyātuhu a a'jamiyyun wa 'ara-
      biyyun*]) Fatani argues that 'we can infer that although it is the meaning of the
      Qur'ān that is all important, this meaning cannot be accessed or explained except
      through knowledge of the Arabic language' (see 'Translation and the Qur'ān' in
      Leaman 2006). Properly, Fatani translates the verse: 'If We had made this Qur'ān
      in a foreign tongue, they would have said if only its verses were explained: What!
      Not in Arabic and [the messenger] an Arab?'. I believe, on the contrary, that *law
      lā fussilat āyātuhu* is a passing comment and not a question. In my view, the verse
      means that the Qur'ānic verses are plainly clear in outward (Arabic) expression
      and in inner meaning, in order to be understood by Arabs who speak Arabic and
      who grasp the clear meaning of the message.

God's ideas are expressed in Arabic words and the same creative act is expressed in an Arab word: *kun* (creation through the word, for example Q. 36: 82; 2:117). The semantics of Qur'ānic Arabic and the very grammatical structure of Qur'ānic Arabic are necessary for understanding the deepest implications of the words' meaning and so to understand the inner intentions of God's speech. Symbolization and metaphorization cannot do without the linguistic substrate, which is unchangeable and is written in Arabic. Only Arabic can disclose the Semitic character of Islamic revelation grounded in monotheism. How could we express other than in Arabic the divine ipseity (*Allāh huwa huwa*) (see Part II), without losing its ontological meaning and substrate?

The hermeneutical issue remains alive for non-Arabs, however. They can have recourse to translations, but if they wish to fathom the deepest meanings of the Book they must turn to Arabic. The translations they use are simply 'interpretations', maybe far from the true meaning of the text. On the whole, the translation of the Qur'ān is both a semantic task and an effort of reconstructing the contextual meaning along with its symbolic interpretation. A great deal more work needs to be carried out on this topic.

# 10

## HERMENEUTICS AND PRAXIS

The common characteristic of contemporary Islamic thought is, in my view, an inclination to praxis (Campanini 2016a). It means that contemporary Islamic thought has a particular political character and aim. I do not mean here 'political science' or the 'science of politics'; rather, the political outcomes of Qur'ānic hermeneutics. Thinking is not solely and exclusively done as a mental exercise, but rather to affect reality and change it. If a relevant part of contemporary Islamic thought is an *idéologie du combat*, as Muhammad Arkoun said (Arkoun 1991), it is evident that the fabric of interpretation refers back to the world of society and history to verify the scope of its application. This fact induces one to suppose that, in the very moment Muslim thinkers concretely perform hermeneutics – i.e. they interpret the holy text – they also theorize it on a methodological level.

This can lead to the emergence of a potential danger: the exploitation of religion for political goals. This happened frequently everywhere in history, in Western and in Islamic history alike. As to Islam, the easiest example to quote is the *fitna*, the civil war between 'Alī and Mu'āwiya that destroyed the mythical unity of the Muslim community. Many Muslim scholars denounced *fitna* as the falsification of Muslim consciousness, allowing Mu'āwiya and the Umayyads to consolidate their secular power at the Muslim *umma*'s unity expense (Abū Zayd 2002; Ghalioun 1997). Contemporary extremism – allegedly "Islamic" – also instrumentalises religion in order to promote *fitna* among the believers This danger must be avoided in hermeneutics: religion must be a real, sincere tool for the conscious transformation of society and history.

The efforts of female and feminist hermeneutics are relevant here, as hermeneutics is an instrument of liberation. This is not the place to discuss the sensitive issue of women's liberation and rights in its ethical or juridical implications. Islamic 'feminism' (as defined perhaps for the first time by Margot Badran) has yielded in recent times a harvest of publications and research.[1] Obviously, hermeneutical confrontation with the Qur'ān was unavoidable.

---

1. I confine myself to quote Barbara Stowasser 1994, Kecia Ali 2006 and Renata Pepicelli 2010. The issue of the Qur'ān is sensitive mainly because it helps Muslim women fighting for female rights (who often do not like to be called 'feminist') to keep themselves within the limits of religion.

Amina Wadud's (b. 1952) exegetic work stands out perhaps as the most meaningful attempt in this direction. Her intention has been supported by the belief that Islam may offer a promising route in the fight for women's liberation and the acknowledgement of women's rights within a society where patriarchal and chauvinist attitudes are increasingly being questioned. The imperative is not only theoretical since Wadud has taken daring direct action, such as leading prayers in New York in 2005, a highly symbolic act that challenged the convention that this function is reserved for men only. Staying on a theoretical level, though, the work that made Amina Wadud famous, *Qur'an and Woman* (Wadud 1999, first edition 1992), which the author presents as a 'gender' study related to the tradition of *cultural studies*, reveals her mature awareness of the need to exploit linguistics and hermeneutics so as to offer not an atomistic, but rather a theme-based reading of the holy text. The author admits her debt to Fazlur Rahman and more generally to Gadamer's philosophical hermeneutic method, suggesting that the modernized and historically aware reading of the Qur'ān uses a process of analysis of words and their context in order to derive an understanding of the text (*nass*). Hermeneutically speaking, every reading partially reflects the intentions of the text and partially the *a-priori* of the person performing the reading. Every exegete makes subjective decisions: some details of their interpretation reflect these subjective decisions and not necessarily the intentions of the text. By this method, Wadud 'demolishes' the male chauvinist interpretation of certain sensitive passages of the Qur'ān (such as the famous and controversial verse Q. 4:34 which appears to institutionalize the husband's 'right' to 'correct' his wife even with physical violence) claiming that Islam's God transcends gender, it is a loving God who wants the best for its creatures who are equal before Him (It in Wadud's term). It is an audacious exegesis, founded on semiotics, even if it does not question the universality of the text, *as it is*, at any time and in any place. Only exploiting arguments such as those of Nasr Abū Zayd or Muhammad Mahmūd Tāhā, however, can the thorny issue of female subordination really be solved. Nevertheless, Wadud shows she appreciates the difference between the Qur'ān's universal prescriptions and those historically determined, e.g. those concerning the Prophet's family or wives. In a wider sense, a typically feminine point of view should be applied to Qur'ānic hermeneutics – a necessity which the author now feels more and more vital.

For the most part, Wadud's work is arranged in three levels:

1.  The first level is linguistic. A thorough examination of Qur'ānic language allows Wadud to 'dismantle' patriarchal interpretations. As we have stressed many times before, the study of language is eminently hermeneutical. With the *caveats* that, on the one hand,

language is a moving and evolving structure, and that, on the other, the Qur'ān is a compact linguistic system with its particular rules and grammar, with multiple meanings. The interpretation of which must be carried out *within* the same text.

2. The second level is philosophical. Philosophical hermeneutics provides Wadud's theoretical framework. Philosophy enriches the interpretive approaches to the text, but it must be managed carefully. I mean that philosophical hermeneutics too must be conscious of the difficulty of penetrating the complex and well-consolidated edifice of tradition (the *pensée* in Arkoun's terms). And act accordingly.

3. The third level is practical. Wadud's interpretation is essentially a weapon to re-discuss gender relations. This immediate, revolutionary goal of her approach must enlarge its horizons towards a long-term commitment in favour of future generations.

A South-African Muslim who personally experienced the hardships of apartheid, Farid Esack (b. 1957), said that the Qur'ān must be the means of liberation. First, from a methodological point of view, Esack privileges the dimension of historicity in the religious approach and introduces the concept of 'progressive revelation' (*tadrīj*). Revelation was not an event given in a single moment; it unfolded over time in connection with precise circumstances and precise events. This is why the text is bound to a context. The fact that the Qur'ān is a contextualized text makes the activity of interpretation more and more fundamental. The features of this interpretative activity concern the interpreted, the interpreter and the interpretation. The interpreted, i.e. the text, often sidesteps the author's intentions. God is the Qur'ān's author, but humans may in no way claim they know His ends and His motives. In this way, the text assumes a solid objective character. As far as the interpreter is concerned, in Gadamer's footsteps, Esack thinks that each interpreter enters the interpretative process with some pre-comprehension of the questions treated in the text. Six hermeneutic keys allow the interpreter to work out an interpretation developing a philosophy of praxis. They are the following: *taqwà*, literally in Arabic 'pity' or 'fear of God', which the author means as 'assumption of liability'; God's Uniqueness, in Arabic *tawhīd*, which Esack does not mean in an ontological sense, but rather as a symbol of the interconnection Islam establishes between the various aspects of reality; the people (*nās*): humanity, which is the heir of God's will; the concept of 'the oppressed' (*mustad'afūn*), contained in several Qur'ānic verses (Q. 28:5; 34:31–33; etc.), opposed to those who are arrogant and oppress (*mustakbirūn*). The interpreter has a duty to side with the oppressed because so did God and the prophets; the concept of justice (*'adl* o *qist*) which engages all men to fight to redress wrongs; and finally *jihād*, which Esack defines as 'fight and praxis'. Certainly, the goal of the *jihād* is to eradicate injustice, but in no way must its aim be the realization of a religiously connoted 'Islamic' state: it must not exchange one form of oppression for another. In addition to that, it is an acknowledgement, a way to understand and to know, it almost has an 'epistemological' value (Esack 1997). The road to a reading of the Qur'ān emphasizing its releasing value is open.

Esack is particularly interested in inter-religious dialogue. All religions can contribute to liberation. This is very interesting in the perspective of philosophical hermeneutics. How to find a common philosophical ground in order to enhance dialogue? Philosophy is fitted for this task because it is an open instrument (theology much less so, although philosophy is, in a sense, the main support of theology). Philosophy can operate without the chains of presupposed truths. Philosophy is seeking for truth, but truth is a never-ending and asymptotic objective (as I will try to show in Part II of this volume).

# 11

## SUMMARY OF PART 1

Looking back over the previous paths, it becomes clear that many threads interweave. First of all, although a number of traditionalist thinkers have argued that there is no need to interpret the Qur'ān, the Holy Book, in its very wording, stimulates and indeed *compels* interpretation. The 'signs' (*āyāt*), of the Scripture and the universe, must be decoded, disclosed, manifested, showed, as we have discussed at length. Thus, hermeneutics became a neglected task for many researchers, while, according to the Qur'ān, every human being has the duty to reflect and draw his/her conclusions (see for example Q. 3:190–91: 'Indeed, in the creation of the heavens and the earth and in the variation of the night and the day there are signs (*āyāt*) for men provided with intellect, who remember God while standing or sitting or lying down and reflect on the creation of the heavens and the earth [saying]: Our Lord, You did not create all this without purpose'). Throughout the first part of this book, I have tried to stress a crucial point: truth is disclosure (*a-letheia*), and disclosure is not simply *ostensio* ('showing') and *unveiling* (*kashf*), but also *orientation* of the text ('orientation' means: 'producing meaning'). This highly phenomenological aim involves the necessity to decodify the symbols of which the Qur'ān is replete; to find a language that can truly capture the flexibility of meaning without losing the adherence to the (literal) text; to direct the meaning towards a (practical) goal.

Contemporary hermeneutics – especially contemporary philosophical hermeneutics (like that of Iqbāl, Rahman, Abū Zayd, etc...) – seeks new methodologies and horizons. The practical outcomes of these efforts on the mentality of ordinary people, and above all on the alleged besieged fortress of traditionalism and traditionalist *'ulamā'*, has not yet been assessed.

However, something that seems urgently needed – and appears as potentially contrary to traditionalism – is *contextualization* (see also Abdel Haleem 2011). No flexible hermeneutics can do without references to historical (timed) circumstances. The hermeneutics of figures like Arkoun, Nasr Abū Zayd as well as Shahrūr and Rahman imposes contextualization. Abdullah Saeed has been a recent, keen supporter of this view – clearly influenced, I believe, by these exegetes. Already in his book *Interpreting the Qur'ān: Towards a Contemporary Approach* (Saaed 2006), Saeed put forward the idea that a contextual approach must be used in order to overcome the literality of the 'textual' approach which asserts that the text bears a single and unique message, obviously immutable. Now (Saeed 2014) he confirms this hermeneutical key, proposing to analyse the Qur'ān within a broad 'macro-context':

> This refers to the social, political, economic, cultural and intellectual settings of the Qur'ānic text under consideration. The macro-context considers also the place in which the revelation occurred and the people to whom it was addressed. In addition it includes the ideas, assumptions, values, beliefs, religious customs, and the cultural norms that existed at the time. An understanding of these elements is important to the process of interpretation' (Saeed 2014: 5).

This is fine as far as it goes, and Saeed is able to apply his method successfully to sensitive issues like men's authority over women or *shūrā* and democracy. I disagree with him, however, when he says that linguistic context is not the primary focus of the contextualist (Saeed 2014: 5). On the contrary, as I have tried to show throughout Part 1 of this book, language and linguistic hermeneutics is the starting point of any other hermeneutics, even philosophical.

I hope Part 1 has succeeded in setting out a number of urgent problems. Not all of them have a ready and fast solution. Part II will put forward a possible thematic interpretation of a circumscribed Qur'ānic aspect.

# PART II

# THE QUR'ĀN AND PHENOMENOLOGY

# 12

## PHENOMENOLOGY

Phenomenology is one of philosophy's interpretative keys. But why, from the many keys to interpretation used in philosophy, choose phenomenology for a study of the Qur'ān, rather than – for example – idealism or existentialism? The reason is that, in my view, phenomenology is an instrument that is more useful than others in allowing a philosophical interpretation of the Qur'ān, thanks to its flexibility and, particularly, as will be seen in this section, its ability to render the subject active and agent and to place it within an ongoing process (historical or intellectual etc.). Many philosophers have studied the Qur'ān, including those working in a Muslim context.[1] And numerous Muslim philosophers have used the Qur'ān to support their arguments. But not many scholars have attempted to read the Qur'ān

---

1. The problem of the status of philosophy in Islam is particularly delicate. From a certain point of view, it can be argued that, as a discipline, philosophy is alien to the intellectual and cultural Muslim world where the dominant disciplines are law (*fiqh*), dialectic theology (*kalām*) and linguistics (*lugha*). It is the case that, in the classical period of Islam (8th–14th centuries), philosophers such as Kindī, Alfarabi, Avicenna and Averroes were marginal figures. They were not marginal as such, as thinkers, physicians, men of state or jurists, but properly as philosophers. It is not casual that in Medieval Islam the profession of philosopher did not exist as existed in the Art faculties of Medieval western universities. The same philosophical inheritance of Avicenna in the East, with thinkers like Sohravardī and Mulla Sadrā, was more a theosophy than a philosophy in the strict sense of the word. Kindī, Alfarabi, Avicenna and Averroes, nevertheless, analysed and studied the Qur'ān through a constructive and positive method and a theologian-jurist-philosopher like al-Ghazālī, although hostile to Greek-influenced *falsafa*, could not avoid using philosophical categories to support his own theological arguments. What is being proposed here is a notion of philosophy as a science based on reasoning and on the use of rational tools, something very different from – or perhaps even the opposite of – the so-called 'philosophy' inspired by mysticism or the essentially theosophical approach, the chief representative of which was perhaps Mulla Sadrā Shirāzī (d. 1640). This type of mystical or theosophical approach to philosophy is practised particularly by those historians or scholars who tend to put forward an 'Oriental' metaphysics, according to which Islam, Buddhism, Hinduism and Taoism share the same basic 'philosophical' principles. This approach is very far from that which I wish to take.

in the light of philosophy as a book (also) of philosophy.[2] This is in part because in the conservatism dominating the concept of the contemporary Muslim world (somewhat convoluted compared with the open-mindedness of classical Islam) there is the widespread idea that it is not reason but tradition alone (*ma'thūr*) that is capable of carrying out an exegesis of the Holy Book. A narrow approach of this kind fails to examine God's word with the methods and tools of systematic argument (described in Arabic as *burhān*), which is to say with the methods and tools of a faculty that characterizes man *qua* man. The time is overdue, then, for the Qur'ān to be examined and explained in the light of philosophy and, particularly, of phenomenology.[3] This part of the present book is an attempt to move in this direction, putting forward not so much specific exegetic analyses as methodological pathways to pursue.

Phenomenology, as used here, cannot be separated from hermeneutics. From the point of view of method, phenomenology shows that *truth is intention, telos, asymptotic direction.* It means that truth is something that cannot

2.   A recent example is a book by Shabbir Akhtar (Akhtar 2008). Perhaps, in Europe, Baruch Spinoza was among the first to promote a philosophical hermeneutics of the Bible. But in Islam the situation is different. Akhtar's book represents a complex and well-argued attempt to discuss the Qur'ān in the light of the main tendencies of contemporary 'secular' thought, with the aim of demonstrating the Holy Book's inexhaustible vitality and ability to confront the modern world. It is not, however, a philosophical study *of* the Qur'ān such as is proposed here. The Qur'ān is not dealt with in the same way as a philosophical work. The opening up of contemporary Islamic thought to phenomenology must probably be ascribed to Hasan Hanafī (b. 1935) and for this writer I would refer the reader to my two articles: Campanini 1994 and Campanini 2005a. As well as Hanafī, mention should be made of Muhammad Arkoun who, as we have said, has sought to apply the methods of the social sciences to the study of Islam and the Qur'ān. In Arkoun, however, philosophy occupies only a minor place in the human sciences: a bit of Derrida – although personally I think that Derrida has more brilliance than substance – and a bit of Foucault. Perhaps closer to my point of view is Ian Richard Netton, but his book *Allah Transcendent* (Netton 1989), imposed onto a semiological and structuralist critique, is a book about the history of philosophy and theology, not a study of the Qur'ān. Unfortunately I was not able to take in account here Leaman 2016.

3.   It is important to emphasize here that, when referring to phenomenology, what is meant is a very precise philosophical attitude, the first founder and exponent of which was Edmund Husserl. The 'phenomenological approach' to Islam put forward by Annemarie Schimmel (Schimmel 1994) is, however, something profoundly and radically different. For Schimmel, phenomenology is essentially symbolism and thus has nothing to do with the path taken by Husserl relating to the refoundation of experience and the transcendentalization of the objects of the mind (with the related consequences in the discussion of the problem of truth, the reconstruction of the historical world and the theological discussion).

be fully attained, but only pointed to, like the geometrical straight line which only approaches the circumference but never attains it. Applied to religion, this means that God himself is intention, telos, asymptotic direction. It is something akin to Nikolaus von Kues' (the cardinal Cusanus) idea of God as *implicatio et explicatio*: human mind can only perceive by intuition, but never grasp factually (*intelligere incomprehensibiliter*), that God is *coincidentia oppositorum*, maximum and minimum at the same time (Cassirer 2011). In the field of contemporary Islamic theology – and preparing the ground for the ideas expressed here – this intention has been perfectly expressed by the *imām* and martyr Muhammad Bāqir al-Sadr (1935–1980):

> Having established that God – may He be praised! – is the Absolute One, the path becomes limitless. The path of man towards God is a permanent approaching that depends on a real advance. This approaching is, however, relative, consisting of steps along the way without the possibility of arriving since that which is limited cannot attain the Absolute and the finite being cannot attain infinite Being. The distance here that separates man for his ideal is infinite but, nevertheless, allows for creativity and development towards limitless perfection (al-Sadr 2009: 76).

Bāqir al-Sadr's position, differing from both the incarnationism of the mystics (*hulūl*) and from the theologians' attempts to 'explain', 'understand' or 'know' God, is clearly phenomenological. A detailed discussion of which kind of phenomenology I plan to use will be preliminary to the phenomenological path in the Qur'ān that I will follow in order to outline the Islamic idea of God.

Phenomenology – a philosophical approach involving different fields of research and yielding a wide variety of results, notably in the areas of gnoseology, metaphysics, ethics, but also in theology (see Aguti 2013: 47) – makes it possible to formulate a method with which to understand divinity and which reads it not so much as an ontological reality as an objective of thought, of belief and of action. Vincenzo Costa sums it up as follows:

> [In phenomenology] that which connects psychic experience and ideal objects is the character of intentionality, and that is to say the peculiarity of every conscience's "living experience" (*Lebenswelt*) of being conscious of something that transcends it and towards which it reaches, without really containing it (Costa 2012: 60).

We can interpret this sentence as follows: 'The thing that connects religious experiences and the ideal object of these experiences [i.e. God] is the character of intentionality, that is to say the uniqueness of every religious experience of being conscious of something that transcends it and which we reach out towards – God – without really grasping Him'.

Phenomenology, through reduction, intentionality and eidetic intuition, has the advantage of placing the question of truth within parentheses. Phenomenology poses the question of truth as an endless quest: 'if truth is not something we possess, then it is something to be sought for, *reached out for*' (Costa 2009: 173). Thus, in Edmund Husserl's terms,

> God, the idea of Goodness at work (*die wirkende Idee des Guten*), the *unum verumbonum*, is eternal in that He is entelecheia and the *idea of development*, in that it is *telos* that requires something and that procures satisfaction, doing so in ever higher ways (Manuscript B IV 6/43, quoted in Costa 2009, 202. Husserl's italics).

A viewpoint of this kind demands an approach to reality that is hermeneutic and interpretative rather than apodictic or materialistic. Although touched only in an allusive and unsystematic way, this idea is put forward by the founder of phenomenology, Edmund Husserl, notably in his discussion of the crisis of European sciences.[4] On the one hand, he states his certainty that 'the problem of God clearly contains the problem of 'absolute' reason as the teleological source of all reason in the world – of the 'meaning' of the world' (Husserl 1970: 9). On the other hand, noting that 'the true being of mankind [...] is, necessarily, directed towards a *telos*' (Husserl 1970: 17), he states how one of the tasks of humanity, or perhaps *the* task of humanity, is to 'understand that the world which constantly exists for us through the flowing alteration of manners of giveness is a universal mental acquisition, having developed as such and at the same time continuing to develop as the unity of a mental configuration, as a meaning-construct (*Sinngebilde*)' (Husserl 1970: 113). This second part of the book will seek to examine theoretically to what extent this holds true in relation to God, taking the Qur'ān as a starting point.

I will also seek to identify the point at which the ideas of Husserl and his heretical disciple, Martin Heidegger, meet and converge. As is well known, Heidegger put forward an ontological re-reading of Husserl's phenomenology, in this way moving away from the basis of consciousness and gnoseology of Husserlian phenomenology. But, while he placed an ontological stamp on phenomenology, Heidegger nevertheless preserves its interrogative value and its intentionality. Heidegger's contribution to philosophical research of a hermeneutic viewpoint makes itself apparent in the realm of *demand* and *possibility*. His view on *being* is notable for the way in which it goes beyond the assertive character of traditional metaphysics in the direction of interrogation and an opening out. In this sense, God is the object of the demand insofar as He is the *being [Sein]* of the *being there* (*Da-sein*), or insofar as He is the dimension that guarantees the ontological coming into

---

4.  Husserl's position is markedly Eurocentric. Europe is a universal *idea* that all other peoples should fall in line with. Obviously, Husserl's attempt to subsume the spirit of every civilization into that of Europe is spurious (although perhaps he would have seen things differently if he had witnessed the horrors of the Second World War). His method and approach are, nevertheless, still valid.

being of reality. Yet, at the same time, this demand remains ever unmet, an infinite object of tension and projection, of transcendence from the *Da-sein* to its condition of validity.

The importance of this lesson, originating with Husserl, even if he did no more than sketch out its consequences, was identified by one of the major scholars of Husserl's work, the Italian philosopher Enzo Paci. In 1968, in the midst of the social upheaval and workers' and students' protests of those tumultuous years and at the peak of the Cold War when institutional blocks and models were dangerously opposed, Paci suggested that, in order to undermine the foundations of oppressive regimes, it is necessary to 'weaken' truth, transforming it into an asymptotic *telos*, into a goal that must stimulate human action but never be attained or transformed into a system, a reality: 'Civil society is weak while structures are so strong that they are afraid of their own strength. If we say that truth is real, the structures will triumph. If we allow unreal truth to become the life of truth, victory will belong to all humankind' (Paci 1975: 18).

Thus, deriving the consequences from Paci's view, the Christian message, as it developed into a power embodied in the churches (Catholic and also Orthodox), was transformed into a political structure,[5] losing its teleological role. This outcome was, furthermore, in a sense implicit in the metaphysical principle of the incarnation. Making God immanent in reality cannot fail to promote a strong political theology. This same fate was to befall one section of Islam, particularly Shiism. Here I will seek to show that the fundamental characteristic of Islam is its teleological nature – and this is thanks to a theology of transcendence that acts as a corrective to political immanence.

Even with the basic relationship of communication between man and God that comes about through prayer, Islam shows its phenomenological tendencies. Initially, it is the spatial aspect that prevails where *qibla* or the direction of prayer is mentioned. In Chapter 4 of Part 1, I have already briefly touched on the issue of *qibla*. It is worth repeating here the crucial Qur'ānic verse Q. 2:144, 149–50:

> Many a time We have seen you [Prophet] turn your face towards Heaven, so We are turning you towards a prayer direction (*qibla*) that pleases you. Turn your face in the direction of the Sacred Mosque (*al-masjid al-harām*): wherever you [believers] may be, turn your faces to it. […] [Prophet], wherever you may have started out, turn your face in the direction of the Sacred Mosque (trans. Abdel Haleem).

5. This is true, of course, also for Protestantism. We need only think of Calvin's Geneva which saw the burning of Michael Servetus (Miguel Servet). The Anabaptist and Anti-Trinitarian movements were a cry of freedom in the face of the most intolerant Protestant oppression. Giordano Bruno, who paid for his outspokenness with his life, considered Protestantism to be worse than Catholicism.

As we have noted, on the one hand, the placing of *qibla* towards Mecca marked the break with Judaism and the realization of an awareness of being Muslim. On the other hand, allegorically *qibla* represents the spiritual and also mystical tension of the believer who turns his attention, thoughts and all his adoration towards God. Now, I stress again this view, quoting Nasr Hāmid Abū Zayd who wrote:

> It is from here [from the experience of the Prophet's Night Journey] that the oneness of *salat*, in comparison with all the other rituals, is derived. According to prophetic tradition, it is the very basis of religion. The importance of prayer is further emphasised by a *hadith* that reports that the Prophet said: "God is present in the direction (*qibla*) of prayer"[6] – a clear indication of the communicative function of the latter (Abū Zayd 2012: 135).

In this sense, the whole world is *qibla*: 'Whichever way you turn, there is the face of God, for God is All-Knowing' (Q. 2:115). The whole world is a mosque – and the Qur'ān seems to confirm this: 'Turn therefore your faces with devotion to the Lord in any place of prayer and call on him with sincere piety' (Q. 7:29). The desert with its endless spaces is a perfect expression of the cosmic vastness of the world as a mosque, *masjid*. Many traditions agree on the fact that the Prophet is believed to have said that he perceived the entire world as a *masjid*: 'Wherever you find yourself at the hour of prayer, that place is a *masjid*' (*hadīth* handed down by Muslim). The Temple clearly has something to do with the direction – the physical, exoteric direction – of Mecca represented by *qibla* and with the spiritual – esoteric – direction represented by the heart. In neither case, however, is the physical presence of God envisaged, but rather his phenomenological presence, object of the intention of conscience and the yearning for his Face by the believer.

*Qibla* marks out the spiritual space, giving it a teleological structure by placing it in line with the structures of the Ka'ba and the *masjid al-harām*, both 'houses' in which 'the name of God is much celebrated' (Q. 22:40). But it also relates to the spiritual orientation of the person who turns his/her face to the Sacred Temple to prove to God the sincerity of his/her worship and personal commitment.[7] God is indeed everywhere: 'The East and the

---

6.  *Hadīth* appearing in Mālik Ibn Anas' *Muwatta'*.
7.  Turning towards the 'East' typical of the mystical theosophy of Sohravardī and other similar thinkers (the contemporary mentor of whom was Henry Corbin, author of a fascinating but deeply flawed interpretation of Islam considered from a mainly esoteric and Shiite-oriented viewpoint) does not correspond to the sacred direction of the *qibla*. The allegorical intention ousts all the 'practical' meaning (in the full sense of praxis) of the turn to God and all the legislative implications of the indication of prayer.

West belong to God and He guides whom He will to the straight path' (Q. 2:142). Thus *qibla* maps out space in a metaphysical sense and defines the distinction between the true believers and those (the Jews in the Qur'ānic contexts discussed here) who have betrayed the divine message. In this defined space, direction is an intention implying a *telos* to a cultural and theological time: 'I turn my face towards Him who has created the heavens and the earth, in purity of faith, and I will give Him no companion' (Q. 6:79). This phenomenological 'turning towards' is, furthermore, the most authentic meaning of 'Islam', a word that implies the 'turning' to God, with submission and faith, proclaiming his Oneness:

> Say: O humans, if you are doubtful about my religion, I say I do not worship those that you worship in the place of God, for I worship God who will lead you to death. In truth, I have been commanded to be one of the believers. Turn your face then to the faith as a pure mono-theist (*ḥanīfan*) and do not be one of the associators (*mushrikūn*)' (Q. 10:104–105).

This teleological directionality seeking the spiritual perfection of the 'heart' of the believer, the house of God that welcomes the visit of the Most High, is feelingly expressed in the following words by the martyr Muhammad Mahmūd Tāhā (1909 ca.–1985):

> The goal of the slave [of God] in Islam is to achieve the perfection of God, and the perfection of God is infinite. God says: "Man has nothing except his own achievement. What he achieves, he shall meet. Then he shall receive the fullest payment. And to your Lord is the ultimate goal" (Q. 53:39–42). This means that God is the purpose of the whole endeav-our. As stated above, progress to God is not through travelling distances, but rather through the longing of the slave to achieve the qualities of God. God says: "O man, you are toiling along towards your Lord and you shall meet Him" (Q. 84:6), whether you want to meet Him or not. And where shall this meeting be, is it on earth or in heaven? God said: "I am neither contained in my heart nor in my heavens, but rather contained in the heart of my true slave" [*hadīth qudsī*] (Tāhā 1996: 65).

The yearning towards the infinite, the reaching out by the believer towards that God, approaching asymptotically without ever touching or entirely reaching Him, is a profoundly phenomenological objective. It is the transcending of the real towards the *telos*; going beyond possessing to seeking. The 'process and evolution towards God (*tasyīr*)' is, furthermore, according to Tāhā, the authentic meaning of determinism, or 'compulsion by the Will [of God] which prompted life towards God and incited it to be close to Him, so it evolved and developed' (Tāhā 1996: 118).

It is in the light of these premises that the study of the Qur'ān becomes a goal of phenomenological research.

# 13

## A PHENOMENOLOGICAL PATH IN THE QUR'ĀN

Since my first book, published in 1986, *Sūrah della Caverna: Meditazione filosofica sull'Unicità di Dio* [*The Sūra of the Cave: Philosophical Meditation on God's Oneness*] (Campanini 1986), I have undertaken the exploration of the possibility of a philosophical exegesis of Islam's holy text (see also Campanini 2005b). I propose here to return to this philosophical exegesis, starting from a phenomenological standpoint. I should add that a comparison with Paolo Dall'Oglio's book *Speranza nell'Islam: Interpretazione della prospettiva escatologica di Corano XVIII* [*Hope in Islam: an Eschatological Interpretation of Sūra18*] (Dall'Oglio 1991) seems particularly stimulating for the theoretical view I assume here.

As I explained in Chapter 6 of Part I, my aim in commenting on the *sūra*, was to point out that it contains, starting from the Islamic concept of God's Oneness (*tawḥīd*), a developed theodicy, a justification of being, good and evil in God's actions and in the Law established by God (*sharī'a*). Dall'Oglio's main thesis is different. His aim is the application of a spiritual, not philosophical hermeneutics (Dall'Oglio 1991,138); his methodological source is derived from the ideas of the Catholic thinker Louis Massignon (Dall'Oglio 1991, 14). Thus, the Qur'ānic text is read firstly from the point of view of faith experience: 'Our religious consciousness asks us to enter in dialogue with Islamic religious consciousness…; and faith experience obliges us to confront and compromise with the faith experience that the text subtends and that the text expresses and continues to nourish to this day' (Dall'Oglio 1991, 127). Moreover, Dall'Oglio emphasizes the eschatological meaning of the whole *sūra*, far beyond any 'speculative' boundary:

> Louis Massignon has been the orientalist who most acutely grasped the crucial importance of this Qur'ānic text for Islam… Through him, this text…which he called "Islam's Apocalypses", a founding text for the eschatological hope of Muslims…became a vital text for the hope of those people who have been called to exercise the Abrahamic vocation of intercession and hospitality (Dall'Oglio 1991, 150).

Dall'Oglio quotes my book in his bibliography (Dall'Oglio 1991, 346), but never in footnotes: I do not know therefore if he took it into account. In his *Introduction*, however, he strongly denounces phenomenology arguing that this philosophical methodology would aim to build up an 'objectivity' removed from 'subjectivity'.

> We may not find refuge in an "objective" study, even in the form of a "phenomenology", because to deny the text its claim to convey a truth, a truth concerning all, a truth about God, man and the world, means to overlook its essence (…). The only way not to fall in such an empty "objectivity" is to let oneself be involved in one's own faith experience. (…) In order to avoid naive readings, which are not unusual, or to accept the naïveté of one's reading, it is necessary to acknowledge that our comprehension is itself historical, and the text does not stand before us in a sort of original purity (…). Our hermeneutic effort is a moment in the text's history and effects. And all this has got a sense inasmuch it eventually tends to be an expression – experience of truth. The text has its own claim of truth (Dall'Oglio 1991, 11–12).

Now, Dall'Oglio's critique does not address the phenomenological reading of my own interpretation of God's existence:

> From a phenomenological point of view, if we wish to arrive at a vision of the divinity as "immediately offering", we must reduce it to its pure essence. Such an essence…is His *existence*. (…) The God of Islam is a God of absolute reality, but who lives, however, separated from the human world of corruption and flux… Now, if, phenomenologically, we identify His essence with His existence, we would be able to find the key that would unlock the meaning of *tawḥīd*: God is One means, in fact, that He is the totally and necessarily existent (Campanini 1986, 14–15),

But rather with the phenomenological approach which opens the way to a new consideration of the Qur'ān:

> We must interpret the meaning of the words according to that which they indicate. That is to say that in a word there is an immediate offering of a meaning… The criterion of truth of the premises in the Qur'ān must be inherent in the Qur'ān itself, since every element of a language […] is part […] of a system supported by particular rules immanent in it. As the revealed word of God, eternal and uncreated, the Qur'ān can be considered as an axiomaticized theory in which the meaning of every concept is only what it takes on within the particular, determined language of the Qur'ān. (…) There is no need to fear offending the Holy Text – it is more a matter of convincing oneself of the opportunity of an approach in which the immediate meaningfulness of the words establishes the truth and the reality of the words, one in relation to the next, and how they constitute and weave the Holy Text (Campanini 1986, 15–16).

These are the premises of the previous discussion (Part I, Chapter 7) of the Qur'ānic thematic interpretation. However, in my book on the *Sūra della Caverna,* I took as a premise a reading of the existence of God that I asserted was only phenomenological, even if today I might be inclined to describe it as phenomenologically determined by ontology and hermeneutics: I also sought to apply a particular approach to the problem of the language used in the Qur'ān, an approach that I might today term as *linguistic-hermeneutic.* I will leave for another occasion any consideration of the matter of Qur'ānic language, since it involves a complex combination of textual exegesis and hermeneutics. As we have seen, the Qur'ān is a linguistic system in which God shows himself as Being: the very opening up of God to human comprehension is linguistic and hermeneutic (in the sense spelled out by Heidegger: If language is the home of being, the place where the event opens, the verbal expression of being can only be interpretative, hermeneutic). A historic or even philosophic-phenomenological approach could be potentially dangerous for the sacredness of the text, especially in conservative thinkers' view. However, although we examine from an exegetic and hermeneutic perspective the dictation of the Qur'ān, although we evaluate the veracity and plausibility of its assumptions, the historical value of the document and the possibility that it might have been added to or falsified and the acceptance or not of its revealed nature – in any case, in point of fact none of these elements have any bearing on its truthfulness as a code of dogma and morals that regulates and directs the daily life of believers. The Qur'ān lives and is *authentic* in that it is daily *put into practice* in the acts of worship and the rules of behaviour followed by Muslims.

Instead, I wish here to reiterate the validity of a reading that takes phenomenology as its point of departure but which integrates a phenomenological perspective with a hermeneutic one (understood, as explained earlier, as tension and open demand). We need therefore to make a distinction. As far as phenomenology goes, in fact, while in *La Sūrah della Caverna* I was still very much influenced by Husserl, in this present chapter I will try to integrate Husserl's phenomenology and its ideas on consciousness and subjectivity with an eminently ontological vision inspired by Heidegger, thus making the best use of the methodological suggestions made by the two philosophers in the way I propose to set out. Husserl's phenomenological reduction has the advantage of bracketing existence without denying it. That is to say, it makes it possible to deal with simple essences (*èidos*), their universal value being removed from the arbitrariness of subjectivity. This position adopted by Husserl was corrected by Heidegger who, to his master's pure transcendentality, added an ontological dimension by seeking to define *being*. If we now go beyond Heidegger and posit that God is Being, we deduce phenomenologically that, by putting the existence of God (which is philosophically indemonstrable) in parentheses (*epoché*) not only do we not deny it, but we transform God into pure essence, the certainty of which no one can doubt.

I am aware that this ontological extension represents a different way of considering phenomenology, compared to the originally logical and consciously aware point of departure. It is possible, however, that the place where phenomenology and ontology find a point of connection is, in fact, hermeneutics. Paul Ricoeur has described how there are two ways of basing hermeneutics in phenomenology. The first, shortest route is the strictly Heideggerian route:

> Such is the revolution brought about by an ontology of understanding. Understanding becomes an aspect of Dasein's "project" and of its "openness to being". The question of truth is no longer the question of method; it is the question of the manifestation of being for a being whose existence consists in understanding being (Ricoeur 1974: 10).

The second route, longer but that preferred by Ricoeur, arrives at the same ontological goal but passes firstly through the stages of semantics and linguistic analysis and then of reflection:

> But a semantics of expressions with multiple meanings is not enough to qualify hermeneutics as philosophy. A linguistic analysis which would treat these significations as a whole closed in on itself would ineluctably set up language as an absolute. This hypostasis of language, however, repudiates the basic intention of a sign, which is to hold "for", thus transcending itself and suppressing itself in what it intends. Language itself, as a signifying milieu, must be referred to existence. By making this admission, we join Heidegger once again: what animates the move of surpassing the linguistic level is the desire for an ontology; it is the demand this ontology makes on an analysis which would remain a prisoner of language ((Ricoeur 1974: 16).[1]

Ricoeur concludes that this surpassing comes about in the fields both of interpretation and hermeneutics, so that hermeneutics, based on phenomenology, moves towards ontology.

All this is fundamental when approaching the study of sacred texts in general and the Qur'ān in particular. Traditional exegesis, eminently linguistic in approach, remains indispensable but should be seen as no more than the beginning of the long path leading to ontological hermeneutics. The most important question is the question of understanding. *Tafhīm al-Qur'ān*, the 'understanding' of the Qur'ān (this is the title of Mawdūdī's commentary), is a matter much discussed in the world of contemporary Islamism, particularly because understanding is no longer simply regarded as knowledge of the text, but as a tool for the transforming of reality. To quote Heidegger, 'understood as existential structure, comprehension projects the possibility of human existence' (Bleicher 1986: 129). The intriguing paradox of the Qur'ān lies precisely in the fact that, with an understanding of God's Being, it is possible to project the possibility of human existence

---

1.    I do not, however, share Ricoeur's enthusiasm for psychoanalysis. Psychoanalytic interpretations will remain outside our investigation, since they are invalidated by potential elements of irrationality that are not, moreover, consonant with the Islamic way of thinking.

(see Fazlur Rahman's politically and socially influenced analysis in *Major Themes of the Qur'an*, where we read: '[God's] existence [...] is strictly functional', because the Qur'ān is not a treatise about God and His nature – and yet 'God is that dimension which makes other dimensions possible' (Rahman 1989: 1, 4).[2]

The line followed here, no more than a preparatory introduction to the practical intention of a transformation of the reality inherent in every concrete phenomenological-hermeneutical-humanistic project, can be summarized – although this is no more than an initial approximation anticipating further research – as follows. Phenomenologically, we consider God to be pure essence, but, since the essence of God is existence (God is existent for essence – Avicenna said that He is the Necessary Existent – thus, if He does not exist, there would be a contradiction), we are venturing into the field of ontology. The Qur'ān allows us to understand (and this is the hermeneutics) the Being of God as pure essence. The understanding of the Being of God as pure essence can pave the way – for a number of contemporary Muslim writers at least – to revolution. This is not the place to discuss this pragmatic aspect thoroughly, not least because I have written about it in a number of essays elsewhere. It is my intention here rather to pursue a line of enquiry that is exclusively philosophical but which will surely be the prelude to more practical developments.

Both views – the phenomenological and the ontological – provide particularly useful tools for a philosophically constructive in-depth analysis on the Qur'ān and a hermeneutics with full philosophical value. On the one hand, it is possible to bring out the aspects of intentionality and teleology; on the other, the ontological element can be shown, something that is clearly essential when discussing God, His essence and His attributes. What we should not do is attempt mechanically to impose Husserl and Heidegger's philosophical categories on the Qur'ān – something that would, in any case, be impossible since neither Husserl nor Heidegger regarded phenomenology as the key to a reading of a sacred text. Neither did they claim to identify being with God as we shall do here (indeed, it is likely that, for Heidegger, God would come into the category of an entity). Instead, what is required is the establishment of a *hermeneutics*, drawing on both ontology and phenomenology that, applied to the Qur'ān, and representing

---

2.   There is maybe a bit of contradiction between these two statements, and I believe, on the contrary, that the Qur'ān *is* a treatise on God. To say that God is the dimension that makes all other dimensions possible, however, is to translate into modern terms an idea that can be traced back to Aristotle: God is the 'reason', the 'Logos' of the natural world. And this not only or perhaps not so much in the sense that God is the creator while nature is what is created, but in the sense in which God is the logical principle that explains the order of nature.

something of a new approach, to see if this hermeneutics, by revealing the content of the sacred text, can be used to express intentionality and ontology traced from a phenomenological viewpoint.

Phenomenology constructs an 'objectivity',[3] but never in the sense of the existence of something that is unrelated in relation to the subject that understands and experiences – from the subject that has-to-be in its relationship to the world – neither from the point of view of perception nor from the point of view of the linguistic or mental expression of such a perception. Rather, phenomenology, by reducing objects to their eidetic essence, draws them all into the ambit of consciousness that experiences and manifests the object according to how it grasps it in its actuality. In this respect, the Qur'ān pursues a potentially linear path. Many routes could be gone down and a multiplication of quotations produced, but one example will suffice. Human beings grasp reality in its existential concreteness, in its 'being given' that at the same time reveals the world of entities: 'But do they never consider (*yanzurūna*) the camel and how it was made; the heavens and how they were raised; the mountains and how they were set down; the earth and how it was made flat?' (Q. 88:17–20). From here they deduce the existence of God and grasp that Truth which is a transcendental sign of His presence:

> Behold God your Lord. There is no god but He, Creator of all things, so worship Him. He is Guardian over all things. No mortal eyes can see Him, though He sees all eyes. He is all-wise, all-knowing. Momentous signs have come to you from your Lord. He who sees them shall himself gain much, but he who is blind shall lose much indeed. I am not your keeper. Thus have we made plain our revelations that they may say: "You [Muhammad] have seen them. This we have made clear to people who understand (Q. 6:102–105).

The recognition by human beings of the existence of God is accompanied by the belief that all things tend towards God: 'God has sovereignty over the heavens and the earth, and all that lies between them. And all shall return to Him' (Q. 5:18: I quote only one example of many such verses).

Here it might be useful to restate the scheme of a possible phenomenological hermeneutics of the ontology of the Qur'ān, taking the structure of the text as a starting point. This can be divided into three essential

---

3.   A. Schimmel, in Schimmel 1994, claims to detect a phenomenological key in the fact that our experience of everyday reality consists of signs of divine reality. I would argue that the advantage of the phenomenological methodology lies in the fact that it allows believers in a religion to take on the content of their faith while setting aside the 'objectivistic' approach that brings the phenomena of religion under the scrutiny of impersonal and abstract categories. Thus are safeguarded the 'subjective' character and the spiritual 'experience' of the text apparently so dear to Dall'Oglio.

moments. First, there is the *establishing of the presence of the entities* – what in Heidegger might be called '*Da-sein*'. This is perhaps the most difficult stage and this for two concomitant reasons. The Qur'ān insists on the subordination of all creatures to God: God is the Omnipotent producer of the universe and nothing has reality compared with Him, in the sense that they all derive their ontological concreteness from the demiurgic action of God, who creates without cease (numerous verses mention this, as, for example: Q. 23:14; 29:20; 36:78–81). Classical Islamic theology, particularly Ash'arite theology, has emphasized a sort of occasionalist atomism: God creates, destroys and recreates reality in every single moment in time, so that it resembles a filmstrip, one frame being projected after another, giving an impression of continuity and stability. The real world seems in this way as being subject to an absolute contingency. Nevertheless, once created, the entities are not illusory, but possess their own well-determined quiddity: the contingency does not negate the concreteness of their existence. This view is energetically corroborated in the Qur'ān. It would be useful to carry out a systematic analysis of the verses and expressions containing the verbs *nazara* and *ra'a*, both meaning 'to see', with the implication of 'to realise' and 'to verify' the objectivity of an event: 'Perhaps they have not seen (*yanzurū*) the kingdom of heaven and of the earth and all that which God has created?' (Q. 7:185). Or: 'And even if they see (*yarau*) all the signs, they will not believe' (Q. 6:25; 7:146). And, as we have seen, 'signs', *āyāt*, is another key term, since the 'signs' of God are manifest in the heavens and on earth, the effects of His creative power and the 'openings' of His being.[4] The words *āya*, *āyāt* appear frequently in the Qur'an. The *āyāt* of God are absolutely real and existent. To 'see' or 'contemplate' God's signs means not only to verify His existence, but also to have a concrete proof of the veracity of the world and of the opening of the entities in the clearing/glade (*Lichtung*) of Being.

---

4.  Openings that are both ontological and linguistic, as is also possible with the semantic meaning of the word *āya*. It implies the complete rejection of any identification of God with reality, whether with the doctrine of the oneness of existence (*wahdat al-wujūd*), the chief theoretician of which was Ibn 'Arabī of Murcia (d. 1240), or with Mullā Sadrā Shīrāzī's (d. 1640) transcendent theosophy (*al-hikma al-muta'aliya*). According to the doctrine of the oneness of existence, God is the only existing being, a view that leans towards pantheism; according to Mullā Sadrā's theosophy, synthesis and culminating point of a highly complex doctrinal argument combining together philosophy and Sufism, post-Avicennian ontology and illumination, reality is the graduated and gradual manifestation of a single existence (*wujūd*), so that quiddities, which is to say individual existing things, are but mental abstractions. For a summary, see S. H. Nasr (2006), chapters IV and V, esp. pp. 89–90. Cf. also note 5 in this chapter.

Secondly, the phenomenological route means *tracing back from the entities to their Being* and this happens on two levels. The first is the recognition of the permanence of God. The key term in this context is *wajh*, 'face', a word that requires an allegorical interpretation, as in the verses: 'To God belongs the East and the West. Whichever way you turn, there is the Face (*wajh*) of God' (Q. 2:115). Or again: 'All that lives on earth is doomed to die, but the Face (*wajh*) of your Lord will abide forever' (Q. 55:27). The 'face' (repeated in other Qur'ānic verses that will be examined below) is used allegorically to indicate, both here and elsewhere, the permanence of Being, the stability beyond the transitoriness of entities; it is invoked to offset contingency. Becoming is directed towards this enduring Being, all entities turn towards it as to their goal. The key word in this case is the verb *raja'a* in the sense of 'to return', a verb occurring so frequently in the Qur'ān that an excess of quotations would be redundant. To give just one: 'God alone has knowledge of what the heavens and earth conceal and all things revert to Him' (Q. 11:123).

As can be seen, phenomenological hermeneutics does not confine itself within an 'objective' study, nor does it deny that the text seeks to convey a truth on God and about God. By showing truth as a *manifestation of* and *tension towards,* this approach seeks rather to emphasize that certainty and reality establish themselves as telos and purpose. *Certain* truth is not always *real*, in the sense that the objective experience of entities must anyway transcend from entities into Being, which is the authentic reality. Phenomenological hermeneutics respects the transcendent value of the text, while at the same time revealing its historical (and historicizable) content and tracing the spatial-temporal frame of reference that posits the existence of God and His message as something contemporaneously *given* once and for all and *intended* in that it is both the final objective and the teleological aim. Thus the Qur'ānic text becomes the linguistic translation of the lived experience of the believer who *grasps* the Truth (*al-haqq*), that is 'disclosed' and 'showed' to him/her, in its evident immediacy: 'This then is God, your True Lord; and that which is not true must be false' (Q. 10:32). In the light of the most recent discoveries in physics, chemistry or astronomy, it is now impossible to attempt to demonstrate the existence of God as cause, whether efficient, formal or final. The causal system is not even any longer epistemologically convincing. Instead, in the light of phenomenology, God must be verified as obvious and self-evident (*Allāh huwa al-haqq*), seized in its immediate evidence as the form of Truth. God 'shows', 'discloses' Himself as evident, and we *grasp* Him as pure essence.

In Arabic philosophical terminology, *haqq* means both 'truth' and 'reality', and both these meanings can be inferred from the Qur'ān. The word *haqīqa* has a similar meaning, but while *haqq* is a Qur'ānic term, *haqīqa* is not. *Haqq* is repeated more than 200 times in the Sacred Book.

Most importantly, several verses testify that God is Truth (*Allāh huwa al-haqq*) (for example, Q. 10:32; 22:6; 24:25), and this means that God is reality in the highest and most absolute sense of the word. If God is reality in this full meaning, His Being coincides with His self, His essence with existence: the Arab phrase is '*Allah huwa huwa*' ('God is God' or 'God is Himself'). He is the divine identity expressed in philo- sophical and mystical terms, parallel to the (alleged) biblical 'I am who I am' (Exod. 3.14).[5]

The great theologian, al-Ghazālī, refers several times to divine ipseity and the meaning of the Truth of the Being of God. In the *Niche of the Lights*, for example, he says:

5.    The Christian theologist-philosopher Thomas Aquinas (d. 1274) allegedly devel- oped a metaphysics of ipseity very similar to the Islamic one described here and particularly that of al-Ghazālī. Taking as his starting point the two premises: a) that 'God is that whose essence is His same being' [*ipsum esse suum est sua quidditas- Liber de philosophia prima I*], and b) that the word be[ing] ends up by basically meaning 'exist', Aquinas concludes by asserting [the fact] that God is pure existence fits perfectly with His indefinability and His ungraspableness. According to human reason, God cannot be spoken of but with a tautologi- cal proposition: '*Ego sum qui sum*'. We can say that God *is* exclusively in the sense that He *exists* in Himself. If with 'being' we mean genera and forms, it is necessary to say that God is the principle of all genera and of all forms, while He does not coincide with any genus and form; in this sense, He *is not* [...]. Recently, somebody commented: 'The proposition "God is not a genus" means: He is absolutely not an entity.' We can express the same concept even more radically: 'God "is" not for the simple reason that "being" is not something God is, because God *is* already Being' [Welte, p. 610] (A. Masullo 1980: 111). Leaving aside the obvious scriptural reference, the question that almost immedi- ately comes to mind is whether Aquinas's idea was inspired by that of Avicenna, the latter obviously emerging within a Muslim conceptual context. Aquinas's distinction between essence and existence certainly owes a debt to Avicenna, but here I would like to go further and suggest that Aquinas's entire doctrine on being is descended from Avicenna. Pasquale Porro, for example, speaks of a 'fundamental debt with regard to Avicenna' and explains the Thomist identifica- tion of God and being with the 'metaphysics of Exodus' ('God is He who is'), to quote the famous phrase coined by Etienne Gilson (see Gilson 1948 and P. Porro 2012: for e.g. pp. 69–72). L. Gardet and G. Anawati (1980) argued that Islamic ontotheology is 'weaker' than Christian ontotheology precisely because it lacks a 'metaphysics of Exodus'. The argument put forward here in relation to the Qur'ān and al-Ghazālī – and the potential for further research on Avicenna (and Ismaili theology) and the Qur'ān – demonstrates that, on the contrary, Islamic ontotheology comes to the same conclusions as the 'metaphysics of Exodus', basing itself not so much on the verb 'be' as on the intrinsically Qur'ānic ideas of *haqq* and ipseity.

In the phrase *lā ilāh illā huwa* [There is no God but He], *al-ilāh* [God] means that towards which the face of the believer turns in worship and in confession that He is the Divine One. I mean the faces of their hearts, for they are lights. And I say further: just as "there is no God but He", so there is no "he" but He [ipseity: *kamā lā ilāh illā huwa lā huwa illā huwa*], since "he" indicates something that, however indicated, can only indicate Him. Indeed, everything that we indicate cannot but be, in reality, an indication of Him, even if you did not know this through your ignorance of the truth of truths that we have mentioned. We do not point to the light of the Sun, but to the Sun. Thus, everything that exists does so in relation to Him, just as, to make a clear analogy, light relates to the Sun. Therefore "There is no God but Allah" (*lā ilāh illā Allāh*) is the profession of the Oneness of God by the common people; "There is no God but He" [ipseity: *lā ilāh illā huwa*] is the profession of Oneness by the élite, since this expression is more complete, more exclusive, more comprehensive, more exact, more subtle and more apt to admit those who use it into the pure Uniqueness and most absolute Oneness (Al-Ghazālī 1987: 144).

Thus, in his treatise *The Ninety-Nine Beautiful Names of God* (1995), al-Ghazālī says, after the affirmation according to which 'the Truth is the [name] who is the antithesis of falsehood', that God is *haqq* because He is 'the One truly existing in itself, from which every true thing gets its true reality'. If the characteristic of being is Oneness, being can only be expressed as 'one one' (*huwa huwa*).[6]

An interesting comparison can be made between two pages from works by al-Ghazālī, again drawn from the treatise on *The Ninety-Nine Beautiful Names of God* and from the *Niche of the Lights*.

The treatise on the *Beautiful Names* tackles the matter of the divine name *haqq*, basing its discussion on Avicennian premises. Like Avicenna, al-Ghazālī distinguishes the necessary from the impossible and the possible from what, in its turn, is possible in itself but necessary through the intervention of an agent outside it. Applied to this metaphysical distinction is the logical distinction between absolute truth, absolute falsity and the relativism between what is true and what is false:

---

6. Here too, as in many other cases, there is an apparent similarity between al-Ghazālī and Avicenna (or at least a certain type of Avicennian thought). For Avicenna too, in commenting on sura 112 *al-Ikhlās* (*Oneness*) (on the affirmation of divine unity and Oneness, *tawhīd*), comes to the conclusion that nothing can be said of God except that He is and that He is what He is (*huwa huwa*), (see, with the accompanying bibliography, O. Lizzini 2012: 151 n. 122). Modern historiography is more and more inclined to underline the philosophical presuppositions and outcomes of al-Ghazālī's theology (see for e.g. Griffel 2009). I agree that al-Ghazālī was a 'philosopher', but in the sense of St. Augustine not in the sense of Ibn Rushd (see my Introduction to al-Ghazālī's *Jawāhir al-Qur'ān*, 2000).

> *Al-Haqq* – the Truth – is the one who is the antithesis of falsehood, as things may become evident by their opposites. Now, everything of which one is aware may be absolutely false, absolutely true, or true in one respect and false in another. Whatever is impossible in itself is absolutely false, while that which is necessary in itself is absolutely true, and whatever is possible in itself and necessary by another is true in one respect and false in another. For this last has no existence in itself and so is false, yet acquires existence from the side of what is other than it, so it is an existent in this respect that acquired existence is bestowed upon it – so in that respect it is true while from the side of itself it is false. For that reason, the Most High said: "Everything is perishing but His face" (Q. 28:88). He is forever and eternally thus; not in one state to the exclusion of another, for everything besides Him – forever and eternally – is not deserving of existence with respect to its own essence but only deserves it by virtue of Him, for in itself it is false; it is true only in virtue of what is other than it. From this you will know that the absolutely true is the One truly existing in itself, from which every true thing gets its true reality (al-Ghazālī n.d.: 79–80).[7]

Similarly, in the *Niche of the Lights*, al-Ghazālī starts from a strictly Avicennian affirmation that echoes the same metaphysics of existence:

> The existing can be divided into that which has existence in itself and that which derives its existence from something else.

He goes on to distinguish between truth and absolute reality. God and his 'face', and truth and reality in relation to living beings who derive their ontological value from the fact of comparing themselves with the totality of the Being of God:

> For each several thing other than God is, when considered in and by itself, pure non-existence. If considered in relation to the existence that flows from the Prime Reality, it can be seen as existing, but not in itself, but solely depending on Him who made it exist. Therefore, the only existing thing is the Face of God the Most High. For everything has two aspects, one turned towards itself and the other to the Lord. In respect of the first, it is not-existing; in respect of the second, it is existing. Therefore, there is no existent except God the Most High and his Face, and therefore "Everything is perishing but His Face" [Q. 28:88] (al-Ghazālī 1987: 137–38).

Here not only can we reassert what was said earlier about the ontological nullification of the world, albeit regarding the sovereign omnipotence of God, stressing above all how existing entities are a manifestation of the divine Being.

---

7.  For an English translation see Burrell and Daher (1995) *The Ninety-Nine Beautiful Names of God*.

The link between the two extracts quoted above can be found in the Qur'ānic verse Q. 28:88, one of the main verses that support the so-called theory of '*wahdat al-wujūd*' ('oneness of being').[8] According to this well-known doctrine of metaphysical Sufism, fully argued and 'vulgarised' by Muhyī al-Dīn Ibn 'Arabī (d. 1240), nothing exists but God, in the sense that living creatures have no ontological reality in relation to God. Despite the fact that this doctrine leans dangerously towards pantheism,[9] al-Ghazālī

8.  This verse has been the subject of endless theological debate. The great Sunni Qur'ānic commentator Fakhr al-Dīn al-Rāzī (d. 1209), for example, claimed it to be the scriptural basis making it possible to give God – surreptitiously – the attribute of being a 'thing' (*shayy'*): 'Rāzī explains [the verse] like this: by *wajhahu* [His face] we must understand *dhātahu*, which is to say God himself [His essence]; saying *illā* [except] God means to declare an exception: "everything perishes except God Himself". Rāzī goes on by saying that which is made an exception is necessarily part, so far as type goes, of that of which it is an exception. Therefore God himself is a "thing"' (Gimaret 1988: 146). Whatever the case, in my interpretation the Qur'ānic verse does not mean that existing beings are God or that, like the theosophy of Mullā Sadrā, gradations of a transcendental *wujūd* (existence), in which the multiplicity of levels of existence is reduced to a single Being. It means rather that existing things are transient compared to the stability of God in Whom essence and existence coincide. The world, as we have said, is a 'sign' of God (*āya*), not merely a mirror reflection but the concrete indication of His presence, power and personality.

9.  Upholders of the mystical and theosophic character of Islamic philosophy maintain that the doctrine of *wahdat al-wujūd*, made to fit with Hindu or Buddhist doctrines, is *not* pantheistic, thereby safeguarding the dualism between God and world. Among the many authors that could be quoted, I will limit myself here to a consideration of a major Japanese scholar, Toshihiko Izutsu, whose work can usefully be considered here. According to Izutsu (see, in particular, Izutsu 2007), the so-called mystical philosophers of Islam, including Mulla Sadrā (but Izutsu cites particularly 'Ayn al-Qudat Hamadhānī, Haydar Āmulī and Mahmūd Shabestārī), considered reality to be a single 'existence' (*wujūd*), within which can be discerned a stable and enduring existence, God, and an ephemeral and transient existence, that of entities. This is the alleged non-pantheistic dualism of the concept of the Oneness of existence. There is no need to embark on a systematic refutation of this idea, since Izutsu's very arguments are self-contradictory. When, for example, he explains the details of this concept with expressions like 'the world of multiplicity is essentially of the very nature of the Absolute; it is the Absolute itself' (Izutsu 2007: 30), or again: 'existence is the sole absolute Reality clothed in visible forms' (Izutsu 2007: 481) he cannot avoid using formulations that are clearly and decidedly pantheistic. Language does not restrict thought, it reveals it! It is a real *a-letheia* (disclosure)! But this challenge to and denial of the Muslim vision of the world lies at the heart of oriental metaphysics, according to which Islam, Buddhism and Hinduism are nothing more than local versions of the same *philosophia perennis*. Some aspects of this can be summarized as follows: (1) the most macroscopic and obvious is that, whereas in orien-

avoids this risk by demonstrating how the things of this world, living creatures, are not mere appearances. Even if God is perfectly capable, should He
wish it, to wipe out the world in the blink of an eye, He does not do it; and,
for so long as the world lasts, the realities that make it up are factual, not
mere shadows, even if they do not possess qualities that are ontologically
inherent in their essence (and this, after all, is the premise of al-Ghazālī's
famous doctrine of causality). As we shall see, other Qur'ānic verses can be
found supporting this concept.

Returning to the matter of 'truth', verses 32–36 of *sūra* 10 (*'Yūnus'*,
Jonah) use at least four subtly different meanings for the word *haqq*: (a)
as a divine attribute, this being the most obvious variant; (b) as 'good', the
alternative of 'evil'; (c) as the goal of human life: 'God leads to Truth'; (d)
and, from an epistemological point of view, as an assertion of absolute, true
knowledge, as opposed to subjective opinion (*zann*). Subjective opinion
leads the ignorant to believe of God that which is not true (Q. 3:154: *ghayr
al-haqq*). Avoiding the dangers of deviating from the straight path, the faithful know that the Qur'ān is *haqq*, since God says: 'All those to whom the
Book was given know that it is the Truth' (Q. 2:144). The Qur'ān is the
direct word of God; therefore all can find in its Truth a guide for the just
path. Furthermore, a number of verses contrast that which is true (*haqq*)
with that which is vain and false (*bāṭil*). For example: 'We shall hurl Truth
at falsehood until Truth (*haqq*) triumphs and falsehood (*bāṭil*) is no more'
(Q. 21:18); and again: 'God knows well what you do, because God is the
Truth (*Allāh huwa al-haqq*) and false (*bāṭil*) is that which you call on in

tal philosophy God is essentially an indeterminate Absolute, in Islam He is most
definitely a *person* with will, knowledge and acting capacity, who through will
and ability *creates* and imposes civil and social *law*; (2) this open relationship
with social life is an essential characteristic of Islam that, as *dīn wa dunyā* (religion and world) sets itself up to regulate human social relations and the historical
relations between individuals, peoples and nations; (3) the *philosophia perennis*,
by minimizing/cancelling out the role of human creatures in society, stands in
the way of the development of ideas, because it makes thought into – as Hegel
put it – a 'night in which all cows are black' without conceptual distinctions and
ideal varieties and pluralities. Islam, by contrast, lays claim – and rightly – to
its own doctrinal and legal structures; (4) Therefore saying that the *fanā'* of the
'orthodox' mystics like al-Ghazālī is tantamount to the vacuity of Buddhism
(Izutsu 2007: 12), is not only to misrepresent the ideas of these mystics but is also
entirely anti-Islamic! The loss or the nullification of the Self as a rational instrument with which to perceive the infinite transcendence of God is a useful bait to
lure false philosophers, but in reality it has no meaning in Islam. If the external
world were in fact only a 'veil of *maya*' it would render meaningless not only
acts of worship and the five principles but also *fiqh* and *sharī'a*. In other words,
we are being led into a context that I would not hesitate to describe as alien to the
authentic Muslim mental viewpoint.

the place of God' (Q. 31:30). The first of these two verses emphasizes the fact that God did not create the world and the cosmos without a predetermined plan: 'It was not in sport (*lā 'ibīna*), that We created the heavens and the earth and all that lies between them but according to the Truth (*haqq*)' (Q. 44:37–38). The cosmos is absolutely true and real and even if God can change it or destroy it whenever He wishes, the world is rational and coherent. These affirmations can be used to support a philosophical concept different from '*wahdat al-wujūd*' (we shall return to this key point because it is what distinguishes it from a whole other interpretative tendency in Islamic philosophy).[10] The opposition of *haqq* and *bātil* is also evident in al-Ghazālī's writing,[11] as where he maintains that the divine essence is necessary in so far as it is true and real ('The necessary in itself [i.e. God] is the absolutely true': *la-wājib bi-dhātihi huwa al-haqq mutlaqan*), contrasted with the nullity of the world. In the Jalālayn's *Tafsīr*, the word *haqq* of Q. 31:30 is explained as '*al-thābit*', that is, 'He who is permanent', or who 'remains' and is 'firm'. By contrast, the vanity of the world (*bātil*) that the misbelievers worship in place of God, is rendered as '*al-zā'il*', or that which is 'ephemeral' or 'transient'. Similarly, in Q. 34:49, we find: 'Say: Truth has come, while falsehood can create nothing and will never return'. On the one hand, no one can doubt the Being of God the Creator and the Truth of His word; on the other, creatures possess a reality that is a reflection of divine reality. In the two Jalāls' *Tafsīr*, therefore, and in similar theological treatises, the opposition between the eternal existence of God and the ephemeral contingency of the world is clearly shown and rooted in the Holy Book.

From a phenomenological point of view, the Qur'ān describes Truth as something given and certain. God makes the world evident ('shows', 'discloses' it) to human beings who live the experience of it, on the level of perception and consciousness: 'Do you not see that God has created the heavens and the earth according to Truth?' (Q. 14:19). There is no room for doubt. The Qur'ān that believers recite every day represents the linguistic space of the unequivocal evidence of the world and its meaning – evidence

10. That of Henry Corbin, Toshihiko Izutsu and Seyyed Hossein Nasr whom we have several times mentioned previously.
11. It is possible that al-Ghazālī deduced this conceptual dichotomy from the thinker who is likely to have most influenced him in his intellectual *bildung*, the philosopher Avicenna. For Avicenna too takes up the distinction between *haqq* and *bātil*, probably basing himself on the Qur'ān, in the *Ilāhiyyāt* or *Metaphysics* of the *Book of Healing*. Distinguishing the Necessary Existent, that he identifies with God, from the possible, Avicenna asserts that 'the necessarily existent (*wājib al-wujūd*) is that which is uninterruptedly true (*haqq*) in itself, while the possibly existent (*mumkin al-wujūd*) is true by virtue of that which is different from itself and in itself is false (*bātil*)' (*Metaph.*, I, 8 in Avicenna 2002: 107; For an English translation see Marmura, *The Metaphysics of the Healing* (2005).

that derives from the fact that the world and its meaning are guaranteed by the Being of God. Consequently, the prophets are not the guardians of any 'secret' (*sirr*), something that would seem to represent a specific difference from Christianity. Only God – and not the prophets or priests – possess 'the keys of that which is hidden' (Q. 6:59), the prophets confining themselves to enunciating and interpreting God's signs. Thus, as we have said in Chapter 6 of Part I, Joseph, after interpreting the dreams of Pharaoh's ministers, adds: 'Did I not tell you that God made known to me things that you know not? [...] O my father, this is the interpretation (*ta'wīl*) of my former dream; my Lord has made it True' (Q. 12:96–100). God is Truth and He testifies to the truth in revelations as He does in the world that He has created.

This is a very difficult topic and one that, particularly for Muslims, could give rise to significant conceptual difficulties. This is what I wrote in *La Surah della Caverna*:

> God in that He exists, seems to be a non-entity. God is not substance, and not being substance, will not occupy any place. The affirmation of the *existence* of God passes through the negation of His *presence*, of his reality in relation to the world (Campanini 1986: 32–33).

By this I meant that God is so transcendent and separated from worldly things that it is not possible to confer on Him attributes that can in some way be assimilated into a *concrete* existence, which is why He appears as a non-entity in that He has an existence that is entirely irreducible to that which is (or perhaps only 'appears' to be) according to the measure of human understanding. 'That which is' is interpretable only as the effect of God's creative action, even if a yawning gulf is thus opened up between the two worlds (divine and creatural).

As we have seen, the theoretical high point of this metaphysical idea can probably be found in Ismailite theology with one of its most important representatives, Abū Yaʿqūb al-Sijistānī (d. after 941). Two passages by this author that are of particular interest come, firstly, from the introduction to *Kitāb al-Yanābīʿ* (*Book of Well Springs*):

> Glory to God whose sanctity transcends all the descriptions of that which the primordial beginning (ibdāʿ) [the intellect] has caused to be; who remains beyond any characterizations that fall within the possibilities of speech and hearing; who, in the hiddenness [absconditus] of His oneness, goes beyond any representation that could depict Him; who in the power of his Word stands beyond any category that might define or describe Him. He lavishes on His creation all that which words can describe and the mind can imagine. But He Himself, in His sublimity, remains inaccessible to the powerless mass of creatures held below the level needed to truly come to know Him (al-Sijistānī in Corbin 1994: 19).

And, secondly from *Kashf al-mahjūb* (*Unveiling of the Hidden*):

> If in the present work we lay stress on the fact that a true knowledge
> of the Creator consists in excluding from Him the modes of being and
> the previously listed qualifications, and that consequently we declare
> that He is not-existing, not-limited, not-qualifiable, not-in-space, not-in-
> time, not-being, then we can say that we have achieved a true knowl-
> edge, since this first negation (that which excludes the Creator from
> bodily qualifications) fulfils the unification that places the One in his
> transcendence. Such authentic unification does not, however, necessarily
> follow yet. For, in fact, a true knowledge will not be achieved except by
> means of a second negation. The former negation consists in establishing
> the transcendence of the One by isolating it from all the characteristic
> marks of living creatures. But it is with the [latter] negation that one can
> reach a true knowledge of the Creator, in such a way, however, that there
> is no suggestion of "depriving" Him [of His positive attributes] (*ta 'tīl*).[12]
> Therefore, our affirmation will take the following form: the Creator is
> not-existing and not not-existing; He is not-limited and not not-limited;
> He is not-qualifiable and not not-qualifiable; He is not-in-space and not
> not-in-space, not-in-time and not not-in-time, not-being and not not-
> being. In this way we will have avoided equally both anthropomorphiza-
> tion (*tashbīh*) and "deprivation" (*ta 'tīl*). We shall avoid comparing Him
> [to creatures] with the first negation and avoid depriving Him thanks to
> the second negation (al-Sijistānī 1988: 44).

God is not only not-being but also not-not-being: *al-hamdu li'llāh al-ma'būd bi-lā wa lā lā,* 'praise be to God, worshipped with not and not-not'.

The theology of the negation of the negation is constructed so as to avoid 'nullifying' God[13] and to keep Him present in human consciousness and understanding, while at the same time distancing Him from compromise with the real and material world in an entirely radical way. In this way, al-Sijistānī himself says, it is possible to avoid both *ta 'tīl*, the taking away of every element of God's essence to the point of – impiously – denying

12. This word is, of course, particularly significant in Mu'tazilite theology.
13. The risk of 'nullifying' God is run not only by the Mu'tazilites but also by Ismai-
    lite thinkers, even more radical than al-Sijistānī, such as Hamīd al-Dīn al-Kirmānī
    (d. *circa* 1021). He asserts that the 'God' of the Qur'ān (*Allāh*) is not *really* 'God',
    but the first being created by a God who lies beyond all definition, understand-
    ing and even beyond all ontological dimensions (God is not even a 'being'). The
    fundamental characteristics of God are his otherness and his unknowableness,
    two characteristics that are reciprocally connected. This kind of extreme nega-
    tive theology is, above all, non-Qur'ānic (where we read, for example, that God is
    'nearer to man than his jugular vein' [Q. 50:16]), and it is regarded by al-Ghazālī
    as 'clear disbelief' (see the discussion in Griffel 2009: 260–64. And mention must
    of course be made of D. De Smet 1995, esp. pp. 195–96).

their existence, and *tashbīh*, the reduction of God to anthropomorphism. I am well aware, of course, that to define God as the negation of negation or as 'non-essential' might seem to be a blasphemous negation of His very reality, a sort of Mutazilite *ta'tīl*: indeed it was to the Mutazilites that I was explicitly referring in my book.

Naturally, God cannot be a non-being (*ma'dūm*), but He can be 'absent' (*ghā'ib*). *The absence of God is His negativity, His non-being, or being-other, in relation to the world*, His irreducibility to the things of the world: 'He is the First and Last, the Manifest and the Hidden' (Q. 57:3). *The absence of God is His establishment of Himself as the telos of the world:* 'God has sovereignty over the heavens and the earth, and all that lies between them. And all shall return to Him' (Q. 5:18). And again: 'He governs the Cause (*amr*) from the heavens to the earth and it ascends back to Him in one day' (Q. 32:5). And again in many other verses we cannot quote fully.

This means that God is eminently existent in the transcendence that distances Him from any similarity or contact with the material world: 'Nothing resembles Him' (Q. 42:11). All that lives on earth is doomed to die, but the Face of your Lord will abide forever' (Q. 55:27). God, in relation to the corporeal and the material, is a non-essential; but, though He is the negation and the opposite of materiality and corporeality, He is the highest and total existence. God, as the totality of being, is He who causes to be: 'We do not confer on the divine power (*qudra*) any other effect, while it acts making [things] existent (*ījād*), than that of existence (*wujūd*)' (al-Shahrastānī 1977: 82).

Al-Ghazālī's metaphysical journey leads him to the recognition of the fact that God is evident in things but hidden in essence. *Therefore He is the Being that manifests itself in entities but yet preserves its transcendence.* Using Fazlur Rahman's image of God as the dimension that makes all other dimensions possible (Rahman 1989: 4, as I quoted above), we can perhaps state that God is Being in essence, not as a presence but rather as a dynamism: God is Being as the realization of all potentialities, the Being that lies behind an entity and which reveals itself in the entity. In this sense, it is the object of questioning and seeking, and never of grasping (intellectually or mystically) and incarnation. This view renders less important both the Christian idea of God's incarnation in Christ and the belief of Muslim mystics in *hulūl*, the 'inhabitation' of God in the person's body.

Again in the *Niche of the Lights*, Al-Ghazālī writes:

> Were anyone to ask, "What is the intelligible image of He who is?", it is inconceivable that anyone could reply. He who transcends all relations is the One Truth. For this reason, when a certain Bedouin asked God's Messenger: "What is the origin of God?", this reply was revealed to the Prophet: "Say: God is One, the Unknowable to whom we direct our prayer. He begat not nor was he begotten and none can be His peer" (Q.

112), the meaning of which is that He is raised up in sanctity (*taqdīs*) and devoid of all relation (*munazzah*). And for this reason, when Pharaoh said to Moses: "Who is the Lord of all humankind?" (Q. 26:23), as if wishing to know His quiddity (*māhiyya*), Moses, in his reply, defined Him through His works (al-Ghazālī 1987: 154–55).

Which is to say, if it is permissible to use Heideggerian terms, 'God is the Being revealed through entities'.

In his treatise *The Ninety-Nine Beautiful Names of God*, al-Ghazālī explains how entities hide, or rather 'veil', the essence of Being, despite the fact that Being manifests itself in these entities themselves. In this way, the essence of God, of Being, remains hidden from the perception of the human mind, even though the human mind can grasp its being shown openly and put into reality through reason and induction: from entities to Being. Far from being denied, God stands outside the reach of definition: in this sense He is a non-entity. He is apparent to the intellect not in Himself but as a light visible in His effects (like the things are visible through the light):

> Al-Zāhir, al-Bātin – the Manifest, the Hidden – these two attributes are also to be taken relatively, for what is manifest can be evident to one thing and hidden from another. Yet it cannot be manifest and hidden in one and the same respect; though it may be manifest in relation to a perception and hidden in another respect. For things are manifest or hidden only in the relation to modes of perception. Now God – may He be praised and exalted – is hidden when He is sought by sensory perception or using the resources of imagination, yet manifest when sought by way of inference using the resources of reason. But if you say: "So far as His being hidden with respect to sensory perceptions, that is evident; but as to His being manifest to reason, that is obscure, since what is manifest is that which is not in doubt and about whose perception men do not differ; yet this subject is one over which much doubt arises among men, so how can it be evident?". But you should realize that He is hidden in His manifestations by the intense way in which He is manifest, for His manifestness is the reason for His being hidden, as His very light blocks His light. So it is that whatever broaches its limits is turned into its opposite (al-Ghazālī 1995: 134).

Here, I believe, we have reached a point of central importance in phenomenological hermeneutics applied to ontology. God is grasped, at one and the same time, as a presence and an absence: as a presence in that He is an immanent providential force and Being that manifests itself in entities; as an absence in that He is a reality than cannot be assigned to the categories of enticity actually present. In that He is an absence, God must be considered as a *telos*, a goal to be attained. In that He is a presence, God is the guarantee of cosmic optimism, in the certainty of the best that is realized in the rationale of *this reality*. God is Being in the fullest sense. The transcendence of God is the withdrawal of Being that opens the clearing (*Lichtung*) [the world] where the entities (humans and other creatures) predominate.[14] And yet the Qur'ān does not hide Being in the entity, it does not reduce – as might happen with Feuerbach – God to man, nor does it attribute all the Being of creatures to God as Sufism does. Creatures are ontologically determined. Rather, it is that God, absent in transcendence, remains present as telos and truth.

We are dealing with a viewpoint that is intrinsically Islamic. It can be demonstrated by reference to Muhammad 'Abd al-Karīm al-Shahrastānī whose Shiite or even Ismailite leanings have been established by scholars (and it would be interesting on this subject to compare him with al-Sijistānī). In his *Mafātīh al-asrār* (*The Keys of the Secrets*), al-Shahrastānī discusses divine ipseity and its quiddity, through a detailed analysis of the word *Allāh* that can not only be compared with that of al-Ghazālī, but once again is centred round the 'Face' of God, interpreted in an ontological sense. As we read in Toby Mayer's reconstruction:

14. The expression is clearly Heideggerian, the Heidegger after his 'turn' or *kehre*. There is not, however, a clearly marked break between the phases of Heidegger's ideas. Even in *Being and Time*, he writes that Being is always pre-understood by us human beings in regards to entity, but it is however never understandable without entity, which is what Heidegger means as (and not long after will call) 'ontological difference'. With this, he makes an ideal connection with the Husserlian theme of the categorical intuition: not only the entity but also the being can in a certain way be given in its original evidence, but it is given precisely in that it is hidden. As Heidegger puts it in *Being and Time*, being is the most concrete phenomenon imaginable, yet it, or rather *precisely because* it 'above all and for the most part does *not* manifest itself [...] in respect to that which manifests itself above all and for the most part' (Esposito 2013: 59). In Islam, however, God is the being that goes beyond the entity, immediately and automatically pre-comprehended in the evidence of the external world, given in His presence, but nevertheless hidden and veiled by the opaqueness of the entities that occupy the ontological horizon. Heidegger does not, however, reach the level of a full formulation of this viewpoint. Describing the 'flights' of the event (*Ereignis*) in his *Contributions to Philosophy*, or when he is discussing poetry as a way of accessing being, he arrives at the point of denying the likely existence of the Christian God, but limits himself to describing God 'as something that can never effectively be, but only effective in subtraction and rejection' (Esposito 2013: 128). And again: 'God *appears*, not like something hidden that leaves its hidden state, but like the manifestation *of* the hidden state itself and its preservation'. God, basically, is 'the absence of being' (Esposito 2013: 188). Thus, for Heidegger, God is not being and is pure hiddenness, pure retraction. But, as well as the retraction of transcendence, God also possesses a positive manifestation of unveiling. The Qur'ān says this in several places; as we have seen also in the first part, He is apparent in the effects of His creative activity because the entire cosmos and the Qur'ān itself are 'signs' (*āyāt*) of God. See also Fabris-Cimino 2009 for an insightful overview.

The most gripping of [Shahrastānī's] interpretations takes the pronoun *huwa* (He) as its starting point. The pronoun is implied by the final *h* of the word *Allāh* which, fully vowelled in the nominative, would be *Allāhu*. *Huwa* would then be yielded from the final *hu* by adding the consonantal "consort" (*qarīna*) of *u* namely *w*. Shahrastānī says that this seed of the divine name stands for a first reification of the godhead, acknowledging its "thingness" (*shay'iyya*). More particularly, it refers to God's majesty (*jalāl*) or utter transcendence, given that it acknowledges, by implication, that *only* God's "He-ness" (*huwiyya*) or quoddity (the fact *that* He is) is known, not His identity (*māhiyya*) or quiddity (*what* He is), which stay wholly outside understanding.

Next, the *l*, central to the name as a whole, is added to this basic *hu* and great meaning is again found in this. In Arabic, the propositional form *li* signifies that what adjoins it has the status of possession (or perhaps responsibility). Shahrastānī renders it with the stock grammatical term, the "*lām* affirming possession" (*lām al-tamlīk*). Prefixed to the pronoun – *hu* to make *lahu* (i . "His" or perhaps "due to Him"), it acknowledges that everything other than God is His possession (*milk*) and dominion (*mulk*). This then is held by our author to refer to the great complement to God's attribute of majesty or transcendence, namely, His "bounty" or "creative largesse" (*ikrām*) – a complementary rooted in Q. 55:26–27: "All that is in the world will pass away and your Lord's face (or 'self') alone will endure in His majesty and bounty" (*dhū'l-jalāli wa'l-ikrām*). The impact of these two attributes of majesty and bounty is later spelt out in Shahrastānī's statement: "He is veiled from them through His majesty, so they may not perceive Him, and He manifests Himself to them through His bounty, so they may not deny Him". So it is that these two affirmations – one through the final *h* and one through the medial *l* of the name – capture the paradox that God is at once incomprehensible *and* undeniable, or as Shahrastānī puts it: "Insofar as He is He (*huwa*) He is ungraspable and insofar as all belongs to Him (or is due to Him, *lahu*) He is undeniable". Lastly the *a* is prefixed to the *l* to give *al-*, the Arabic definite article. For Shahrastānī, the true meaning of grammatical defini-tion (*ta'rīf*, literally "making known") in regard to God is to get across that He is indeed *better* known (*a'raf*) than all else.

So it is that through this ingenious understanding, the divine *nomen-proprium* voices synthetically the deus *absconditus* and the deus *revela-tus*. For it enshrines in its extrema the paradox that God is both wholly hidden (i.e. through-*hu*) *and* unhidden (i.e. through-*al*). Moreover, through its median (i.e. *l*), the name shows precisely in *what* way the hiddenness does not contradict the apparentness (Mayer 2009: 37–38).

This clearly critical, rather than literal, reconstruction by Toby Mayer of al-Shahrastānī's ideas based on his commentary on the Qur'ān shows how the dialectic between the presence and absence of God, between *Deus revelatus* and *Deus absconditus*, represents one of the most notable fea-tures of the Islamic theological outlook, and how it is phenomenological in character.

In fact, the positions taken by al-Ghazālī and al-Shahrastānī agree in that they admit the possibility, in some way, of *speaking of being*. At the end of his philosophical career, Heidegger arrived at the conclusion that it is not possible to know Being. He did not identify anything with Being. He merely sought to find a linguistic approach to a discussion of it. I, on the other hand, identify Being with God. Ismailite and Ghazalian philosophy, insofar as their interpretation of the Qur'ān is metaphysically correct, place God as Being beyond human understanding, even if not entirely outside expression in words: when we say that God is *huwa huwa*, which is to say that everything perishes except only His Face, we are trying to say something about Being, even if we do not claim to be able to understand it or explain it (as Christianity claims to explain God through the Trinity). *Deus revelatus* is the God about whom we are able to say something, whose ipseity we can affirm as being that-which-is-within-the-entity, as He who reveals himself through His names and through the works of His creation. *Deus absconditus* is the God whose essence we are not able to comprehend, Whose definition is – and must be – beyond the reach of the limited abilities of intelligence. He is *samad*, unknowable and object of our invocations (Q. 112), and nothing resembles Him (Q. 42:11). It is in this dialectic between the veiled and the hidden, presence and absence, immanence and transcendence that the full phenomenological meaning of the Islamic vision of God is to be found. If we remember what was said in Chapter 4 of Part I regarding Ibn Rushd, once more we attain a plurality of approaches to Being through language and realize a real metaphysical hermeneutics.

I hope to have shown that phenomenology allows a coherent, latitudinal, philosophical interpretation of a number of important Qur'ānic verses. Admittedly, this might appear easier because the verses involved are in themselves metaphysical, that is philosophically oriented. However, this is precisely the point: the Qur'ān contains philosophical truths, it is a book of philosophy. The Qur'ān is *bahr muhīt*, deep ocean, and also philosophy lands on its shores. Muhyī al-Dīn Ibn 'Arabī was a thinker who presented a philosophical hermeneutics of the Qur'ān, for instance in his *Fusūs al-Hikam (Bezels of Wisdom)*, while Nasr Abū Zayd (Abū Zayd 1998) made a thorough study of this hermeneutics. An in-depth analysis of the metaphysical texture of Ibn 'Arabī's interpretation (maybe contrasting it with al-Ghazālī) is urgently needed. Phenomenology is a more recent method, however, and nowadays metaphysics is exploring new fields of application, very different from the metaphysics of an Aristotle or a Descartes. Thus, the theoretical effort deployed in this small book is a first step. I leave it to others to judge whether it is worthy to pursue this approach further.

# 14

## CONCLUSION
## FROM HERMENEUTICS TO PRAXIS

To grasp the phenomenological characterization of the idea of God in Islam involves an inner dynamics of God's concept. Now, it might be argued that only in Christian theology and philosophy is the concept of God dynamic and that this dynamism is shown in the idea of the Trinity. In the idea of the Trinity, we deify the relationship and not the substance. Deifying the relationship (as St Augustine did) means that God is activity and an incitement to activity. Deifying the substance (as St. Thomas Aquinas did) means making rigid the idea of God with respect to dogma.[1] This 'prejudice' directly affects the meaning of Islamic monotheism, so it is worthy of discussion. There are problems of method and problems of content.

As to the method, an intriguing judgement about Islamic philosophy has been advanced by my colleague at Milan University, Massimo Parodi, who is not an *islamologue*:

> In the Islamic world there has not been an actual philosophical elaboration, but rather a very lively interest by a number of thinkers in the philosophical reflections developed by the Greeks, or rather by Plato and Aristotle [...] One wonders then whether it may be envisaged that philosophy is a Western literary genre and that Islamic culture has never actually had its own specific philosophical reflection, but rather a specific and fruitful interest in Greek philosophy. If, at a certain point, this interest has ceased to be and the connection to philosophy has been interrupted, we may wonder at the reasons for this, but we are talking about the ending of an interest in Greek philosophy that no longer exists, and not of the ending of Islamic philosophical reflection. The idea of a fracture and a centuries-long break looks a lot less dramatic and much less difficult to explain. It raises, however, an even deeper underlying question leading back to the all-important themes of time and history. Both the Islamic intellectuals and the Western intellectuals who engage in these topics should not *go back to Averroes*, nor continue referring to the

---

1.  This interpretation of St Augustine and St Thomas's theologies is obviously questionable. A long analysis and discussion of primary and secondary literature would be needed. In any case, what is useful for my perspective is the contraposition of two precise metaphysical categories: that of relationship and that of substance, the first involving plurality, the second acknowledging the soundness of Being.

great bloom of Muslim thought, but should rather clarify by which paths and schedule cultural reflection was addressed. It is precisely on this ground that Western reason is unable to imagine that time, in that civilization, may in some way have developed according to its own particular principles, rhythms, paces and connections – elements that we must attempt to understand, without the need to envisage breaks, slowdowns or halts, all of which we measure of course in the light of our own time (Parodi 2006b: 17–18).

The problem that arises here is a challenge: what are we speaking of, when we discuss Islamic philosophy or theology? If the theoretical pillar of Islam is God's Oneness (*tawhīd*), God's Oneness must be the yardstick by which we understand the deep meaning – as authentic as possible – of Islamic philosophy and theology. On the other hand, the issue of the rupture – of the suspension, as it were – of the period of philosophy must be reconsidered *within* the context of the history of theological and philosophical Islamic thought itself. Did philosophy and theology die after Ibn Rushd's death? Did a suspension and a stagnation of roughly four centuries really take place before the renaissance of Islam and its theoretical and cultural tradition in the eighteenth and nineteenth centuries? Is the theosophical tradition of Mullā Sadrā and other metaphysical thinkers, true *philosophy*? Is the illuministic re-reading of Ibn Rushd really progressive and capable of opening new ways to Islamic thought? Many other similar questions can be formulated. Ibn Taymiyya is the major figure whose ideas definitively buried philosophy; his thought was a point of no return where the parallel histories of speculative theology and philosophy were both swallowed up in the same gulf.[2] This attitude further coincides with the philosophy of *praxis*, but the classical age was by now over.

From the point of view of content, Parodi set out the issue as follows:

> The very fact of incarnation, as Vattimo has stressed, weakens the metaphysical component of the Christian religion and sets in motion a theological reflection in which the ethical and knowledge components, which are often closely interconnected, as in Augustine, are to be central. The idea of incarnation is decisive into filling up the ontological gap separating God – one and transcendent – from the multifarious created world,

---

2.   I am perfectly aware that this contention is bold and needs justification. Unfortunately, I cannot develop the argument here. Recent historiography has tried to put a positive gloss on Ibn Taymiyya, but I believe that his ideas marked a real turning point. His incitation to re-open the door of *ijtihād* meant the definitive rejection of philosophy in the Sunni world for at least four centuries. Admittedly, a sort of philosophy (theosophy?) flourished in Shiite world, but Western/European modernity clashed strongly with traditional Islamic ideology. It is no accident, in my view, that Ibn Taymiyya became the *maitre-à-penser* of contemporary hyper-conservative Salafism.

but from a certain point of view it can also put transcendence at risk. What may be even more *dangerous*, in this perspective, is the idea of a Trinitarian God, an idea that arose as a way of proving, as far as possible, Christ's divine nature but later becomes, particularly as in Augustine's reflection, the content and the instrument for a real revolution in the way of conceiving God, the world and their relationship. The Trinitarian structure becomes the pure form of the analogical relationship that, in Augustine, connects the various levels of being with one another and also makes it possible to see in God the source of the variety and the movements that featured in the *region of dissimilarity*. And once again we are led back to the topic of diversity, movement, time; a strictly monotheistic and absolutely transcendent conception of God, or, philosophically, of the absolute principle, will inevitably be suspicious faced with a way of conceiving God that raises doubts about both features (Parodi 2006b: 21–22).

Parodi argued perceptively that the 'Augustinian paradigm' (as he calls it) inspired the best part of European (Medieval) thought (not all the historians of philosophy would agree with his interpretation of St. Augustine, however; I discuss it because it is stimulating). In Parodi's view, the fundamental character of the Augustinian paradigm is the concept of *relationship*.

> The idea of process, the dynamics of research, the route leading the knowing subject towards the boundless ideas of unity and totality turn substantially into the individuation, reconstruction and proposition of links and relations.

thus,

> Trinity intimately is [...] dialectics of unity and relationship. [...] In this context, Trinity arises almost as a musical rhythm, a kind of rhythmical texture of reality (Parodi 2006a: 107, 35 and 110 respectively).

Parodi puts forward here a solution from the point of view of transcendence. In his opinion, if I understand it correctly, Christianity, read through the lens of St. Augustine, worships the Trinity as *relationship* and this represents an application of the dynamic principle (I have myself acknowledged as phenomenological) that holds up and gives life to all the universe. Parodi is perfectly right in putting forward the problem from the point of view of transcendence. All Islam is based on transcendence. Monotheism is transcendence or it is not monotheism. But Islam actually *breaks* radically with the *Logos*, breaks radically with the ideas of relation, mediation, analogy or similarity between God and the creatures, or between God and Himself, from the point of view of God's unique ontological reality. It is well-known that the Qur'ān argues energetically against the Trinity (the main *locus* is in my view Q. 4:171). But we have to remember above all those verses which emphasize God's absolute alterity and His firm grip over the universe. Many verses are worth quoting, but I restrict myself to the following:

> [It is He] who created the Earth in two days… He is the Lord of all the universe. He placed on it [the Earth] solid mountains, gave it His blessing and in equal measure (*qaddara fīhā*) provisions [for humans and animals] in four days. Then He turned to the sky – and it was smoke – and said to it and to the Earth: Come willingly or under compulsion. They said: We come obediently. Then He completed them (*qadāhunna*) with seven heavens in two days and imposed to any heaven its order (*amr*). We[3] adorned the terrestrial sky with lamps and We keep it [in existence]. This is the determination (*taqdīr*) of the Powerful and All-Knowing One (Q. 41:9–12).

God's eminence is overwhelming: He determines nature's laws (*qaddara/taqdīr*) and the universal rational order (*amr*) through His omnipotent decree (*qadā'*). It follows patently that any eventual dimension of relation, mediation, multiplicity in God compromises or even destroys this kind of monotheism.

Obviously, we might quote a great number of *loci* wherein Muslim thinkers described monotheistic ideas. Particularly pregnant, I believe, are the following verses of the mystical poet al-Ansārī who accurately expressed the intrinsic compactness of the monotheistic concept:

> There is no one who can attest to the oneness of the One
> For anyone who attest to that One denies It.
> The attestation of oneness by One who describes It,
> Is but an empty thing, annulled by the One.
> His oneness is that which is His oneness,
> And the one who describes Him is an apostate (*lāhid*) (quoted in Keeler 2006: 125).

Oneness – metaphysically outlined in divine ipseity (Oneness is Oneness that is *huwa huwa*) – is so ineffable that it is absolutely impossible to know it and describe it, as Christian theology claims to know and describe the very essence of God (i.e. the Trinity). Oneness is a tautology, as it were: thus, any hypostatical mediation or any plurality (even through relationship) is excluded. In the Islamic view, reducing the highness of divinity at the human level through the incarnation in Jesus Christ – making him one member of the Trinitarian relation – is tantamount to the multiplication of God's Oneness and can be therefore considered idolatrous. On the other hand, it is not true that the absolutely transcendent God of Islamic theology and philosophy is necessarily an inactive God. In a sense, al-Fārābī's and Ibn Sīnā's God is inactive after creation, or, better, released from His pro-

---

3.    There is an abrupt change of subject here, a common feature in the Qur'ān.

duction (better than 'creation'): He is transported in an absolute transcendence – in order to guarantee His oneness also risks making Him totally separated from the world. He thinks only of Himself and emanates by spontaneous energy, like a lamp that spontaneously emanates light. Al-Ghazālī's God is different, however: in his thought, God is really the Omnipotent One who keeps the universe alive and ordered in every instant of time, and who, in every instant of time, attracts to Himself the believer's will. The inert God is more philosophical than theological.

In my view, therefore, *we have to deify neither the relationship nor the substance, because God is far higher and beyond relationship and substance*. 'Say: [He] is God and leave them engrossed in their vain talk (Q. 6:91)'.

Al-Ghazālī grasped, perceptive as always, the theological centrality of this point:

> If somebody asked: "What does that concept represent that we cannot succeed in grasping it in its truest inner meaning?", well it would be necessary to answer that He Who transcends any kind of relation is God, the True (*haqq*). Thus, when a Bedouin asked the Messenger of God what was the origin of God, the following revelation came down as answer: "Say: He, God, is One, God, [the Being] to whom we direct our prayers (*samad*). He did not beget nor was He begotten and nothing is like Him" (Q. 112). The meaning of God's Holiness (*taqdīs*) is precisely to transcend any relation (*munazzah*), and this is why, when Pharaoh asked Moses "Who is the Lord of the universe?" (Q. 26:23), as though he asked about His quiddity (*māhiyya*), Moses cannot answer but by referring to His works (al-Ghazālī 1987: 154–55).

This purity of the Islamic idea of God is on the whole conceptually different from either the Neoplatonic or the Aristotelian traditions of Christian thought. An asymptotic solution to Heidegger's metaphysical problem (the concealment of Being through entities) can perhaps be found in Q. 57:3: 'He is the First (*awwal*) and the Last (*akhir*), the Manifest (*zāhir*) and the Hidden (*bātin*)', and in al-Ghazālī's commentary to this verse in *The Ninety-Nine Beautiful Names of God* I have quoted earlier. God is Manifest in things, that is in entities, but at the same time He – the supreme Being – withdraws Himself and remains hidden.

Phenomenological hermeneutics (or hermeneutical phenomenology)[4] must become an active instrument in the interpretation of history. The hermeneutical developmental thread starting with Nietzsche and arriving

---

4.  Hasan Hanafī (Hanafī 1977 and 1977a) grasped the specular interaction of the two methods. They are not simply methods, however, The conquest of consciousness, not only through speculation but also through political praxis, means the conquest of a place in history.

at Gianni Vattimo through Heidegger formulated the category of 'weak thought'. 'Weak thought' means that metaphysics is deprived of its potentially alienating strength, while Perspectivism erected into system represents the main epistemological key of knowledge. As we said at the very beginning of this book, there are no facts but only interpretations. However, weak thought seems restricted to the presupposition of multifarious truths: it is Perspectivism erected into system. Philosophy becomes hermeneutics insofar as, acknowledging the interpretative character of human existence, it gives up any foundational thought and accepts its own finitude. As Gianni Vattimo put it: 'Before Heidegger, Nietzsche connected the theories of interpretation and nihilism. Nihilism means in Nietzsche "devaluation of the supreme values" and fabulation of the world: there are no facts, only interpretations, and this also is an interpretation. [...] The tendency to weaken [the concept of Being] shown in this path of thinking...is the truth of Nietzsche's nihilism, the very meaning of God's death, that is the dissolution of truth as peremptory and objective evidence. Up to now, philosophers believed they were describing the world. Now, it is the time to interpret it' (Vattimo 2002: 17–18).[5]

God must remain an objective, an objective that will probably never be attained, in order to keep alive the universal value of truth which makes of Him the living reality *within* human history.[6] In this perspective of liberation, I have interpreted Hasan Hanafī's (b. 1935) thought as a particularly fulfilled expression of a progressive contemporary Islam. In Hanafī's thought, the metaphysical essence of God matters only on a purely speculative level: ontologically it has been weakened. It is necessary to put God between brackets through the phenomenological *epoché* in order to avoid a theological–political creation of oppressive institutions and in order to suppress any temptation of 'violent' metaphysics. In today's secularized world, Hanafī argues, the only way to safeguard God's transcendence and His theological presence in politics is to translate theology into anthropology, that is to 'neutralize', as it were, the idea of God. In Hanafī's view, Islam is more fitted than Christianity for this end, because the metaphysics of incar-

5.    Another tendency of Nietzsche's critique, rather than emphasizing the interpretative dimension, emphasized the dimension the defeat of nihilism by Superman (*Uebermensch*) (see Volpi 2004).

6.    Enzo Paci's words introducing Husserl's *Krisis der europäischen Wissenschaften*, quoted in the first paragraph of this Part II, are worth repeating: 'If we say that truth is real, the structures will triumph. If we allow unreal truth to become the life of truth [*vita della verità* in Italian], victory will belong to all humankind'. God is truth but is not 'real': He is existent but not as a metaphysical reality, but as a *telos*, a phenomenological direction. So He becomes 'life of truth', a force animating the universe and human action without being embodied in a super-structural institution.

nation involves God's immanence in the world and subsequently a rigid form of political theology.

It is important to stress that this weakening of God's essence has nothing to do with nihilism. For, even though God's essence is weakened, His existence is not weakened. Even though essence has been put between brackets, God continues to live, to be existent in human consciousness. Being existent in this way, God becomes the phenomenological *telos* of human practical and political action, and at the same time the theorization of the philosophical truth. God is above all a value, not a metaphysical reality. As Hanafī put it: 'Returning to the Qur'ān, source of all religious thought, both theological and otherwise, God does not present Himself on a theoretical level but on a practical level. God is not Logos, but Praxis. God is not rational object, concept, category or idea, but behavior or conduct' (Hanafī 1972: 241).

Rather, implicit in this perspective is an open invitation to humans to lay aside their dogmatism. Putting God between brackets weakens the metaphysical solidity of being. Being is eminently possibility, openness. At the very moment social justice is demanded, at the very moment we demand food for the hungry and clothes for the naked, we proclaim God as existence and value. Islam is more fitted to do this, because Islam, on the one hand, extols Oneness, while, on the other hand, it urges the faithful to struggle for the oppressed (and this is the real meaning of *jihād*) (Hanafī 1972, 1983, 1995). Islam makes God a value absent/present and this absence/presence of God is phenomenologically and teleologically oriented to practical and political action within history.

I believe that Hanafī succeeded in constructing – on a phenomenological basis – a philosophy that re-reads in a highly original way both Islam's authentic role as a religion and ideology, and the future perspectives (hopefully not destroyed by terrorism) for the history of Muslim peoples in particular, and for the history of the so-called Third World countries in general. Hanafī understands the subject as the consciousness of the 'passing through' the objectivity of the world in order to project a future where the Islamic profession of faith (*lā ilāh illā allāh wa Muhammad rasūl Allāh*) can mean the fulfillment of a universal code of ethical behaviour and the declaration of an acquired independence of reason and the autonomy of the human will.

Hanafī's teleological phenomenology is based on a re-elaboration of the concept of *tawhīd* – God's Oneness – that presupposes the idea that theology is not science. Sciences have an 'object' of study, but God cannot be an 'object' of study because His essence is unknowable. Cataphatic theology (i.e. the attribution to God of positive qualities – Being, omnipotence, omniscience, goodwill and so on) is a mere transposition on Him of human qualities. God must remain a desire and a perspective; His idea must be removed from any compromise with anthropomorphism. For God is first of all a principle of equality representing the goal of the whole of humanity in its daily social and historical praxis. If the profession of faith (*shahāda*) is action ('*amal*) and opposition (*mu'ārada*) and revolution (*thawra*), God's Oneness and Uniqueness (*tawhīd*) means the process of unification of God's essence as the goal and end of human social praxis – in the same way that freedom means liberation (*al-hurriyya taharrur* – Hanafī's icastic affirmation). The phenomenological (Husserlian) 'infinite goal of humanity' consists for a Muslim in the anthropological re-foundation of Islam (remember that Hanafī was the teacher of Abū Zayd). Human consciousness tends to divine reality.

In Hanafī's view, the fundamental duty of Muslims is to transform the ancient discipline of '*ilm usūl al-dīn*, that is the science of the religious principles regarding the '*ibādāt* (worship) and the *mu'āmalāt* (society), from a juridical science into an instrument of social action and practical re-orientation of the masses. The science of God, on the other hand, will become a science at the service of men/women, losing any purely abstract characterization. If, as Hanafī says, ignorance is blind obedience while knowledge is revolution, knowledge must acquire as soon as possible a practical value, must become praxis in order to transform and change present society and the *status quo*. This is the authentic relation between the man/woman fully aware of himself/herself and the phenomenological God. Obviously, intellectuals have an even more binding duty to engage themselves in society, because life's experience (*Lebenswelt* in Husserlian terms) is the place wherein knowledge loses its reified character, loses its abstractness so far removed from concrete reality and discloses itself (*a-letheia*) to the subject, opening new ways.

At the very end of Hanafī's intellectual parabola, the Egyptian philosopher returns again to his creature: the Islamic Left (*al-yasār al-islāmī*). The Islamic Left is a method connecting religious thought (*fikr dīnī*) with political and social fact (*al-wāqi' al-siyāsī al-ijtimā'ī*). The true illuminated religious thinker knows that the text (the Qur'ān in this case) must be put at the service of reform and action in order to make the word of God operative among humans (*rajul al-dīn mustanīr yantaqil min al-nass ilā al-wāqi', wa min kalām Allāh ilā awdā' al-bashar hattā yakūn khitābuhu akthar dalāla wa awda' 'inda al-nās*) (Hanafī 2012: 12). Interpreting the Qur'ān means moving from the level of commentary to the level of engagement: from theology to anthropology (Hanafī 1972), from dogma to revolution (*min al-'aqīda ilā al-thawra*, Hanafī 1989), from the text to the fact (*min al-nass ilā al-wāqi'*, Hanafī 2012).

Hanafī's dream appears to go so far beyond the boundaries of the Qur'ānic text that he has been accused by fundamentalists of being an 'atheist' and by the seculars of being an 'integralist'. The phenomenological hermeneutics of the Qur'ān I have proposed here can have this kind of outcome, however. A revolutionary Shiite theologian like 'Alī Sharī'atī (1933–1977) also moved in the same direction (see for e.g. Sharī'atī 1980 and Sharī'atī n.d.). Intellectuals must be militant. Their mission, however, is not political leadership, but 'production of consciousness'. The goal must be the production of a human prototype in order to *orient* the social philosophy and the ethical thought directing everyday life. Sharī'atī shows here a clear – albeit not fully aware – phenomenological inclination. The human prototype to be achieved is a *telos*, not an already predetermined and fixed reality. As such as for God, the idea of humanity is dynamic and growing step by step in time.

The Qur'ān at the service of humanity; the Word of God as a dialogue between God Himself and humanity; the Qur'ānic phenomenological idea of God as the inspiring motive of human action and praxis. These are the final outcomes of the present philosophical effort of Qur'ānic interpretation. Hermeneutics as a science stands out as an unavoidable duty overcoming literality.

# BIBLIOGRAPHY

AA.VV. (1991). *Masdjid*, in *Encyclopedie de l'Islam*, 2nd ed. Leiden: Brill, vol. VI, 629–95.

'Abd al-Bāqī, Muhammad. (1988). *Al-Mu'jam al-Mufahras (Dictionary and Index of the Qur'ān)*. Cairo: Dār al-Hadīth.

Abdel Haleem, Muhammad. (2004). *The Qur'ān*. Oxford & New York: Oxford University Press.

Abdel Haleem, Muhammad, & Badawi, Elsaid. (2008). *Arabic-English Dictionary of Qur'ānic Usage*. Leiden: Brill.

Abdel Haleem, Muhammad. (2011). *Understanding the Qur'ān*. Cairo: American University in Cairo Press.

'Abduh, Muhammad. (1978). *Rissalat al-Tawhīd. Exposé de la Religion Musulmane*, ed. M. Abdel Razik & B. Michel. Paris: Geuthner.

'Abduh, Muhammad & Ridà Rashīd. (2002). *Tafsīr al-Manār (Commentary of the Lighthouse)*. Beirut: Dār Ihyā' al-Turāth al-'Arabī.

Abul Fadl, Mona. (1998). *Ittijāhāt jadīda fī tafsīr al-Qur'ān (New Trends in Qur'ānic Exegesis)*. Qum: Qadāya Islāmiyya Mu'āsira.

Abū Zayd, Nasr. (1998). *Falsafat al-ta'wīl: Dirāsa fī ta'wīl al-Qur'ān 'inda Muhyī al-Dīn Ibn 'Arabī (The Philosophy of Hermeneutics: Essay on the Qur'ānic Hermeneutics of Ibn 'Arabī)*. Beirut: Dār al-Tanwīr.

— (2000a). *Mafhūm al-nass (The Concept of Text)*. Beirut-Casablanca: Markaz al-Thaqāfī al-'Arabī.

— (2000b). *The Qur'ān: God and Man in Communication*. Leiden: Universiteit Leiden.

— (2002). *Islam e storia*. Torino: Bollati-Boringhieri.

— (2004). *Rethinking the Qur'ān: Toward a Humanistic Hermeneutics*. Leiden: Humanistics University Press.

— (2006). *Reformation of Islamic Thought. A Historical Critical Analysis*. Amsterdam: Amsterdam University Press.

— (2010). *Muqāraba jadīda li'l-Qur'ān: min al-nass ilā al-khitāb, nahwa ta'wīliyya insānawiyya (From the Text to the Discourse, towards a Humanistic Hermeneutics)*. In: *Al-Tajdīd wa'l-tahrīm wa'l-ta'wīl: bayna al-ma'rifa al-'ilmiyya wa'l-khawf min al-takfīr (Renewal, Prohibition and Hermeneutics: between Scientific Knowledge and Fear for the Charge of Unbelief)*. Beirut-Casablanca: Markaz al-Thaqāfī al-'Arabī.

— (2012). *Testo sacro e libertà. Per una lettura critica del Corano*, ed. F. Fedeli. Venezia: Marsilio.

Afsaruddin, Asma. (2008). *The First Muslims. History and Memory*. Oxford: Oneworld.

Aguti, Andrea. (2013). *Filosofia della religione*, Brescia: La Scuola.

Akhtar, Shabbir. (2008). *The Qur'ān and the Secular Mind. A Philosophy of Islam*. London & New York: Routledge.

al-Azmeh, Aziz. (2009). *Islams and Modernities*. London & New York: Verso.

al-Ghazālī, Abū Hāmid. (n.d.). *Maqsad al-asnà fī-sharh ma'ānī asmā' Allāh al-husnà (Commentary on the Beautiful Names of God)*. Cairo: Maktabat al-Qāhira.

— (1974). *Kitāb al-Arba'īn fī'usūl al-dīn (The Forty Principles of Religion).* Cairo: Maktabat al-Jindī.

— (1987). *Mishkāt al-anwār (The Niche of the Lights).* Beirut: 'Ālam al-Kutub.

— (1995). *The Ninety-Nine Beautiful Names of God,* ed. D. Burrell & N. Daher. Cambridge: The Islamic Texts Society.

— (2000). *Le perle del Corano (Jawāhir al-Qur'ān),* ed., M. Campanini. Milano: Rizzoli.

al-Hallāj, Husayn Ibn Mansūr. (2007). *Il Cristo dell'Islam. Scritti mistici,* ed. A. Ventura. Milano: Mondadori.

al-Jābrī, Muhammad 'Ābid. (1994a). *Introduction à la critique de la raison arabe.* Paris: La Découverte.

— (1994b). *Takwīn al-'aql al-'arabī (The Shaping of Arab Intellect).* Beirut: Markaz Dirāsāt al-Wahda al-'Arabiyya.

al-Na'im, Abdullāhi. (1990). *Toward an Islamic Reformation: Civil Liberties, Human Rights and International Law.* Syracuse, NY: Syracuse University Press.

al-Sadr, Muhammad Bāqir. (2009). *Lecture Thématique du Coran.* Beirut: Dar Albouraq.

al-Sijistānī, Abū Ya'qūb. (1988). *Le Dévoilement des Choses Cachées,* ed. H. Corbin. Verdier: Lagrasse.

al-Shahrastānī, Muhammad Ibn 'Abd al-Karim. (1977). *Kitāb al-milal wa al-nihal (Book on Religions and Sects).* Cairo: Maktaba al-Anglū al.Misriyya.

— (2009) *Mafātīh al-asrār (Keys to the Arcana. Al-Shahrastani's Esoteric Commentary on the Qur'ān)* ed. Toby Mayer. Oxford, New York & London: Oxford University Press and the Institute of Ismaili Studies.

al-Tabarī, Muhammad Ibn Jarīr. (1956–1957). *Jāmi' al-bayān 'an ta'wīl āy al-Qur'ān (The Comprehensive and Clear Commentary of the Qur'ān).* 30 volumes. Cairo: Dār al-Ma'ārif.

Ali, Kecia. (2006). *Sexual Ethics and Islam: Feminist Reflections on Qur'ān, Hadith and Jurisprudence.* Oxford: Oneworld.

Arberry, Arthur. (1964). *The Koran Interpreted.* Oxford: Oxford University Press.

Arkoun, Mohammed. (1982). *Lectures du Coran.* Paris: Maisonneuve.

— (1991). *La Pensée Arabe.* Paris: Presses Universitaires de France.

— (2002). *The Unthought in Contemporary Islamic Thought.* London: al-Saqi Books.

'Attār, Farīd al-Dīn. (1990). *Poema celeste,* ed. M. T. Granata. Milano: Rizzoli.

— (1999). *Il verbo degli uccelli,* ed. C. Saccone. Milano: Mondadori.

Averroes, Ibn Rushd. (1976). *On the Harmony of Religion and Philosophy (Fasl al-maqāl).* ed. G. Hourani. London: Luzac.

Avicenna, Ibn Sīnā. (2002). *Metafisica [Ilāhiyyāt of the Shifā'],* ed. O. Lizzini & P. Porro. Milano: Bompiani, with Arabic and Latin texts.

Aristotle. (1996). *Poetics.* London: Penguin Classics.

Barlas, Asma. (2002). *Believing Women in Islam: Unreading Patriarchal Interpretations of the Qur'ān,* Austin, TX: University of Texas Press.

Bausani, Alessandro. (1959). *Persia religiosa.* Milano: Il Saggiatore.

— (1980). *Il Corano.* Milano: Rizzoli.

Bearman, P.J., Th. Bianquis, C.E. Bosworth, E. van Donzel, & W.P. Heinrichs (1991). *Masdjid,* in *Encyclopedie de l'Islam,* 2nd ed. Leiden: Brill, vol. VI, 629–95.

Berg, H. (2000). *The Development of Exegesis in Early Islam. The Authenticity of Muslim Literature from the Formative Period.* London: Curzon Press.

Bigliardi, Stefano. (2014). Islam and the Quest for Modern Science: Conversations with Adnan Oktar, Mehdi Golshani, Mohammed Basil Altaie, Zaghloul El-Naggar, Bruno Guiderdoni and Nidhal Guessoum. *Transactions,* no. 21.

Bint al-Shāti' 'Abd al-Rahmān, 'Ā'isha. (2004). *Al-Tafsīr al-bayānī li'-Qur'ān al-Karīm (The Explicative Commentary of the Qur'ān).* Cairo: Dār al-Ma'ārif.

Bleicher, J. (1986). *L'ermeneutica contemporanea.* Bologna: Il Mulino.

Bori, Pier Cesare. (1987). *L'interpretazione infinita. L'ermeneutica cristiana antica e le sue trasformazioni.* Bologna: Il Mulino.

Bori, Caterina. (2014). *Un caos senza speranza? Studiare il Corano oggi.* Introduction to A. De Prémare, *Alle origini del Corano.* Roma: Carocci.

Buchman, D. ed. (1998). *The Niche of Lights.* Provo, UT: Brigham Young University Press.

Burckhardt, Titus. (1979). *Introduzione alle dottrine esoteriche dell'Islam.* Roma: Edizioni Mediterranee.

Burton, John. (1990). *The Sources of Islamic Law. Islamic Theories of Abrogation.* Edinburgh: Edinburgh University Press.

Burrell D., & N. Daher (eds). (1995). *The Ninety-Nine Beautiful Names of God.* Cambridge: The Islamic Texts Society.

Campanini, Massimo. (1986). *La Surah della Caverna. Meditazione filosofica sull'Unicità di Dio.* Firenze: La Nuova Italia.

— (1994). 'Hasan Hanafī e la fenomenologia:per una nuova politica dell'Islam'. *Oriente Moderno* 13 (74): 103–20.

— (2005a). *Dall'Unicità di Dio alla rivoluzione. Un percorso fenomenologico di Hasan Hanafī*, in *Teologie Politiche. Modelli a confronto*, ed. G. Filoramo, 215–30. Brescia: Morcelliana.

— (2005b). 'Qur'ān and Science: a Hermeneutical Approach'. *Journal of Qur'ānic Studies* 7(1): 48–63.

— (2007). *The Qur'ān, the Basics.* London & New York: Routledge.

— (2011). *The Qur'ān: Modern Muslim Interpretations.* London & New York: Routledge.

— (2016a). *Il pensiero islamico contemporaneo.* Bologna: Il Mulino.

— (2016b). *Islam, religione dell'Occidente.* Milano-Udine: Mimesis.

Cantwell Smith, Wilfred. (1980). 'The True Meaning of Scripture: An Empirical Historian's Non-Reductionist Interpretation of the Qur'ān'. *International Journal of Middle Eastern Studies* 11(4).

Carré, Olivier. (1984). *Mystique et politique. Lecture revolutionnaire du Coran par Sayyid Qutb.* Paris: Presses de la Fondation Nationale des Sciences Politiques.

Cassirer, Ernest. (1985). *Philosophy of the Symbolic Forms.* 3 vols. New Haven, CT: Yale University Press.

— (2011). *The Individual and the Cosmos in Renaissance Philosophy.* New York: Dover Publications.

Cooper, John, R. Nettler & M. Mahmoud. (eds) (1998). *Islam and Modernity. Muslim Intellectuals Respond.* London: I.B. Tauris.

Corbin, Henri. (1971–1972). *En Islam Iranien. Aspects spirituels et philosophiques.* 4 vols. Paris: Gallimard.

— (1994). *Trilogie Ismaèlienne.* Verdier: Lagrasse.

Costa, Vincenzo. (2009). *Husserl.* Roma: Carocci.

— (2012). *Edmund Husserl*, in *Storia della fenomenologia*, ed. A. Cimino & V. Costa. Roma: Carocci.

Cragg, Kenneth. (1971). *The Event of the Qur'ān: Islam and its Scripture.* London: George Allen & Unwin.

Cuypers, Michel. (2007). *Le Festin: Une Lecture de la sourate al-Mā'ida.* Paris: Lethielleux.

— (2011). 'Semitic Rhetoric as a Key to the Question of the *nazm* of the Qur'ānic Text'. *Journal of Qur'ānic Studies* 13(1): 1–24.

Dall'Oglio, Paolo. (1991). *Speranza nell'Islam. Interpretazione della prospettiva escatologica di Corano XVIII*. Genova: Marietti.

Dante. (1991). *Divina Commedia*, ed. A. Leonardi Chiavacci. Milano: Mondadori.

De Smet, Daniel. (1995). *La Quietude de l'intellect*. Leuven: Peeters.

Di Branco, Marco. (2011). *Alessandro Magno, eroe arabo nel Medio Evo*. Roma: Salerno.

Donner, Fred. (1998). *Narratives of the Islamic Origins: The Beginning of Islamic Historical Writing*. Princeton, NJ: Darwin Press.

— (2010). *Muhammad and the Believers. At the Origins of Islam*. Cambridge, MA: Harvard University Press.

Eco, Umberto. (1986). *Postille* to *Il Nome della rosa*. Milano: Bompiani.

Eco, Umberto, & Fedriga, Riccardo. (2015). *La filosofia e le sue storie. L'età contemporanea*. Milano-Roma: Encyclomedia and Laterza.

El-Desouky, Ayman A. (2013). '*Nazm, I'jāz*, Discontinuous Kerygma: Approaching Qur'ānic Voice on the Other Side of the Poetic'. *Journal of Qur'ānic Studies* 15 (2): 1–21.

— (2014). 'Between Hermeneutic Provenance and Textuality: The Qur'ān and the Question of Method in Approaches to World Literature'. *Journal of Qur'ānic Studies* 16(3): 11–38.

Emon, Anver M. (2012). *Religious Pluralism and Islamic Law: Dhimmis and Others in the Empire of Law*. Oxford & New York: Oxford University Press.

Ennaifer, H'mida. (1998). *Les Commentaires Coraniques contemporains*. Roma: Pontifical Institute of Arab and Islamic Studies (PISAI).

Esack, Farid. (1997). *Qur'ān, Liberation and Pluralism*. Oxford: Oneworld.

— (2005). *The Qur'ān: a User's Guide*. Oxford: Oneworld.

Esposito, John. (ed.) (1983). *Voices of Resurgent Islam*. Oxford & New York: Oxford University Press.

Esposito, Costantino. (2013). *Heidegger*. Bologna: Il Mulino.

Fabris, Adriano & Cimino, Antonio. (2009). *Heidegger*. Roma: Carocci.

Ferraris, Maurizio. (1997). *Storia dell'ermeneutica*. Milano: Bompiani.

— (2014). *Spettri di Nietzsche*. Milano-Parma: Guanda.

Frye, Northrop. (2000). *Northrop Frye's Notebooks and Lectures on the Bible and Other Religious Texts*, ed. R. D. Denham. Toronto: University of Toronto Press.

Gadamer, Hans Georg. (1960). *Wahrheit und Methode*. Tubingen: Mohr.

Gardet, Louis & Anawati, Georges. (1980). *Introduction à la Théologie Musulmane*. Paris: Vrin.

Gätje, Helmut. (1976). *The Qur'ān and its Exegesis*. London: Routledge & Kegan Paul.

Ghalioun, Burhan. (1997). *Islam et politique. La modernité trahie*. Paris: La Découverte.

Giami (1980). *Yusuf and Zulaykha*, abridged prose version by D. Pendlebury. London: Octagon Press.

Gilson, Etienne. (1948). *L'Esprit de la philosophie médiévale*. Paris: Vrin.

Gimaret, Daniel. (1988). *Les Noms divins en Islam*. Paris: Cerf.

Gordin, Jean & Weinsheimer, Joel. (1997). *An Introduction to Philosophical Hermeneutics*. New Haven & London: Yale University Press.

Griffel, Frank. (2009). *Al-Ghazālī's Philosophical Theology*. Oxford & New York: Oxford University Press.

Guessoum, Nidhal. (2011). *Islam's Quantum Question. Reconciling Muslim Tradition and Modern Science*. London & New York: I.B. Tauris.

Guillaume, Alfred. (1982). *The Life of Muhammad. A Translation of Ibn Ishaq's Sirat Rasul Allah*. Oxford & New York: Oxford University Press.

Hallaq, Wael. (2009a). 'Groundwork of the Moral Law: A New Look at the Qur'ān and the Genesis of Sharī'a', *Islamic Law and Society* 16(3–4): 239–79.

— (2009b). *Sharī'a. Theory, Practice, Transformations*. Cambridge: Cambridge University Press.

Hanafi, Hasan. (1972). 'Théologie ou Anthropologie?', in AA.VV., *Renaissance du monde arabe*, 233–64. Duculot: Gembloux.

— (1977a). *La Phénomenologie de l'Exègese. Essai d'une Hermeneutique existentielle à partir du Nouveau Testament*: Cairo: Dār al-Fikr al-'Arabī.

— (1977b). *L'Exègese de la Phénomenologie. L'Etat actuel de la méthode phénomenologique et son application au phénomene religieux*. Cairo: Dār al-Fikr al-'Arabī.

— (1983). *Al-tajdīd wa al-tardīd fī'l-fikr al-dīnī al-mu'āsir (Renewal and Stagnation in Contemporary Religious Thought)*. In: *Fī Fikrinā al-mu'āsir (Our Contemporary Thought)*. Beirut: Dār al-Tanwīr.

— (1989). *Min al-'aqīda ilā al-thawra (From Dogma to Revolution)*. 5 vols. Cairo: Madbūlī.

— (1995). *Method of Thematic Interpretation of the Qur'ān*. In: *Islam in the Modern World*, I: 407–28. Cairo: Anglo-Egyptian Bookshop.

— (2012). *Al-Wahy wa'l-Wāqi' (The Revelation and the Factual Reality)*. Cairo: Al-Maktab al-Misrī li'l-Matbū'āt.

Heidegger, Martin. (1959). *Unterwegs zur Sprache*. Pfullingen: Neske.

— (1998). *Pathmarks*, ed. W. McNeill. Cambridge: Cambridge University Press.

Husserl, Edmund. (1970). *The Crisis of European Sciences and Transcendental Phenomenology*. Evanston, IL: Northwestern University Press.

Ibn 'Ashūr, Muhammad Tāhir. (1979). *Tahrīr al-ma'nà al-sadīd wa tanwīr al-'aql al-jadīd fī'l-kitāb al-majīd (Explanation of the Correct Meaning and the Illumination of the New Intellect in the Glorious Book)*. 30 vols. Tunis: Dār al-Tunisiyya li'l-Nashr.

Iqbāl, Muhammad. (2013). *The Reconstruction of Religious Thought in Islam*. New Delhi: Kitab Bhavan.

Izutsu, Toshihiko. (2004). *Ethico-religious Concepts in the Qur'ān*. Kuala Lumpur: Islamic Book Trust.

— (2007). *Concept and Reality of Existence*. Kuala Lumpur: Islamic Book Trust.

Keeler, Annabel. (2006). *Sufi Hermeneutics. The Qur'ān Commentary of Rashīd al-Dīn al-Maybūdī*. Oxford & London: Oxford University Press & the Institute of Ismaili Studies.

Khalafallāh, Muhammad Ahmad. (1999). *Al-Fann al-Qasasī fī'l-Qur'ān al-Karīm (The Art of Story-telling in the Qur'ān)*. London, Cairo & Beirut: Mu'assasat al-Intishār al-'Arabī.

Kinberg, Lea. (1988). '*Muhkamāt* and *Mutashābihāt* (Koran 3:7): Implication of a Koranic Pair of Terms in Medieval Exegesis'. *Arabica* 35: 143–72.

Lawson, Todd. (2009). *The Crucifixion in the Qur'ān: A Study in the History of Muslim Thought*. Oxford: Oneworld.

Leaman, Oliver. (1988). *Averroes and His Philosophy*. Oxford: Clarendon Press.

— (2004). *Islamic Aesthetics. An Introduction*. Edinburgh: Edinburgh University Press.

— (2016). *The Qur'ān. A Philosophical Guide*. London: Bloomsbury.

— (ed.) (2006). *The Qur'ān. An Encyclopaedia*. London: Routledge.

Lings, Martin. (1988). *Muhammad: His Life Based on the Earliest Sources*. London: Allen & Unwin.

Lizzini, Olga. (2012). *Avicenna*. Roma: Carocci.

Liverani, Mario. (2003). *Oltre la Bibbia. Storia antica di Israele*. Roma & Bari: Laterza.

Luxenberg, Christoph. (2007). *The Syro-Aramaic Reading of the Koran: A Contribution to the Decoding of the Language of the Koran*. Berlin: Hans Schiller.

Madigan, Daniel. (2001). *The Qur'ān's Self-Image*. Princeton, NJ: Princeton University Press.

Malti-Douglas, F. (1991). *Woman's Body, Woman's Word: Gender and Discourse in Arab-Islamic Writing*. Princeton, NJ: Princeton University Press.

Marlow, Louise (1997). *Hierarchy and Egalitarianism in Islamic Thought*. Cambridge: Cambridge University Press.

Martin, Richard. (1980). 'The Role of the Baṣrah Muʿtazila in Formulating the Doctrine of the Apologetic Miracle'. *Journal of Near Eastern Studies* 39(3–4): 175–89.

Marmura M. ed. (2005). *The Metaphysics of the Healing*. Provo, UT: Brigham Young University.

Massignon, Louis. (2012). *I sette dormienti di Efeso*. Milano: Mimesis.

Masullo, Aldo. (1980). *Metafisica*. Milano: Mondadori.

Mawdūdī, Abū'l-Aʿlà (1988). *Towards Understanding the Qur'ān. English Version of Tafhīm al-Qur'ān*, ed. Z. I. Ansari. Leicester: The Islamic Foundation.

Mayer, Toby. (2005). 'Shahrastānī on the Arcana of the Qur'ān: A Preliminary Evaluation'. *Journal of Qur'ānic Studies* 7(2): 61–100.

— (2009). *Introduction* to *Keys to the Arcana. Shahrastānī's Esoteric Commentary on the Qur'ān*. Oxford & New York: Oxford University Press & the Institute of Ismaili Studies.

McAuliffe, Jane. (ed.) (2001–2006). *Encyclopaedia of the Qur'ān*. 6 vols. Leiden: Brill.

Merad, ʿAli. (1998). *L'Exégèse Coranique*. Paris: Presses Universitaires de France.

Mir, Mustansir. (1986). *Coherence in the Qur'ān: A Study of Islāhī's Concept of Nazm in Tadabbur-i Qur'ān*. Indianapolis, IN: American Trust Publications.

— (1990). 'Bāqillānī's Critique of Imruʾ al-Qays'. In: *Studies in Near Eastern Culture and History in Memory of Ernest T. Abdel Massih*, ed. James Bellamy, 118–31. Ann Arbor, MI: Centre for Near Eastern and North American Studies, University of Michigan.

Moosa, Ebrahim. (2003). *Introduction* in Fazlur Rahman, *Revival and Reform in Islam*. Oxford: Oneworld.

Motzki, Harald. (2000). *The Biography of Muhammad: The Issue of the Sources*. Leiden & Boston: Brill.

Naguib, Shuruq. (2015). 'Bint al-Shāti''s Approach to *tafsīr*: An Egyptian Exegete's Journey from Hermeneutics to Humanity'. *Journal of Qur'ānic Studies* 17(1): 45–84.

Nallino, Carlo Alfonso. (1963). *Chrestomathia Qorani Arabica*. Roma: Istituto per l'Oriente.

Nasr, Seyyed Hossein. (1966). *Ideals and Reality of Islam*, London: Allen & Unwin.

— (2006). *Islamic Philosophy from its Origin to the Present. Philosophy in the Land of Prophecy*. Albany, NY: State University of New York Press.

Netton, Ian R. (1989). *Allah Transcendent*. London: Curzon Press.

Neuwirth, Angelika. (2007). 'Orientalism in Oriental Studies? Qur'ānic Studies as a Case in Point'. *Journal of Qur'ānic Studies* 9(2): 115–27.

Neuwirth, Angelika & Nicolai Sinai. (2011). *Introduction* to Id. Michael Marx (ed.), *The Qur'ān in Context*. Leiden & Boston: Brill.

Nietzsche, Friedrich. (1999). *La volontà di potenza [Wille zur Macht]*, eds. M. Ferraris & P. Kobau. Milano: Bompiani.

Paci, Enzo. (1975). *Prefazione* to E. Husserl, *La crisi delle scienze europee e la fenomenologia trascendentale*, eds. W. Biemel & E. Filippini. Milano: Il Saggiatore.

Parodi, Massimo. (2006a). *Il paradigma filosofico agostiniano*. Bergamo: Lubrina.

— (2006b). *Il tempo del confronto e dell'ascolto*, in AA.VV., *L'Islam e la filosofia. Tradizioni, identità e confronto*, ed. M. Bianchetti. Milano: Edizioni Alboversorio.

Penrice, James. (2004). *A Dictionary and Glossary of the Koran*. New York: Dover.

Pepicelli, Renata. (2010). *Il femminismo islamico*. Roma: Carocci.

Porro, Pasquale (2012). *Tommaso d'Aquino, un profilo storico-filosofico*. Roma: Carocci.

Privitera, G. Aurelio. (2005). *Il ritorno del guerriero. Lettura dell'Odissea*. Torino: Einaudi.

Qutb, Sayyid. (1999). *In the Shade of the Qur'ān (Fī Zilāl al-Qur'ān)*, ed. M. A. Salahi & A. A. Shamis. Leicester: The Islamic Foundation.

Rahman, Fazlur. (1984). *Islam and Modernity*. Chicago & London: University of Chicago Press.

— (1989). *Major Themes of the Qur'ān*. Minneapolis, MN: Bibliotheca Islamica.

— (2003). *Revival and Reform in Islam*. Oxford: Oneworld.

Ramadan, Tariq. (2006). *In the Footsteps of the Prophet. Lessons from the Life of Muhammad*. Oxford & New York: Oxford University Press.

— (2009). *Radical Reform: Islam, Ethics and Liberation*. Oxford & New York: Oxford University Press.

Reynolds, Gabriel Said. (2010). *The Qur'ān and its Biblical Subtext*. London & New York: Routledge.

Ricoeur, Paul. (1974). *The Conflict of Interpretations*. Evanston, IL: Northwestern University Press.

— (1980). *Essays on Biblical Interpretation*, ed. L. S. Mudge. Philadelphia, PA: Fortress Press.

Ries, Julien. (1994). 'Le symbole'. In *Catholicisme, Encyclopédie*. Paris: Letouzey et Ané, vol. XIV, coll. 636–54.

Rippin, Andrew. (ed.) (1988). *Approaches to the History of the Interpretation of the Qur'ān*. Oxford: Clarendon Press.

— (ed.) (1999). *The Qur'ān: Formative Interpretation*. Ashgate: Aldershot.

— (ed.) (2001). *The Qur'ān: Style and Contents*. Ashgate: Aldershot.

— (2001a). *The Qur'ān and its Interpretative Tradition*. Ashgate: Aldershot.

Rūmī, Jalāl al-Dīn. (1980). *Poesie mistiche*, ed. A. Bausani. Milano: Rizzoli.

Sabetta, A. (2015). *La Cristologia filosofica nell'orizzonte della modernità*. Roma: Studium.

Saccone, Carlo. (2008). *Alessandro Dhu'l-Qarnayn, in viaggio tra i due mari*. Alessandria: Edizioni dell'Orso.

Saeed, Abdullah. (2006). *Interpreting the Qur'ān*. London & New York: Routledge.

— (2014). *Reading the Qur'ān in the Twenty-first Century: A Contextualist Approach*. London and New York: Routledge.

Scarcia Amoretti, Biancamaria. (2009). *Il Corano: Una lettura*. Roma: Carocci.

Schimmel, Annemarie. (1985). *And Muhammad is His Messenger. The Veneration of the Prophet in Islamic Piety*. Chapel Hill, NC & London: University of North Carolina Press.

— (1994). *Deciphering the Signs of God: A Phenomenological Approach to Islam*. Albany, NY: State University of New York Press.

Shah, Mustafa. (ed.) (2013). *Tafsir: Interpreting the Qur'ān: Critical Concepts in Islamic Studies*. 4 volumes. London & New York: Routledge.

Shah-Kazemi, Reza. (2012). *The Spirit of Tolerance in Islam*. London & New York: I.B. Tauris in association with the Institute of Ismaili Studies.

Shahrūr, Muhammad. (1990). *Al-Qur'ān wa'l-Kitāb: Qirā'a Mu'āsira (The Qur'ān and the Scripture: a Contemporary Reading)*. Damascus: Dār al-Ahālī.

— (2012). *Al-Qasas al-Qur'ānī: Qirā'a Mu'āsira (The Qur'ānic Tale: a Contemporary Reading)*. Beirut: Dār al-Sāqī.

Shalabī, Hind. (1985). *Al-Tafsīr al-'Ilmī li'l-Qur'ān al-Karīm bayna al-Nazariyyāt wa'l-Tatbīq (The Scientific Commentary of the Qur'ān between Theory and Application)*. Tunis: n.p.

Sharī'atī, 'Alī. (n.d.). *School of Thought and Action*. Albuquerque: Abjad.

— (1980). *On the Sociology of Islam*. Berkeley, CA: Mizan Press.

Smith, Mark. (2002). *The Early History of God: Yahweh and the Other Deities in Ancient Israel*. Grand Rapids, MI & Cambridge: Eerdmans.

Spinoza, Baruch. (2004). *Tractatus theologico-politicus*, ed. A. Dini. Milano: Bompiani.

Stowasser, Barbara. (1994). *Women in the Qur'ān, Traditions and Interpretation*. Oxford: Oxford University Press.

Tabātabā'ī, Muhammad Husayn. (1983). *al-Mīzān: an Exegesis of the Qur'ān*, trans. S. Akhtar Rizvi. Tehran: World Organization for Islamic Services.

Taji-Farouki, Suha. (2004). *Modern Muslim Intellectuals and the Qur'ān*. Oxford & London: Oxford University Press and the Institute of Ismaili Studies.

— (ed.). (2015). *The Qur'an and its Readers Worldwide. Contemporary Commentaries and Translations*. Qur'anic Studies Series, 14. Oxford & New York: Oxford University Press in association with the Institute of Ismaili Studies.

Tāhā, Mahmud Muhammad. (1996). *The Second Message of Islam*. Syracuse, NY: Syracuse University Press.

Tilliette, Xavier. (1993). *Le Christ des Philosophes*. Namur: Culture et Vérité.

Varzi, Achille. (2005). *Ontologia*. Roma and Bari: Laterza.

Vattimo, Gianni. (2002). *Oltre l'interpretazione*. Roma and Bari: Laterza.

Ventura, Alberto, & Ida Zilio Grandi (ed.) (2012). *Il Corano*. Milano: Mondadori.

Volpi, Franco. (2004). *Il nichilismo*. Roma and Bari: Laterza.

Von Kuegelgen, Anke. (1994). *Averroes und die Arabische Moderne*. Leiden: Brill.

Wadud, Amina. (1999). *Qur'ān and Woman. Rereading the Sacred Text from a Woman's Perspective*. Oxford & New York: Oxford University Press.

— (2006). *Inside the Gender Jihad: Women's Reform in Islam*. Oxford: Oneworld.

Wansbrough, John. (1977). *Qur'ānic Studies*. Oxford: Oxford University Press.

— (1978). *The Sectarian Milieu: Context and Composition of Islamic Salvation History*. Cambridge: Cambridge University Press.

Watt, William M. (1962). *Muslim Intellectual: A Study on al-Ghazālī*. Edinburgh: Edinbugh University Press.

— (1991). *Muslim-Christian Encounters. Perceptions and Misperceptions*. London & New York: Routledge.

Welte, B. (1968). La métaphysique de Saint Thomas d'Aquin et la pensée de l'histoire de l'etre chez Heidegger. *Archiv der Philosophie*.

Wensinck, Arnt, & Jacques Jomier. (1978). 'Ka'ba'. In: *Encyclopedie de l'Islam, 2nd edition*, vol. IV, 331–37. Leiden: Brill.

Wild, Stefan. (ed.) (1996). *The Qur'ān as Text*. Leiden: Brill.

Xella, Paolo. (1982). *Gli antenati di Dio. Divinità e miti della tradizione di Canaan*. Verona: Essedue Edizioni.

# INDEX

CPSIA information can be obtained
at www.ICGtesting.com
Printed in the USA
BVOW06*0748161216

469687BV00007B/4/P

9 781781 792308